State of Defiance

UNIVERSITY PRESS OF FLORIDA

Florida A&M University, Tallahassee
Florida Atlantic University, Boca Raton
Florida Gulf Coast University, Ft. Myers
Florida International University, Miami
Florida State University, Tallahassee
New College of Florida, Sarasota
University of Central Florida, Orlando
University of Florida, Gainesville
University of North Florida, Jacksonville
University of South Florida, Tampa
University of West Florida, Pensacola

# STATE of DEFIANCE

Challenging the Johns Committee's
Assault on Civil Liberties

**Judith G. Poucher**

University Press of Florida
Gainesville | Tallahassee | Tampa | Boca Raton
Pensacola | Orlando | Miami | Jacksonville | Ft. Myers | Sarasota

A Florida Quincentennial Book

Library of Congress Cataloging-in-Publication Data
Poucher, Judith G. author.
State of defiance : challenging the Johns Committee's assault on civil liberties /
Judith G. Poucher.
pages cm
Includes bibliographical references and index.
ISBN 978-0-8130-4993-9
1. Civil rights—Florida—History. 2. Florida. Legislature. Legislative Investigation
Committee. 3. Communism—Florida—History. 4. Johns, Charley. 5. Homosexuality—
Florida—History. 6. Culture conflict—Florida—History. 7. Gays—Abuse of—Florida.
8. Gay rights—Florida—History. 9. Florida—Politics and government—1951– I. Title.
KFF411.P68 2014
323.092'2759—dc23    2013051135

University Press of Florida
15 Northwest 15th Street
Gainesville, FL 32611-2079
http://www.upf.com

In memory of Audrey Flynn (1935–2009) and Carmen Avila (1940–1994): leaders, warriors, pioneers, sisters, and friends. The lives of women in Jacksonville and Tallahassee are better today because they lived. We are their legacy.

# Contents

# Figures

# Preface

*One ... [person] with courage makes a majority.*

Andrew Jackson

Courage empowered by conscience often makes heroes of ordinary people; their cumulative efforts also generate groundswells for political change and social progress. In Florida, such a gathering momentum was created by five people who never knew each other: civil rights activists Virgil Hawkins and Ruth Perry; college professor Sig Diettrich; lesbian bartender G. G. Mock; and university administrator and professor Margaret Fisher. However, these people had one major experience in common: When Florida was in the grip of its own brand of McCarthyism, these individuals challenged the prejudices of the legislature's investigating group, the Florida Legislative Investigation Committee. Because of the influence of its creator, Senator Charley Johns, that committee soon became known as the Johns Committee and is referred to as such throughout this book.[1]

A study of these Floridians' battle with their own government is long overdue. Few published works exist that focus entirely on the Johns Committee, and very little has been published on the people who defied the committee.[2] While certainly selective and not a comprehensive study, the profiles in this book illuminate the impact of ordinary people—black and white, women and men, gay and straight—who risked careers and lives because they saw beyond the politics of the moment.[3] By drawing upon primary sources (particularly the unsealed records of the Johns Committee) and previously unpublished materials, this book examines the stands taken by these five people against the Johns Committee and its witch hunts.

The Johns Committee was an "equal opportunity abuser." As a result, it produced survivors who championed a variety of civil rights. Each survivor fought against Florida's "little McCarthyism" while simultaneously battling an additional form of bigotry, be it racism, homophobia, or threats to teachers and academic freedom.[4] The duality of these battles made them very demanding, for the risk of failure—as well as the effort required—was doubled. These individuals not only insisted on the right to live their lives as free citizens but they also resisted the committee's tactics, by enduring questioning by the committee and its staff (either in a public hearing or privately, with a record of such questioning still extant), not cooperating with the committee, and not living like victims after being persecuted by the committee. To defy the McCarthy-like tactics of the committee was difficult enough, but to challenge their prejudices as well took extra resolve.

Major leaders are not featured in *State of Defiance*, although they are included to some extent. The reason is simple: their stories are in no danger of being lost, unlike those of their less well-known colleagues. The stories of recognized leaders have already been preserved through their own autobiographies, contemporary accounts, and secondary sources. For example, the chapter on Ruth Perry includes information on Father Theodore Gibson, president of the Miami chapter of the National Association for the Advancement of Colored People (NAACP), and his U.S. Supreme Court case, but only from the standpoint of Perry's having written about her friend's case in her newspaper column. Also, Robert Saunders, an important figure in the history of the Florida NAACP, appears in Perry's chapter primarily because he had a major role in determining his organization's response to the Johns Committee's treatment of Perry. Gibson's and Saunders' narratives have already been published; Perry's full story has not. It is the stories of these "ordinary" people that this book will preserve.

*State of Defiance* uses the stories of five citizens to illustrate the Johns Committee's bigotry and abuse of civil rights and civil liberties in its targeting of integrationists, Communists, homosexuals, and liberal teachers in Florida from 1956 to 1965. Chapter 1 introduces the committee's creator, Charley Johns, and its first target, Virgil Hawkins. Their lives intersected when Hawkins' determination to attend the University of Florida (UF) College of Law collided with Johns' scheme to stop integration and destroy the Florida NAACP through the committee. A description of the Johns

Committee's origins and strategies concludes the chapter. Chapter 2 resumes the confrontation between Johns and Hawkins, with Hawkins as the first witness at the committee's first hearing, which focused on Hawkins' suit to integrate UF. Hawkins was the first of this book's subjects to defy the Johns Committee, thwarting its barratry strategy and continuing his lawsuit. Chapter 3 tells the story of Ruth Perry, a Miami NAACP officer, and how she worked as an activist, journalist, and witness to fight the committee. She foiled the committee's strategy, which was to destroy the Florida NAACP by portraying it as Communist influenced. Chapter 4 presents the story of Sig Diettrich, caught in the wide net of homophobia cast by the Johns Committee during its sting operations at UF. Threatened, coerced, and humiliated by the committee, he refused to cooperate, but the Johns Committee continued to affect UF. Chapter 5 relates the story of G. G. Mock, arrested in a local sting operation in Tampa during the committee's hunt for gay and lesbian teachers. She was harassed by the Johns Committee both before and during her years in prison. Chapter 6 presents the story of Margaret Fisher and her University of South Florida (USF) colleagues. They defended USF's vision and policies against the Johns Committee's assault on liberal teaching and academic freedom. Fisher and her colleagues also dealt with the aftermath of the investigation while the Johns Committee was coming to an end. Chapter 7 concludes the book by first examining the cold war fears that the Johns Committee exploited for nine years and the reasons the committee flourished in Florida after the height of McCarthyism had passed in the United States. After reviewing the gathering momentum of resistance that ended the committee, the chapter briefly surveys examples of other Americans who refused to relegate their conscience to their government. The chapter ends by analyzing the individual strengths of Hawkins, Perry, Diettrich, Mock, and Fisher that empowered their acts of conscience and produced majorities of one.

Finally, because Florida's public records laws (sunshine laws) are retroactive, they cover past Senate, House, and joint committees. Thus any legislative committee's papers are considered public records. However, in order to protect further the people who were wronged by the Johns Committee investigations, *State of Defiance* contains only names already included in sources other than the committee's documents, such as contemporary newspaper accounts that published witnesses' names.

# Acknowledgments

Despite the solitary nature of writing, no one writes a book alone—or without the assistance of librarians and archivists. The staff of the Florida State Archives was very helpful from the beginning of my research. Beth Golding advised me to start my adventure through the Johns Committee's thirty thousand pages by studying the committee's administrative files first. That turned out to be excellent advice. Further along, Boyd Murphree offered help as well as encouragement. Near the end, Miriam Spalding found the missing box 9 of the Clerk of the House Papers, to my great relief. At USF, Gayle Penner, now retired, was the first to show me the Ruth Perry Papers and the Robert and Helen Saunders Papers, and Mark Greenberg's staff later offered additional help with documents from the university's archives. Archivists at Florida State University (FSU) and Florida A&M University also assisted with files from their respective Special Collections departments. Finally, if it is possible for a Florida historian to have a favorite library, mine would have to be that of the University of Florida, particularly the Special Collections department. Jim Cusick, Flo Turcotte, and other staff members clearly love their work and are an asset to UF and to any researcher.

I am also indebted to Reverend Ruth Jensen-Forbell, one of the youngest Johns Committee survivors. If not for her, I would never have written this book. I was intrigued by her story, examined the committee's papers for the first time, and soon realized that Jensen-Forbell's interrogation transcript was missing or had been destroyed. Since no written record exists of her approximately fifteen-hour interrogation as a nineteen-year-old sophomore at FSU, I could not include her story in *State of Defiance*, even though she refused to name lesbians at FSU and was subsequently forced to leave the university. Fortunately, the committee delayed but did not destroy her dream of becoming a minister. Today Jensen-Forbell is the pastor of First Coast Community Church in St. Augustine.

I must also thank my colleague Steve Piscitelli, who read an early version of part of the manuscript. Also, my former campus president at Florida State College, Duane Dumbleton (1939–2006), strongly supported my taking a year's sabbatical. With the exception of the sabbatical year, my teaching duties allowed me to do substantial work on the book only during the summers, so this has been a long project. My first editor at the University Press of Florida, Meredith Morris-Babb, now heads the press, and my second editor, Eli Bortz, is now employed in a higher position at another press. My hope is that whatever good luck springs from working on this book will also fall to my third editor, Sian Hunter, and eventually to the author. In any case, I certainly value their expertise and assistance. Additionally, civil rights scholar Steven F. Lawson reviewed the manuscript, offering many generous and helpful comments, which I not only appreciate but have also implemented.

Finally, on a personal level, I have to thank my mother, June Poucher, not only for instilling an early interest in history and biography but also for being one of my editors and cheerleaders from the beginning. Also, large thanks are due to my partner, Lori Jordan, for everything from proofing, editing, and brainstorming to, above all, encouraging—whether she thought that I needed it or not.

# 1

## Charley Johns and Virgil Hawkins

Ambition Realized, Dream Deferred

On May 17, 1954, Charley Johns turned and faced the television cameras. The U.S. Supreme Court had just made history with the *Brown* decision, eliminating the legal basis for segregated schools. As Florida's acting governor, Johns called a press conference and calmly read to reporters the telegram that he had sent to Florida attorney general Richard Ervin: "Please make exhaustive study of ruling of US Supreme Court today concerning segregation and public schools."[1] Twenty-four hours later, Johns abruptly changed his tone, saying, "My present inclination is to call an extraordinary session of the legislature." By the following day, Johns' erratic responses continued when he announced that a special session was not needed after all.[2]

Throughout his political career, Charley Johns' reactions were usually more consistent, reflecting the conservative and segregationist views of his constituents.[3] When another U.S. Supreme Court ruling ordered that fellow Floridian Virgil Hawkins, an African American, be admitted immediately to the University of Florida (UF), Johns' reaction was more in character: he created a legislative investigation committee to target the National Association for the Advancement of Colored People (NAACP) and other integrationists. Soon after the committee was formed, the lives of Charley Johns and Virgil Hawkins intersected when Hawkins' determination to attend UF collided with Johns' scheme to stop integration and destroy the Florida NAACP.

•

The scion of one of Bradford County's founding families, Johns was only an infant and his brother, Markley, only ten years old when their father, a Nassau County deputy sheriff, was shot in the back a week before he was scheduled to testify in federal court. Charley, Markley, and their mother and sister soon moved back to their hometown of Starke. Although direct descendants of one of Bradford County's founding families, Mrs. Johns and her children struggled financially for several years, even taking in boarders to make money.[4]

Years later, as the family's finances improved, and with young Charley working part time, Markley was able to afford law school. He graduated in 1915 from Virgil Hawkins' intended alma mater, the University of Florida College of Law, with high honors. Markley returned to Starke and established a successful law practice. He then continued a Johns family tradition by serving in the state legislature as his and Charley's grandfather had done in the 1880s. In 1928, Markley ran successfully for the Senate and during the 1931 biennial session was elected president pro tem.[5] At age thirty-five, the age at which his father was killed, Markley died suddenly from pneumonia and never took office as Senate president.[6]

With Markley's death, Charley felt that he had not just lost a brother; he had also, for the second time, lost a father. Charley also grieved for his brother's unrealized potential and "vowed right then . . . to become Senate President—for Markley."[7] Johns was twenty-six years old when he made that vow and was suitably positioned to implement it. He had attended UF briefly, wanting to be an attorney, but he left for financial reasons, and worked for ten years as a brakeman and then conductor for the Seaboard Airline Railroad. Johns had been married to his high school sweetheart, Thelma Brinson, since 1927 and had a young son.[8]

A year after his brother's death, Johns was elected to the Florida House of Representatives for the 1935 biennial session. Two years later, he was elected to the Senate for the 1937 session, representing Bradford and Union counties. Johns soon began to establish relationships with Senate power brokers and chaired several committees. He also supported legislation for local improvements in his district (most often roads) as well as for increased benefits for widows, the disabled, and the elderly and helped to pass a pay raise for public school teachers. Johns' position in the Senate also increased the earnings of an insurance agency he had started several years earlier in Starke. His company made seventy thousand dollars in one year by selling insurance to such state agencies as the Game and Freshwater Fish Commission.[9]

A naturally gregarious, likeable man, Johns enjoyed the socializing and

Figure 1.1. Group portrait of the Pork Chop Gang during the special legislative session of 1956. Senator Charley Johns is back row, far right, in a dark suit. Senator Dilworth Clarke, Johns' mentor and sometime banker, is front row, center, at the microphone. State Archives of Florida, *Florida Memory*, http://floridamemory.com/items/show/35657.

camaraderie of the Senate, and those traits helped him to become a member and later leader of a group dubbed the Pork Chop Gang by the *Tampa Tribune* in 1955. The term described a group of north Florida lawmakers who dominated the legislature. According to the *Tribune*, the Gang not only put "pork [or political spoils] over principle"[10] but also consumed pork as part of the local diet in their small, rural counties. The Pork Choppers and many of their constituents were also native Floridians who were very conservative in regard to religion, education, and their love of the rural lifestyle. Thus they sought to maintain the status quo, particularly in their social structure and politics. One of the most effective ways of doing that was by dominating the legislature.[11]

The Pork Chop Gang was able to control the legislature—and thus tax revenues from the more populous counties in south Florida—because of the state's malapportioned election districts. In the 1950s, a majority of the

Florida House was elected by only 20 percent of the state's population. The Senate was worse, where only 18 percent of the population elected the majority. Thus, the four counties with the largest population, all in south Florida, were grossly underrepresented in comparison to the small, Pork Chopper–controlled counties in north Florida. The Pork Chop Gang also flourished within a legislative mechanism that gave lawmakers only forty-four working days every two years, provided no printing of bills before the legislature voted, and protected a corrupt committee system dominated by lobbyists. The numerous committees, invariably chaired or vice chaired by Pork Choppers, operated under rules that excluded the public and allowed chairmen with multiple proxies to conduct meetings by themselves.[12]

Pork Choppers benefited most from the process for choosing the Senate president. A simple majority of the senators who were not up for reelection, nineteen men in 1951, selected the president from those running for reelection, also nineteen in 1951. Thus, about ten senators often chose the Senate president. Every Senate president from 1947 to 1965 was a member of the Pork Chop Gang. In turn, those presidents controlled virtually all legislation because they created and interpreted Senate rules, determined the Senate calendar, recognized senators during debates, appointed committee chairs and members, and decided which bills would be reviewed by which committees. Such inequities invariably produced a culture clash between legislators from the rural, sparsely populated northern part of the state and those from the urban, populous south, who wanted more equitable representation and greater control of the larger tax revenues produced in their part of the state.[13]

In 1951 Johns' political relationships as a Pork Chopper paid off; at the age of forty-eight he was unanimously elected president pro tem of the Senate and then chosen president of the Senate by unanimous vote for the 1953 session. He had become Senate president for his brother. A month before the 1953 session opened, though, Johns collapsed. Waking up in an oxygen tent, he thought he would die young, like his father and brother, but mostly he feared that he "was going to let Markley down."[14] What Johns thought was a heart attack turned out to be a gallbladder problem. Although it caused him to lose more than forty pounds before the end of the legislative session, he doggedly presided over the Senate for the entire 1953 session.[15] He kept his vow to his brother. From that point on, though,

Figure 1.2. Senate president Charley Johns in 1953, displaying both his (*left*) and his brother Markley's (*right*) presidential portraits. Red Kerce, State Archives of Florida, *Florida Memory*, http://floridamemory.com/items/show/45295.

Charley Johns would work to realize ambitions beyond his promise to Markley.

In February of 1953, only a few days before Johns' gallbladder episode, Governor Dan McCarty had a heart attack. Johns responded by telling the press that, as a McCarty supporter, he would implement the governor's policies with McCarty's appointees if he, as Senate president and thus next in line, ever had to be governor. While McCarty continued to recover during the legislative session, Johns supported a bill to establish a "joint legislative committee to investigate criminal and subversive activities"[16] in Florida. Many senators opposed the bill, feeling it would exaggerate the state's crime problem and thus hurt tourism. McCarty also opposed the bill and had Senator LeRoy Collins from Tallahassee lobby against it. Johns' first attempt to establish what would later be known as the Johns Committee failed by two votes.[17]

During the 1953 session, the legislature also debated the question of succession to the governor's office, with some lawmakers supporting a bill to establish the office of lieutenant governor. Johns, along with other Pork Choppers, managed to defeat the lieutenant governor bill, and the procedure for succession remained unchanged: the Senate president would assume the office of governor. Four months later, Johns was the first to benefit from the bill's defeat when McCarty suffered a second, fatal heart attack.[18]

An hour after McCarty's body was moved from the Capitol, Johns was sworn in as acting governor. In the days that followed, he waited for resignation letters from McCarty's appointees. When they didn't resign, Johns suspended or fired seventeen men, accusing many of malfeasance. Johns insisted that the suspensions and firings were not personal but were necessary to "provide executive leadership."[19] He apparently saw no irony in removing the appointees of a man who, like his brother Markley, died before he could fulfill the duties of his office. Johns' hypocrisy angered McCarty's supporters. Because Johns had said that he would implement the governor's program with his appointees, McCarty supporters felt betrayed. Johns also created a brain trust of Pork Chop Gang leaders and supporters to advise him and then outlined his plans for Florida, which included road building in several areas of the state, expediting welfare payments for seniors and the disabled, and increasing teachers' salaries.[20]

Two months later, Johns was pleased when the Florida Supreme Court ruled that there would be a special election the following year to choose McCarty's successor and that Johns was eligible to run. The winner would take office in January of 1955, giving Johns five months until the May primary to gain the support of Florida voters. If he won, he would be the first Florida governor to succeed himself, but if he lost, he would be a lame duck governor for seven of his total fifteen months in office.[21] Johns wasted no time in appointing more of his cronies to various positions. He was especially helpful to the Florida State Road Department, spurring $7.5 million of construction in central Florida alone in the five months before the special election.[22]

Johns' campaign in the special election began with a political gaff. His announcement that he would run was broadcast live from a rally in Starke via a statewide radio hookup on March 5, 1954. As the crowd finished eating their fried catfish, they waited for Johns. When he did not appear, his influential Pork Chopper colleague, Senator Dilworth Clarke from Monticello, approached the microphone. Clarke was also Johns' creditor. A wealthy banker, he often made loans to legislators and was particularly generous to Johns, loaning him more than seventy thousand dollars in a twenty-year period. Clarke, now attempting to fill the time void for the tardy Johns, blithely told the gathering that he had not "seen a crowd [that] large since the last lynching in Jefferson County."[23] Clarke's coarse humor preceded several mistakes made by Johns' supporters.

As part of the press package for the campaign, staffers had written a brief biography of Johns. After explaining how Johns' father was killed when the acting governor was only nine months old, the biography went on to say that Johns and his brother Markley "were given the burden of supporting their mother and sister,"[24] despite Johns having been an infant at the time and Markley only ten years old. The biography also erred in touting Johns' elimination of "many patronage jobs," for this rejuvenated the issue of Johns' suspension and firings of McCarty's appointees.[25]

Johns' claims of eliminating patronage did not go unnoticed by his chief opponent, Senator LeRoy Collins. A McCarty confidant, Collins had been outraged by Johns' suspensions and firings. Collins was no newcomer to Florida politics. A native of Tallahassee and son of a local grocer, Collins had worked his way through college and law school and then returned home to set up a law practice in the midst of the depression years. He was first elected to the state House of Representatives in 1934, the same year Johns began his political career. Beginning in 1940, Collins was repeatedly elected to the Florida Senate. In the late 1940s and early 1950s, he supported the reapportionment plan for expanding south Florida's legislative representation, which Johns opposed. In the 1951 session, Collins sponsored the law prohibiting secret organizations (that is, the Klan) from wearing masks or burning crosses; Johns voted against the bill, saying that it was not strict enough. Despite representing a north Florida county, Collins was not a member of the Pork Chop Gang. Identifying more with urban, progressive south Florida, Collins benefited from living in a county in which his family ties and the moderately liberal environment fostered by Leon County's two state universities helped to reelect him.[26]

In the 1954 special election, Collins raised the issue of the new appointments Johns made after firing McCarty's men. Johns countered that Mc-Carty's men had "ganged up on [him and tried] to discredit [his] administration," adding that "the road department was a do-nothing department, and [there was] work to be done."[27] In the first primary, votes were divided among Johns, Collins, and a third candidate, Brailey Odham, so a runoff was necessary. After receiving Odham's support, Collins was optimistic. He also knew that if he could carry Dade County, the largest in the state, he could win.[28]

The climax of the runoff campaign—and the worst mistake made by Johns' staff—came on May 13, 1954, in a debate televised live in Miami and broadcast statewide by radio. Collins spoke first, producing a copy of the following day's *Miami Herald*. The newspaper regularly printed an early edition of the next day's paper and distributed it the evening before. Thus the paper Collins showed to the television cameras carried the date of May 14 but was purchased on May 13 shortly before the debate began. In the paper was a Johns campaign ad, which Collins read aloud: "Well, Senator Collins (wherever you are), we told you what would happen. You asked for it on television last night, and you got it. You didn't look so good, Senator. Did you? Neither did your record—when it was put up against that of Governor Johns. Did it?"[29]

Collins then pointed out that the ad was run two hours before the debate began yet described him as having lost the debate. Johns was silent for several seconds, then said he did not know anything about the ad and had nothing to do with the advertising phase of his campaign.[30]

The damage from the newspaper ad was irreparable, although Johns' campaign staff could not admit it. Four days later, desperately trying to salvage the campaign, they ran a second ad that eerily foreshadowed Johns' political legacy:

Senator Collins has reminded us of another senator—Senator Mc-Carthy. Like Senator McCarthy, Senator Collins started out in pursuit of a worthy objective. In Senator McCarthy's case, it was the elimination of Communists in government. In Senator Collins' case, it was a desire to carry out the fine principles of Governor McCarty. But each man lost his way somewhere along the line. Each became irresponsible and reckless in making charges against innocent persons without offering any shred of proof against them.[31]

Figure 1.3. Governor-elect LeRoy Collins (*left*) and acting governor Charley Johns on Inauguration Day, 1955. State Archives of Florida, *Florida Memory*, http://floridamemory.com/items/show/72546.

Even before this ad appeared, the Johns' campaign was over; it had begun with a racist joke and ended with an embarrassing staff mistake, both broadcast statewide. The second ad was merely a redundant requiem. With a large voter turnout, Collins won on May 25, 1954, a week after the *Brown I* decision.[32]

Although Johns reacted erratically to the high court's ruling, Attorney General Ervin responded consistently, emphasizing that there was time to file Supreme Court briefs on how and when *Brown* would be implemented. First, he asked the cabinet to fund a survey about potential problems in Florida if the *Brown* decision were implemented; he planned to cite the survey in his Supreme Court brief. Ervin then chose Florida State University (FSU) sociologist Lewis Killian to direct the study.[33]

Killian's survey, with a 51 percent return rate, found that most Floridians, African American and white, would comply with the *Brown* decision. However, Ervin skewed the survey data in his brief. Despite four of five white groups saying that they would comply with *Brown*, Ervin stated that "white groups differ[ed] . . . in [their] willingness to comply."[34] Ervin also reported results negatively, saying that one-fourth to one-half of the white groups believed African Americans were opposed to integration. (Of course, this also meant that three-fourths to one-half of those groups did *not* believe African Americans opposed integration.) Killian later said that Ervin's data distortions helped create the appearance of "a united front of resistance and delay . . . that [the] research did not show to exist."[35] The FSU professor believed that this false front of resistance, in turn, helped to galvanize the NAACP's push for integration via the federal courts after the *Brown II* ruling in 1955.[36]

In his Supreme Court brief, Ervin not only advised the court to "restrain the use of coercive measures . . . until the hard core of public opinion has softened" but also warned that immediate integration could cause "a tornado which would devastate the entire school system."[37] Apt as the meteorological metaphor may have been for Florida, Ervin's logic was flawed. If defiant public opinion was strong enough—and reason enough—simply to delay integration, then that hard-core resistance might never change. As for actually implementing *Brown*, Ervin's plan was a "blueprint for intransigence,"[38] a series of legal maneuvers so complicated that they would have taken decades or more to achieve integration. Clearly, Florida's official approach to integration was simply to delay. The skewed reporting of the survey results implied as much, but the brief itself confirmed it. Even a year later, in a speech in Miami, Ervin contended that "gradualism was the only answer" to integration.[39]

While awaiting the Court's response to the Ervin brief, Johns completed his term as acting governor. In the fall of 1954, he hosted a small, informal meeting of the Northern Club, which was composed of north Florida senators, the majority of them Pork Choppers. They met at Johns' request to initiate and get the backing of their new members. The club decided to vote as a bloc against reapportionment in the upcoming legislative session, and they divided up the chairmanships of the major Senate committees, with Johns given the chair of the powerful Finance and Taxation Committee.[40]

In December 1954 Johns left office, saying that his fifteen-month term had created "a boom in all directions" and had demonstrated the wisdom of using the "experience of Senate leadership as a backstop for the chief executive."[41] In one of his last statements as acting governor, Johns also told the press that when he returned to the Senate the following spring, he would "introduce and fight for legislation to create a state FBI."[42]

·

Johns' "state FBI" would collide with the goal of one of his contemporaries, Virgil Hawkins. Since childhood, Hawkins had wanted to attend the University of Florida and become an attorney. Despite numerous obstacles, he found hardships to be a catalyst. He grew up in the racist climate of Lake County and lived only twelve miles from Groveland, scene of the infamous 1949 rape case in which the local sheriff, Willis McCall, shot two of the African American defendants. Lake County was also well known as Ku Klux Klan territory.[43]

Virgil Hawkins Jr. had seven siblings, all the children of an industrious African Methodist Episcopal (AME) minister. Virgil Hawkins Sr., after enduring dangerous work in a clay mine, had bought a ten-acre homestead in 1895 before marrying Josephine Brown, the daughter of an AME minister. To supplement their modest earnings from the church and their farm, the family ran a small store near their home. Josephine also washed and ironed white people's clothes, and the whole family worked picking oranges and skinning the bark from pine trees for turpentine. Young Virgil hated the pine tree work in particular; it was dreary, backbreaking labor. He wanted to earn a living with his mind, with words, for he loved to talk.[44]

He also listened. As a young boy, he had accompanied his father to court when two of their church members had been arrested for gambling. The white judge asked the accused men if they were guilty or not. Young Hawkins soon realized that the men "didn't know what the word 'guilty' meant."[45] They received a six-month jail sentence for a ten-cent gambling game. At other times, Hawkins listened when women came to his father with their problems, usually because a husband was in jail for a petty crime. The senior Hawkins would tell the women to pray and not to waste their money on cheating lawyers, but his son noticed that the women with lawyers got their husbands back a lot sooner than the ones who just prayed. It seemed to him that lawyers could protect African Americans better than ministers could, so young Hawkins decided that he would go to UF and become an attorney. He had heard that judges and the best lawyers went there. Thus his dream of attending UF took root.[46]

When Hawkins was about fourteen years old, his goal was reinforced after his cousin was lynched by a white mob. The terrorists forced Hawkins' uncle to watch as they lynched his son and then fired at his dead body. In a separate act of violence, a white neighbor killed another uncle after the men argued over a farm animal. After his cousin's lynching, Hawkins decided that he would become a civil rights attorney and defend other African Americans against white supremacists. Hawkins' father, although not initially pleased with his son's decision, soon began to refer to him proudly as "my little lawyer."[47]

Unfortunately, Hawkins' educational opportunities in Lake County were limited, despite his parents' best efforts. Along with their neighbors, Reverend and Mrs. Hawkins raised enough money to build a school near the family farm. With matching funds from the Rosenwald Foundation, they opened the two-room Okahumpka School in 1917 and hired a teacher, giving local African American children more education than was available in many areas in early-twentieth-century Florida. The school offered classes only through the tenth grade, and Hawkins subsequently attended Edward Waters College, more than one hundred miles away in Jacksonville. While living in the city, he observed local court proceedings and saw that African Americans seldom received effective legal representation. Hawkins graduated with his high school diploma in 1930 and went on to study at Lincoln University in Pennsylvania. After a year he had to return home to make money, not an easy task during the depression years.[48]

Back in Florida, Hawkins found the first job that allowed him to earn a living with words: selling life insurance for the Afro-American Life Insurance Company. He also married Ida Frazier, a teacher from Ocoee, a small town twenty-five miles southeast of Okahumpka. Hawkins became a teacher himself at nearby Groveland Elementary School and later served as the school's principal. He worked there for a number of years, commuting one hundred miles a day from his home in Ocala. Later, he became public relations director at Edward Waters College in Jacksonville and then moved on to the same position at Bethune-Cookman College (BCC) in Daytona Beach.[49]

BCC was the perfect place for Hawkins. Founded by Mary McLeod Bethune, the private African American college had become a vibrant community of faculty and students that fostered social activism. Thus Hawkins was surrounded by young African Americans who were passionate about civil rights. As he worked there and took courses to finish his bachelor's degree in public relations, he often talked to the students late into the evening and then resumed his public relations duties during the day. Despite his being almost forty years old, his boyhood dream was revived. He decided that he would go to law school, but not by taking the state's tuition handout and going north to school (a common practice of southern states that maintained segregation in higher education). He would apply to UF, which he and his family had supported with their taxes for years; he would also remain near his and his wife's families.[50]

In May 1949 UF rejected Hawkins' application, along with those of four other African Americans applying to graduate programs. Seven months later, the state reacted by approving the establishment of a law school as well as graduate programs in mechanical engineering, agriculture, and pharmacy at Florida Agricultural and Mechanical University (FAMU). Although the other applicants did not continue to pursue a legal remedy, Hawkins did.[51]

With the help of an attorney, Hawkins asked Florida's Supreme Court to require the Board of Control (the agency overseeing Florida's state universities) to admit him to the UF law school. From a lawyer's point of view, Hawkins was an excellent plaintiff: cheerful, excited about the case, middle aged, and employed. He also had a supportive wife but no children who could be harmed. Above all, he was tenacious, or, as attorney Horace Hill explained, "Virgil root[ed] in. He [had] a grip like a pit bull."[52]

Alex Akerman, a white attorney from Orlando, was Hawkins' first lawyer. Hawkins soon switched to Hill when the case became mired in the state courts and Akerman was called to military service. Hill, an African American attorney from Daytona Beach, agreed with Hawkins' desire to pursue justice through every level of the court system.[53]

In 1950, the case reached the Florida Supreme Court, where justices literally turned their backs on Hill as he argued the case before them. As he recalled, "I was arguing to just the curtain."[54] The Board of Control metaphorically turned its back on Hawkins also, offering him two equally unacceptable methods for getting his legal education: the state would pay his tuition at an out-of-state law school, or he could attend the newly created law school at FAMU. However, as part of the second approach, the court would allow Hawkins to attend UF as a FAMU student, until FAMU's law school was built. Given the time needed for construction, Hawkins would receive most of his legal training at UF, but his court case would end, thus delaying UF integration for several years or longer. Hawkins rejected both approaches, insisting that, as a Florida citizen and taxpayer, he should not have to leave his home state to get his education and that the newly created FAMU law school was in no way equal to that of UF. The Florida Supreme Court found that the new school, although it existed primarily on paper at that point, was equal to UF.[55]

Florida's official response to the Hawkins case was similar to Texas' initial reaction in *Sweatt v. Painter*. The state rented a few rooms in Houston in 1946, hired two African American attorneys as faculty, and designated the new Prairie View Law School as a separate but equal facility. Two years later, in *Sipuel v. Oklahoma State Board of Regents*, the Board of Regents argued that a roped-off section of the capitol building with three faculty members was equal to the University of Oklahoma School of Law. In 1949, six months after Hawkins was rejected by UF, the Oklahoma Board of Regents' response to George McLaurin's suit was to allow him to enroll at the University of Oklahoma's graduate school, but he was then segregated in a separate anteroom outside his classroom as well as being limited to isolated areas of the library and cafeteria.[56] While McLaurin found his segregation "strange and humiliating," Hawkins' reaction, even years later, to the Florida Supreme Court's ruling was indignation: "You mean to tell me that a brand-new, half-baked law school would be as good as UF, the school where judges went? Did they think I was stupid?"[57]

A year later, in 1951, Hawkins was before the Florida Supreme Court again, claiming that the FAMU law school was unequal and thus violated his Fourteenth Amendment rights to equal protection. The court disagreed and refused to relinquish jurisdiction over the case. In 1952, Hawkins, now with a bachelor of science degree from Bethune-Cookman College, was before the court for the third time, asking for admission to UF and, failing that, for dismissal of the case so that the U.S. Supreme Court might hear the suit. In August of 1952, the Florida court dismissed the case.[58]

While Hawkins sought solutions through the courts, he encountered other problems. Once the UF case began to generate publicity, he received numerous death threats from segregationists. Living like a refugee in his own country, he slept some nights at the homes of friends and family and some in his apartment in Daytona Beach. When the threats were particularly graphic or frequent, he hid underneath his family's or friends' houses. His sister, Hallie, begged him to end the nightmare, telling him that anyone whose last name was Hawkins was in danger. Throughout most of the 1950s, his wife, Ida, feared not only for their lives but also for her teaching job in Lake County, so they pretended to be divorced and saw each other only at night.[59]

He also received hate mail, vicious letters with recurring lines: "Your daddy was a monkey, and you're a nigger; why would we want to go to school with an ape?"[60] The letters stung, but so did the responses of some of his community. When conservative African Americans said that he was going too far in his fight to integrate the UF law school, he was certainly disappointed. However, when one minister insisted that Hawkins' deceased father would have been ashamed of his son, he was deeply hurt.[61]

By 1953, while the death threats and hate mail that had jeopardized Hawkins' goal in previous years continued, their effects lessened. His family had begun to encourage him to continue his fight to attend UF. Although a previous employer had fired him for continuing the UF lawsuit, his current employer, BCC, stood by him. Even when a wealthy white patron offered sixty thousand dollars to fire Hawkins, BCC's president, Richard Moore, told the college's benefactor: "Keep it. We'll get by without your money."[62] Mary McLeod Bethune had become Hawkins' personal advocate. She inspired him, saying: "I want you to fight until it's over. Never stop. If you stop now, it might be a generation before somebody else comes along to take up the fight. Why not this generation?"[63]

For a time, Hawkins also had the support of Ed Davis and the Florida State Teachers Association (FSTA). Davis, a former teacher and principal from Ocala, was a state NAACP officer as well as a former president of FSTA, a professional organization for African American educators in Florida. They raised money for Hawkins' legal costs, as did Harry T. Moore, the outspoken coordinator for the Florida NAACP. When Moore and his wife were assassinated in a dynamite blast to their home, not only did Florida lose a civil rights champion but Hawkins also lost a strong ally. Davis continued his and Moore's work with FSTA through a group he chaired, known as the Steering Committee, which offered to help with legal expenses. Other than the money promised by the Steering Committee, Hawkins' only financial help came from church donations, small amounts given mostly by noneducated African Americans. Notably, his own denomination (African Methodist Episcopal) made no contribution.[64]

By 1954 it was clear that his difficulties had not really ended but rather had taken on an additional dimension: financial hardship. Although the Florida Supreme Court's dismissal of his case was a legal victory that allowed him to petition the U.S. Supreme Court, a case before the high court meant greater expenses. Legal costs had already strained Hawkins' modest salary, and his wife's earnings as a teacher were small. He could not convince a bank to give him a loan, and in 1953 his troubles with the Internal Revenue Service began. Hawkins had not paid all of his income taxes because BCC had not withheld enough money from his salary, and he could not pay the deficit. Soon, his meager assets were at risk.[65]

Fortunately, Hawkins received some good news in the spring of 1954. On May 24, 1954, one week after the *Brown* decision, the U.S. Supreme Court vacated the Florida court's ruling in *Hawkins v. Board of Control* and returned the case to the Florida court in light of *Brown*. Virgil Hawkins was overjoyed. When he heard the ruling, he hugged his wife and laughed out loud with his attorneys. He believed that his long nightmare was finally over and his dream was coming true; even though he was in his late forties, he was sure that he was on his way to UF.[66]

•

Meanwhile, Charley Johns was back in the Senate, still a power broker. He tried for a second time to pass a bill to create an investigative committee or a state FBI as a way to fight integration. The bill failed again. Clearly, Johns needed a different marketing strategy to create what would later become known as the Johns Committee.[67]

While Johns was recuperating from the 1955 session, Hawkins' case, now back with the Florida Supreme Court, was delayed. Although conceding that UF must admit Hawkins, the court withheld its ruling until the U.S. Supreme Court rendered its *Brown II* decision in May of 1955. That ruling, while requiring "all deliberate speed"[68] toward integration, was really a compromise with segregationists because it allowed officials to take local circumstances into account. This concession gave the Florida court another way to delay, as it contended that Hawkins' admission would create "public mischief" (violence), based on a hearing and subsequent report by circuit judge John Murphree. Meanwhile, the Board of Control commissioned another survey to determine if integrating UF would create "public mischief." The survey results showed that students were *not* significantly opposed to integration at UF or FSU. In November of 1955, Hawkins appealed the Florida ruling to the U.S. Supreme Court. On March 12, 1956, seven years after Hawkins had first applied to UF, the U.S. Supreme Court ordered his "prompt admission" to the university.[69] Florida's delay strategy had failed.

The spring and summer of 1956 soon became a desperate time for segregationists. First, the *Hawkins* ruling came during a volatile gubernatorial campaign in which the case and integration became a major issue. When a political newcomer and rabid segregationist, Sumter Lowry, accused the other candidates of avoiding the integration issue, they suddenly became very vocal in supporting segregation. On the day that the *Hawkins* decision was announced, Governor Collins responded in a press release by telling Floridians: "Every legal recourse will be followed to avoid integration. . . . We will not surrender in our battle to protect our State's customs and traditions."[70] Collins' major opponent, former governor Fuller Warren, also was not above using the *Hawkins* case. He even sent a telegram to the Board of Control, accusing Hawkins of beating two children at Groveland Elementary in the 1940s. Hawkins denied the accusations and later said, "All the candidates seemed to . . . [be] running against me."[71] With the candidates trying to best each other as defenders of segregation, the *St. Petersburg Times* characterized the governor's race as "rolling along like a segregation surrey with a lunatic fringe on top."[72]

Governor Collins convened a special conference on segregation ten days after the *Hawkins* decision was announced. The conference was attended by his cabinet, the Board of Control, all of the state university presidents, and some legislators and educators. The attendees adopted the new admission standards initiated by the Board of Control in December of 1955 and recommended that Ervin petition the U.S. Supreme Court to rehear the *Hawkins* case. (The high court denied the petition a month later.) The conference attendees also advised Collins to establish a desegregation commission, and he appointed Judge L. L. Fabisinski of Pensacola to head this effort. The Fabisinski Committee worked diligently through the spring to create a legislative program for fighting integration legally and nonviolently. However, segregationists soon had another reason to fear that they were losing not only the battle for segregated schools but also for segregated transportation.[73]

Only three weeks after the Fabisinski Committee was formed, two FAMU coeds were arrested after being told that they could not remain in the nearly empty white section of a Tallahassee city bus. Two days later, twenty-three hundred FAMU students rallied and voted unanimously "in light of recent events in Montgomery"[74] to boycott city buses. The boycott spread throughout the city's African American community, which constituted the majority of bus patrons, and by July 1956 what had begun as a simple boycott had become a movement: there was no bus service in the state capital. When integrationists threatened to expand the boycott, Collins called a special session of the legislature to act upon the Fabisinski Committee's report. Collins also warned legislators that exceeding the Fabisinski suggestions for new anti-integration laws would weaken their legality.[75]

The Fabisinski Committee made four recommendations: (1) enact a pupil assignment law, allowing county officials to place students based upon individual needs and abilities; (2) pass a similar teacher assignment law; (3) empower the governor to regulate the use of public facilities to prevent violence; and (4) increase the governor's emergency powers. Legislators, desperate to pass strong anti-integration laws, ignored Collins' warning, proposing and creating laws that went beyond the Fabisinski recommendations. After passing a pupil assignment law and expanding the governor's emergency powers, segregationist legislators also introduced bills to establish state-supported private schools and to abolish public schools that were faced with integration.[76]

Segregationists then proposed an interposition resolution that erroneously insisted that no body of the federal government (for example, the U.S. Supreme Court) had the authority to oppose the acts of a state that had created that federal government. Thus the effect of the interposition resolution was to condemn the *Hawkins* and *Brown* decisions and support segregated education. The resolution passed the Senate by late July but then became deadlocked in the House. The stalemate gave Collins an opportunity to defeat the resolution, which he described as a "preposterous hoax": he simply adjourned the special session.[77]

While Johns and his colleagues had been working to pass the interposition resolution, he also began to see a way to pass his state FBI bill. Johns, always a clever backroom politician, simply prepared a new marketing strategy for the bill. His timing was perfect. Into the volatile climate of reactions to the Supreme Court decisions, the crisis created by the two-month-old Tallahassee bus boycott, and struggles between the governor and the legislature, Johns launched another incendiary element. Senate Bill 38, worded more broadly than its earlier versions, provided for a legislative committee to investigate "organizations advocating violence or . . . violation"[78] of state laws, which, of course, included segregation laws. Designated officially as the Florida Legislative Investigation Committee, the group soon became known as the Johns Committee. The final bill did not mention subversives (as prior versions had) or Communists. In other settings, however, Johns, capitalizing on residual hysteria from Senator Joe McCarthy's witch hunts, characterized integration as a Communist plot. Telling reporters that "there was . . . no doubt that Communist people [were] behind all of this racial agitation," Johns began to broker the public's fears of integration and Communism into power.[79] The bill also did not mention the NAACP by name, for fear of legal repercussions. However, Senator Dewey Johnson, one of the bill's sponsors and a future Johns Committee member, admitted to the press that he could think of no other organization that the bill "would fit."[80]

Because of its recent civil rights litigation (particularly the *Brown* and *Hawkins* cases) and its provision of some financial and legal support for the bus boycott, the NAACP was already a favorite target of Florida's segregationist legislators. Also, only six weeks before Johns introduced his bill, the NAACP's chief counsel, Thurgood Marshall, told the organization's national convention that Florida was a target state because its political leaders would not even "consider the possibility of desegregating."[81] Almost simultaneously with Marshall's remarks, six parents in Miami filed a school desegregation suit under the auspices of the NAACP. Shortly after that, the Miami NAACP began to plan a bus suit as well. Thus, Johns designed his bill to respond to these threats and at the same time to pander to two of his colleagues' fears: integration and Communism.[82]

The Senate passed the bill on July 25, 1956, but the bill had less support in the House. Representative Jack Musselman, although a future Johns Committee member, had expressed concerns about the composition of an investigation committee to Governor Collins and to Ted David, speaker of the House, before the legislative session began. Musselman stressed that any such committee should be composed of "stable, moderate" legislators, ones "not easily susceptible to mob or emotional influence and who would not be open to attack because of previous radical statements in either direction."[83] As the end of the special session drew near, the House Rules Committee refused to support Johns' bill and, in the first concerted criticism of it, Representative Lacey Mahon from Jacksonville predicted that the bill would "open the way for 'witch hunts' [because] it was broad enough to provide for investigation of anything that might come along."[84] Unfortunately, the House ignored both Mahon's and the Rules Committee's warnings. On August 1, 1956, the bill passed, 72 to 15, a bare two-thirds majority. Referring to Johns' bill as a legislative and not an executive branch issue, Collins allowed the bill to become law without his signature.[85] If only one representative had voted against the bill, the Johns Committee would not have been established for at least another year. Florida's "little McCarthyism" had begun.

The first chair of the Johns Committee was Representative Henry Land, a real estate and insurance agent from Apopka who had served in the House since 1953. The freshman members of the committee were both from the House: Jack Musselman and J. B. Hopkins, attorneys from

Pompano Beach and Pensacola, respectively. In addition to Johns himself, other members were Senator John Rawls, an attorney from Marianna and senator for one prior term; Senator Dewey Johnson, an attorney from Quincy and legislator since 1938; and Representative Cliff Herrell, a real estate and insurance agent from Miami Springs, serving his second term in the House. Like Johns, both Rawls and Johnson were Pork Choppers, and Herrell, despite representing an urban, south Florida county, often voted with the Pork Chop Gang. Thus legislators with Pork Chopper and/or north Florida interests dominated the first Johns Committee.[86]

In their first meeting, committee members decided that their "staff should immediately secure all information available in other states and in Washington, DC relative to the National Association for the Advancement of Colored People."[87] The committee knew that the NAACP was under attack throughout the South. In addition to Florida, Texas and six other southern states had created legislative committees similar to the Johns Committee, and Texas opened its files to the committee. The same states also established commissions similar to the Fabisinski Committee, whose sole purpose was to devise legal methods to circumvent integration. Texas charged the NAACP with tax evasion; Georgia did the same and fined the organization twenty-five thousand dollars. Arkansas declared the NAACP tax delinquent and dissolved it. Six southern states prohibited state employees from being NAACP members, while five states required the NAACP to register as a corporation. Nine states demanded the association's membership lists. Finally, Arkansas, Georgia, Mississippi, South Carolina, Tennessee, and Virginia, in an effort to limit the association's access to the courts, established criminal punishments for barratry (soliciting or instigating lawsuits). An attorney convicted of barratry could be disbarred, and, since the NAACP was known for its successful litigation (particularly *Brown*), preventing the organization from sponsoring lawsuits would deprive it of its lifeblood.[88]

The committee's chief counsel, Mark Hawes, intended to pursue the barratry strategy. A former marine, he attended the UF law school on the G.I. bill and was admitted to the Florida Bar a year after Virgil Hawkins first applied to UF. Hawes had served in the criminal division of the attorney general's office, working on the Tallahassee police investigation of the local bus boycott before joining the Whitaker law firm in Tampa. Hawes thought that NAACP barratry convictions could also be used to slow down integration and to create a constitutional loophole of sorts. First, the barratry convictions would deprive many African Americans of legal help, forcing them to rely on their own financial resources. As a result, Hawes believed, the integration movement would be impeded. Furthermore, as he told legislators, "Placing these people on the same basis with everyone else . . . would not be discriminatory, and legislation which effected that end should withstand attack on Constitutional grounds."[89]

With the barratry strategy in mind, Hawes began to gather data on the NAACP from other states and Washington, D.C. He solicited numerous public officials and businesses for information on the organization and its attempts at integration, and his staff prepared reports on the *Hawkins* case. Furthermore, Hawes ordered the committee's full-time investigator, R. J. Strickland, to ask all police chiefs in Florida to examine NAACP bank accounts. Strickland had worked with Hawes on the police investigation of the Tallahassee bus boycott, and Hawes hoped that Strickland's information would show that the NAACP was the financial backer of integration suits in Florida. The first part of the committee's strategy would be to show that the NAACP—rather than the plaintiffs—controlled integration lawsuits, making it susceptible to charges of barratry. The barratry strategy was essentially the committee's only strategy in the first hearing.[90]

The second part of the committee's strategy (which was not implemented until the first Miami hearing) was to use a hunt for Communists as a way to attack the Florida NAACP, demanding that the organization release its membership lists and meeting minutes. These records would then be matched against the committee's lists of Communists that were obtained primarily from the U.S. attorney general's list of subversives created during the Truman administration and from the files of grand jury investigations held in Miami in the late 1940s and in 1954. That the committee's lists of Communists were inaccurate was of little concern during Florida's little McCarthyism. Although the Johns Committee could destroy careers and reputations with inaccurate lists, the NAACP with its integration lawsuits was the ultimate enemy in the eyes of committee members and had to be destroyed at any price. They did not mind if they labeled loyal citizens, especially NAACP members, as subversives in the process. If the Johns Committee could portray the NAACP as Communist influenced, it was but a short leap to show that the NAACP's push for integration was really a Communist plot. Charley Johns also knew that his colleagues in the legislature would continue to fund their fears—of both Communism and integration—and thereby extend the life and influence of his committee.[91]

Early in 1957, Mark Hawes made his first progress report to the committee as well as making final preparations for its first hearing. Two weeks before he questioned the first witness, Hawes reached his own conclusions about the NAACP: The organization was illegally instigating integration suits, had financed the *Hawkins* case, and had made a financial profit from its lawsuits for the past fifteen years. Hawes also admitted that the committee's "prov[ing] that the NAACP ha[d] committed . . . barratry [would] . . . depend . . . upon the testimony of witnesses."[92]

The committee subpoenaed NAACP officials to answer questions about their organization, scheduling hearings in Tallahassee and Miami for February. Committee chair Henry Land also solicited advice from Attorney General Ervin, asking if committee members would still have legislative immunity for their actions in Johns Committee proceedings. Ervin assured Land that, as an established part of state government, committee members were immune and that the committee would only exceed its legislative powers if it usurped the functions of the judicial or executive branches. Ervin added that, should it become necessary, he would also represent the committee in any civil suit that resulted from their investigations as he had other legislative committees. Anticipating some defiant witnesses, committee attorney Hawes asked Ervin if (and how) the committee could cite witnesses for contempt. Ervin explained to Hawes that the committee had no legal authority to cite directly but that either the House or the Senate could later cite witnesses for contempt, based upon the committee's recommendations, and then fine or jail the witnesses.[93]

•

With this last bit of advice, the Johns Committee was ready for its first four-day hearing in Tallahassee. Since Charley Johns was absent for half of that hearing, he and Hawkins did not meet until the last day of the hearing,[94] when Hawkins' determination to attend UF collided with Johns' scheme to stop integration and destroy the Florida NAACP.

# 2

## Virgil Hawkins

Pursuit of the Dream Continues

Attorney Mark Hawes' florid complexion became even more red when he was angry or frustrated, sometimes putting him at a disadvantage in the courtroom. Tall and heavyset, he compensated for his complexion by using his physical presence to intimidate witnesses and had so far built a reputation as a brutal but successful interrogator. However, Hawes was now struggling to control his frustration, and his face was turning a deep red. He was having a bad day, and it was only 10 a.m.[1]

It was also the first day of the Johns Committee's first hearing, February 4, 1957. As chief counsel, Hawes had already told the committee that the NAACP was controlling the *Hawkins* case. However, Virgil Hawkins, the first witness, was not cooperating with the Johns Committee's assault on integration; he was thwarting Hawes' barratry strategy and continuing the lawsuit to enter UF. Still, if Hawes' interrogation was not going well, it was not for lack of planning. His strategy was sound, and it hinged on one central question: Who controlled the Virgil Hawkins case? In order to answer that question, Hawes needed to know who paid the costs and who made the decisions in the case. If someone (or some group) other than Hawkins was in control of his case, then barratry (solicitation or instigation of lawsuits) was a distinct possibility and could lead to the disbarring of NAACP attorneys.[2]

•

The NAACP had worked to avoid barratry and ensure that their cases were properly managed. Typically, when a chapter leader contacted association headquarters on behalf of a prospective plaintiff, the staff would conduct a preliminary evaluation to determine if the case entailed not only racial discrimination but also a basic civil right and thus had potential for establishing a legal precedent. If so, the staff would then consider the practical issues of finances and the amount of local support available. If there was backing from the local African American community, the NAACP would proceed with legal advice and would sometimes organize fund-raising campaigns. Local branches raised money as well; for example, one Sunday per month in African American churches was sometimes devoted to collecting special offerings for an NAACP case. Although association attorneys and staff would do further research, the national office would advise the plaintiff to contact a local NAACP attorney for several reasons. First, most southern states required defendants to be represented by lawyers licensed in that state; second, if local attorneys were used, the NAACP could not be accused of being outside agitators; and third, NAACP headquarters lacked the funds, staff, and time to enter all local suits. The local attorneys would then receive advice from the national office.[3]

When the Tallahassee hearings began, Hawes focused immediately on the NAACP's financial role in the *Hawkins* case. Finances were a delicate area for the association because the committee did, in fact, have evidence that the NAACP had paid legal costs and solicited contributions for the *Hawkins* case. Still, when asked about the arrangements for retaining and paying attorneys, Hawkins made it clear that he personally retained his previous attorney, Alex Akerman, and agreed to pay him, but Hawkins didn't recall how much he had paid. He also testified that the primary responsibility for paying Akerman fell to Hawkins himself—not to the Steering Committee (a fund-raising group from the Florida State Teachers Association and not affiliated with the NAACP). When Hawes asked how the Steering Committee raised money, Hawkins cleverly replied that he had nothing to do with their fund-raising methods. When Hawes later asked if the NAACP paid any of the case's expenses, Hawkins said that he never asked the Steering Committee which organizations made donations.[4]

Hawes then shifted his approach, asking how much Hawkins had agreed to pay his present attorney, Horace Hill. Hawkins would not name a specific amount. However, when Hawes asked if the NAACP had agreed to pay Hawkins' attorney fees, his reply was unequivocal: "The NAACP has never agreed to pay anything for me."[5] When Hawes persisted, asking the same question again, Hawkins said emphatically, "No organization has paid any money to my counsel for me."[6] Hawes was only able to achieve a standoff between himself and his witness, with Hawkins repeatedly insisting that he did not know the specific amount paid. When Hawes finally asked if it was true that Hawkins knew little about the financing of his case, he simply said yes but, again, would not elaborate. However, even in saying yes, Hawkins annoyed Hawes and the Johns Committee even further by consulting with Horace Hill for several minutes, which was apparently too long for the committee. Chair Henry Land told Hawkins that he could not even ask Hill to clarify any legal issues.[7]

Hawes then immediately shifted the full focus of his interrogation to the NAACP, asking if Hawkins had an agreement with them about financing his case. Hawkins became more assertive again, saying that he had already answered that question, he had no agreement with the NAACP to pay anything, and it was the second time he had been asked the identical question. Hawes persisted, again asking if the NAACP had paid any of Hawkins' legal costs, and Hawkins again replied: "I have answered that question. For the third time, no."[8] Hawes still continued to ask if the NAACP had ever paid Hawkins any money or had its attorneys from the national office represent him, which Hawkins flatly denied. Hawes then attempted to ask if the NAACP Legal Defense Fund had ever contributed any money, but Hawkins cut him off, saying: "For the fourth time, no sir."[9] When Hawes asked if Hawkins had ever received any money from the Florida branch of the NAACP Legal Defense Fund, he was more defiant: "No, no. That's the NAACP again, isn't it? No, no!"[10] Hawes then asked for a short recess and excused Hawkins for the rest of the day.[11]

Ed Davis followed Hawkins as the next witness and was repeatedly asked many of the same questions. Since Davis was the chair of the Steering Committee and a former president of FSTA, many of those questions were barratry related. Much to Hawes' disappointment, Davis testified that the Steering Committee retained Horace Hill but not Akerman, and that the NAACP had no role in retaining Hill and no agreement with the Steering Committee about financing the case.[12]

The next witness was William Fordham, immediate past president of the Florida NAACP. He had also served as attorney for the Florida NAACP prior to being state president and had known Virgil Hawkins for many years because Hawkins was a friend of Fordham's aunt. Unfortunately, when Hawes produced six checks to Hill, drawn on a Florida NAACP bank account, Fordham was forced to admit that the Florida NAACP paid some of Hill's fees. When Hawes asked about the Florida NAACP's records, Fordham said that the branches' membership records were in New York rather than Florida but that the meeting minutes from the annual state conference were still in Miami with the state secretary, Ruth Perry.[13]

When Hawes asked how the NAACP determined which students would file integration suits, Fordham replied, "We don't stir up litigation. The individual comes to us." Then, in a surprising move, Fordham added: "So if you want to get some information to outlaw us, we can go ahead and stipulate on that. You've got enough of that already."[14] Hawes, apparently surprised, asked if Fordham thought that the Johns Committee had sufficient information at that point to outlaw the Florida NAACP. When Fordham said yes, Hawes then asked if the Florida NAACP had a permit to solicit funds. When Fordham said they did not, Hawes asked a few questions about financial accountability within the state organization but then dismissed Fordham for the rest of the hearing.[15]

Horace Hill, the next witness, had been practicing law since 1948, but Hawes had set a trap for the experienced attorney. Hawes first showed Hill a series of letters, bills, invoices, and checks. Some of the documents, such as checks drawn on NAACP bank accounts, were subpoenaed by Hawes from two banks in Tampa. However, much to Hill's surprise, the Johns Committee also had his entire file on the *Hawkins* case. Nothing in the file had been obtained through subpoena. Thus the committee had his complete correspondence with the national NAACP office about the case, but, most incriminating of all, were five checks written to Hill from the Florida NAACP Legal Defense Fund. Hill responded that the correspondence only showed that he had collaborated with the national office, but he was forced to admit that the checks were for the *Hawkins* case. When Hawes asked if one of the documents came directly from Hill's own files, he was unable to restrain his exasperation over his files being violated and replied: "You would know better than I."[16] Hill then added a qualifying explanation: since no one had asked his permission to examine his files and to make copies of them, he could not vouch for the source or legitimacy of

Hawes' documents. Hawes, stymied again, soon concluded his interrogation of Hill.[17]

How the committee acquired copies of Hill's documents is unclear. One Johns Committee investigator did say that some of them were obtained "by chance" but offered no further explanation. However, an undated, anonymous committee memo, written after 1955, referred to Hill's legal briefs and documents found "in the firm,"[18] which could be taken to mean in the office of Horace Hill. The committee's staff also had access to the files of the Alabama and Texas attorneys general as well as Attorney General Ervin's records. In referring to the Texas files, Hawes had told the committee: "Substantial portions of the Florida NAACP records can be reconstructed from the copies of the records from the Texas file."[19] Johns Committee members and staff also discussed obtaining search warrants for the Tampa NAACP office and for Hawkins' office at Bethune-Cookman College, but whether or not the committee followed through remains unclear.[20]

After the first day of the hearings ended, Hawkins attended a meeting that only served to emphasize his ties to the NAACP. He spoke briefly to members and supporters of the Inter-Civic Council, a Tallahassee group that had kept the local bus boycott viable with help from the NAACP. Hawkins boldly told the eight hundred attendees that UF's repeated refusals to admit him had only ensured that he would continue his legal battle.[21]

When Hawkins was recalled to testify at the outset of the second day of the hearings, Hawes shifted to the issue of who made the decisions in the *Hawkins* case, asking if Hawkins' agreement with his attorneys was not just an authorization for them to use his name and represent him on the Steering Committee's behalf. Hawkins objected, insisting that he never "offered [himself] . . . as an exhibit into something they [the Steering Committee] could use."[22] Hawes then came to the pivotal decision in the case—Hawkins' desire to go to UF law school—and asked why he wanted to attend UF. After Hawkins gave his reasons, Hawes countered that they were the same ones given by his NAACP attorneys, implying that the reasons were not Hawkins' but the NAACP's. Hawkins pointed out that he did not know what the attorneys said because he was not in court and had not read the briefs. He then reminded Hawes that he asked why Hawkins wanted to attend UF, not what was said by someone else.[23]

Clearly hoping to trap or confuse Hawkins, Hawes next had the court reporter read a question from the previous day's testimony about the Florida NAACP Legal Defense Fund giving Hawkins money and his emphatic reply that they had not. However, Hawkins used this opportunity to clarify his prior testimony, explaining that, when the UF case was in the newspapers, everyone to whom he owed money began to pressure him. Also, during the 1956 governor's race, he was under pressure because Fuller Warren accused him of beating two children when he taught at Groveland Elementary School. Thus Hawkins told Ed Davis that he needed a loan, and Davis sent him a check.[24] Hawkins agreed to repay the loan in sixty days.[25]

Most likely in an attempt to embarrass or intimidate Hawkins by exposing personal information, Hawes next delved into Hawkins' finances, asking the amount of his and his wife's annual salaries, which totaled about seven thousand dollars. However, when Hawes asked the amount of their joint income as reported on their 1956 tax return, Hawkins said that he did not remember and did not have his files to refer to. Then, seizing the opportunity to revisit the issue of the committee's violation of his attorney's files, Hawkins made a direct request of Hawes, saying: "If you have it [Hawkins' tax return], I wish you'd give it to me." Hawes ignored the request.[26]

When Senator Rawls wondered why Hawkins could not pay his attorney directly from a seven-thousand-dollar income, Hawkins asserted that he had paid because he had received donations through his speaking engagements. Hawes then became annoyed, since he had already asked Hawkins if he paid Hill personally. However, Hawkins, showing a lawyer-like ability to parse words, contended that Hawes had not used the word "personally." Hawes, frustrated by Hawkins' use of semantics, said that he had asked if paying was Hawkins' primary responsibility, but Hawkins countered that the responsibility was still primarily his because, when he hired Hill, Hawkins did not know if the Steering Committee would be able to raise any funds. Hawes then lost his professional composure, saying, "You are trying to seize on every little cute word that you can in order to evade truthfully answering this Committee."[27] Hawkins replied that if Hawes thought that he (Hawkins) was evading the truth, Hawes should say so and "ask [him] something."[28] Hawes soon concluded his interrogation of Hawkins.[29]

After being excused for the rest of the day, Hawkins asked Chair Henry Land if he knew how long Hawkins would have to stay in Tallahassee. He told Land that the Johns Committee had given him barely enough money for transportation and one night's stay and so far he would have to pay for three nights and was losing salary as well. Land, attempting to be dismissive, said that the committee did not know how long Hawkins would be in town, but Hawkins persisted, saying, "You haven't the slightest idea?" and was told no.[30]

On the fourth and final day of the hearings,[31] there were only two witnesses: Horace Hill and Virgil Hawkins. Hawes attempted to set another trap for Hill. First, Hawes showed Hill the agreement between himself and the Steering Committee, most likely taken from Hill's files without his permission, and he was forced to admit that he represented the Steering Committee because the document clearly stated that he would "represent the Committee aforementioned in the University of Florida cases in the State Supreme Court and the United States Supreme Court."[32] However, the document also showed that Hill, rather than the NAACP, really was in control of the case because the agreement was for representation at both the state and federal levels. Then, in a seemingly benign line of questioning, Hawes sprung his trap, asking if the Steering Committee functioned as an intermediary between Hill and his clients. Hill fell into the trap, saying: "At times they did, sir."[33] Hawes then cited the section of the state's Code of Ethics that prohibits attorneys from using intermediaries when dealing with clients. All Hill could say was that he believed that he had abided by the code.[34]

Not letting up, Hawes produced a bill from Hill's files that noted one hundred dollars as having been paid to him. Hill was forced to admit that it was NAACP money. Hawes next tried to show that Hill had held the Florida and national NAACP accountable for his fees. Hawes produced correspondence from 1955, when Hill had withheld the *Hawkins* case files from the state and national organization until his back fees were paid. After Hill twice refused to admit that the correspondence showed that he had a financial understanding with the NAACP, Charley Johns interrupted, saying that Hill was "fast perjuring himself and [should know] the penalties for such perjury."[35] However, Hill continued to refuse to admit to any understanding with the NAACP.[36]

The final question for Hill was from Charley Johns, asking if Hill was or had been a Communist Party member, to which Hill firmly replied that he never had been nor would be a member. This was only the second time that any Johns Committee member or staff had asked that question during the hearing.[37]

Virgil Hawkins, the first witness in the hearing, was recalled as the last witness. Hawes fared no better with Hawkins on the last day than the first. When Hawes asked why Hawkins had not enrolled at UF via Florida A&M University (FAMU), he made it clear that, in the pursuit of his dream, he would not accept an inferior offer from the state. When Hawes wanted to know if anyone—the NAACP, Davis, or Harry T. Moore—had advised Hawkins to reject that offer, he insisted that the rejection was "his own idea."[38]

Hawes then tried a softer approach, first saying, "We've got so close to the truth that we might as well get it out here, and let's go home."[39] He then repeatedly pressured Hawkins to say that the Steering Committee really made the decisions in the case. Three times Hawkins said no. Finally, he ended his testimony defiantly, saying, "They didn't tell me what to do or what not to do. I made my own decisions in this case."[40] Clearly, another Hawkins' decision would be to continue the UF case, despite his being targeted and interrogated by the Johns Committee.

Charley Johns then asked if Hawkins was a Communist. Hawkins said no and was excused. However, Hawes was not quite finished. In preparation for the upcoming Miami hearings, he entered fifteen exhibits into the record, including a letter from Ruth Perry, secretary of the Florida NAACP, about potential contributors. The Johns Committee then adjourned the Tallahassee hearings. Later that day, committee member Senator John Rawls told reporters that the committee had proof that the NAACP had been "going out and actively soliciting litigants and money to develop lawsuits."[41] Two weeks later, Attorney General Richard Ervin even asked the Florida Supreme Court to delay its ruling in the *Hawkins* case because of testimony given during the hearings. However, the court rejected Ervin's request.[42]

A month later, while updating the legislature on the Tallahassee hearings, Hawes told lawmakers that Virgil Hawkins "had virtually no control over"[43] his case. Hawes also recommended that a copy of the hearing transcripts be given to the Florida Bar to determine if any NAACP attorneys were guilty of ethics violations.[44]

Charley Johns then introduced a package of five bills into the Senate. Since Florida had no laws forbidding an organization from financing or sponsoring lawsuits, four of the bills focused on barratry and the NAACP without mentioning the organization by name. The committee's proposed legislation defined barratry, made soliciting lawsuits illegal, forbade lawyers hired by an association from representing individual members, and prohibited groups who were not plaintiffs from financing litigation. Another bill gave the attorney general the power to examine the records of most Florida organizations. Many legislators found the bill troubling because it meant that the membership, policy, and financial records of any Florida church, lodge, or club would be available for inspection. However, when Representative Fred Karl of Daytona Beach was the only one to vote against the bill, his opponents left a note on his desk advising him that he was now an honorary NAACP member. The final bill extended the life of the Johns Committee for another two years and increased its powers to include the investigation of subversive organizations. Except for the Johns Committee bill, all others in the barratry package failed in the House because legislators feared that the bills were so broad that they could hurt other business, social, and fraternal groups.[45]

•

While the committee was preparing its barratry bills, Hawkins' case reached the Florida Supreme Court, which rejected the U.S. Supreme Court's demand for Hawkins' "prompt admission" to UF. The Florida court cited both Judge Murphree's report and the Board of Control's "public mischief" survey from the previous year, despite their contradicting each other. Although the Florida court acknowledged Hawkins' constitutional right to enter UF, it also affirmed its prerogative to determine when he would enter the university, ruling that Hawkins himself would have to prove that his admission would not cause "great public mischief."[46] Yet again, Hawkins appealed to the U.S. Supreme Court. Having no vehicle for executing its own rulings and faced with state officials who not only ignored their sworn duty to uphold the Constitution but also chose to defy the federal government, the Court instructed Hawkins in October

1957 to file suit where the Court had supervisory jurisdiction: a federal district court.[47] This approach also offered the great benefit of avoiding a federal-state crisis only three weeks after federal troops were sent to Little Rock, Arkansas, to end segregation riots there.

Meanwhile, Hawes followed through on his plan to report NAACP attorneys in Florida to the Florida Bar. In September of 1957, Hawes sent the transcripts from the Tallahassee hearings to the Florida Bar, where officials first decided that five NAACP attorneys had managed school integration suits unprofessionally. However, the Bar later decided that the lawyers were not guilty of ethics violations. Perhaps the Bar chose to let the Johns Committee confront the NAACP instead of having the Florida Bar drawn into a public dispute.[48]

Although the Florida Bar had avoided a dispute, Virgil Hawkins was soon drawn into a controversy that was personal. In December of 1957, his nephew, Melvin Hawkins Jr., was arrested in Lake County by its notorious sheriff, Willis McCall, for the alleged rape of a white woman. On Christmas Eve, Florida NAACP field secretary Robert Saunders and Tampa NAACP attorney Francisco Rodriquez met with Melvin Hawkins Sr. He explained that a friend of the Hawkins family had overheard McCall order one of his deputies to arrest the younger Hawkins because he was the nephew of "that nigger who was trying to get into the University of Florida."[49] At 11 p.m. that night, Saunders called Governor LeRoy Collins, persuading Mrs. Collins to wake him up. Collins talked with the senior Hawkins for almost an hour and promised him that his son would be safe. The younger Hawkins was released the next day and had no further problems with local law enforcement.[50]

In January of 1958, Virgil Hawkins and his attorneys appeared before federal district court judge Dozier DeVane. He first lectured them on what he had done to help "your people in Florida"[51] and commented that, if he had his way, African American students at UF would be required to post bonds to cover the inevitable damages that would ensue when they attended. He then ruled that he would not hear the case. However, the U.S. Court of Appeals for the Fifth Circuit overturned DeVane's ruling, compelling him to hear the case. Meanwhile, the Board of Control used a new requirement against Hawkins: a score of 250 or higher on an admissions test. The standard was retroactive, and Hawkins' score in August of

1956 had been 200; in 1949, when he first applied, there was no test score requirement.[52]

In May of 1958, after attorneys for both sides had presented their arguments to Judge DeVane, he asked Hawkins a pivotal question: Was he prepared to make a new application to UF, or would he seek admission through his original 1949 application? Hawkins took the first option because using his 1949 application would have meant an extended trial about his qualifications and whether he could be exempt from the new test standards, based on the 1949 requirements. This would have forced other qualified African Americans applicants to wait. He had recently included in his case a class action request to require UF to admit any qualified African Americans. By removing the question of his own qualifications, Hawkins forced the federal court to address the race issue directly.[53]

Hawkins' choice made Judge DeVane's ruling of June 18, 1958, possible: UF was prohibited from limiting graduate admissions to whites only. After four rulings from the Florida Supreme Court, three from the U.S. Supreme Court, and three federal court reviews,[54] justice in higher education was rendered to all African Americans in Florida—except Virgil Hawkins. The man who was the first in line to enter UF's law school had stepped out of that line, allowing other African Americans to walk through the doors of UF.

Hawkins later explained his choice. Not only did he wish to prevent other African Americans from being delayed by his reapplying to UF, he also was worn down by his long battle and had little money. Also he wanted to honor his wife's request to end the case because he loved her, and she had continuously supported his quest for nine long years. Hawkins' goal of receiving his law degree from UF was ended for him—although it was beginning for the African Americans who would benefit from his fight. On August 26, 1958, only three months after Hawkins' selfless decision, George Starke became the only African American among UF's twelve thousand students and was admitted to the UF law school. On September 15 while he was waiting in line to register, he received a welcoming handshake from one of UF's student representatives, David Levy.[55] One wonders if Levy thought that George Starke was Virgil Hawkins.

Although he experienced no demonstrable opposition, Starke left UF in the fall of 1958. Fortunately, Hawkins' sacrifice was recognized at the same time. At the annual convention of the Florida State Conference, the NAACP made Hawkins honorary chair of the convention, held, appropriately enough, on the campus of Bethune-Cookman College. Ruby Hurley, southeast regional secretary, also presented Hawkins with an award.[56]

·

A year later, Hawkins started a new life in Massachusetts. He entered Boston University's School of Public Relations at the age of fifty-two and earned a master's degree in public relations. In 1961 Hawkins received a partial scholarship to the New England College of Law. Driving a cab, waiting on tables, and working as a night janitor at the Harvard Club to meet expenses—sometimes even working during the day and attending class at night—he persevered. Meanwhile in Florida, the *Hawkins* case bore fruit. As a FAMU undergraduate, George Willie Allen had been inspired by meeting Hawkins and became the first African American graduate of the UF law school in 1962. Three years later, Hawkins received his law degree in Boston. He was fifty-nine years old and ready to come home.[57]

When Hawkins returned to Florida with his law degree, he discovered that he would not be allowed to take the bar exam. His law school was not accredited by the American Bar Association (at that time a segregated organization) until four years after Hawkins graduated. Thus, he was ineligible. The man who had fought so many battles with the state of Florida chose not to fight this one. At an age that most would consider close to retirement, Hawkins got a job with a grants program for the needy in Lake County and bought a small home in Leesburg. He then became director of the agency administering the grants program.[58]

Although he was no longer attempting to practice law, Hawkins soon found himself at the center of another controversy. Segregationists in Lake County pressured county officials to fire Hawkins. However, he filed a complaint with the Office of Economic Opportunity's Civil Rights Division in Atlanta. The chief of that division was none other than Robert Saunders, former head of the Florida NAACP. When Saunders' staff investigated, they found that Hawkins was indeed discriminated against because of the UF case, and they were able to save his job. During this time, Hawkins tried to suppress his desire to practice law, but it would not die. Approaching seventy, Hawkins appealed to the Florida Bar. They relented:

If he could pass the bar exam, he could practice in Florida. He tried but could not pass the exam; he had been out of school too long.[59]

Had it not been for the brother of former attorney general Richard Ervin, Hawkins' quest might have ended there. In 1974, the Florida Supreme Court admitted Ben Ervin (whose brother was by now a Florida Supreme Court justice) to the Bar, even though Ben Ervin had failed the bar exam four times. Ben Ervin had argued that, had he not been drafted, he would have begun law school in 1951, when he would still have been eligible for diploma privileges: admission to the Florida Bar upon graduation without taking the bar exam. Hawkins saw an opening—and surely the irony—in the Ben Ervin case. Richard Ervin had represented the state in the various *Hawkins* cases in the 1950s, and now his brother's case had revived Hawkins' goal. In November of 1975, Hawkins was again before the Florida Supreme Court, citing Ben Ervin's case as precedent and asking to be admitted directly to the Florida Bar. Two weeks before his seventieth birthday, Hawkins won his first case. In a unanimous ruling, and with the urging of Justice Ervin, the court admitted Virgil Hawkins to the Florida Bar.[60] Fifty-eight years after his quest began, his boyhood dream was finally realized.

Hawkins quit his ten-thousand-dollar-a-year job as director of consumer affairs for a community action agency and opened a law office in downtown Leesburg. Although most of his clients were people on welfare, he turned no one away. He was soon so busy that he "got . . . tired and didn't even know it."[61] The cumulative effects of operating a one-man law firm, as well as the paperwork, the research, and the pace of his profession, were too difficult for a man in his seventies. In 1980, he defended a man pro bono for aggravated assault and was found guilty of attorney errors. The Florida Bar then asked the Florida Supreme Court to suspend him. Once again, Hawkins was before the Supreme Court, this time as an attorney fighting to remain so. In November of 1983, he made a dramatic plea to the court: "On the 28th of this month, I'll be seventy-seven years old, and all of us know that, at age seventy-seven, the sand in the hourglass of time is swiftly running out. I would hate very much to be suspended on a little thing and leave here not a member of the Florida Bar."[62] Hawkins won his case, but he was reprimanded and put on probation for two years.[63]

Figure 2.1. Virgil Hawkins, ca. mid-1980s. State Archives of Florida, *Florida Memory*, http://floridamemory.com/items/show/36072.

Unfortunately, Hawkins had other problems. During his two-year probation, some of his opponents in the Lake County legal profession set up a scheme to undermine him: a person would come to Hawkins' office, posing as a potential client, and soon after he or she would file a legal proceeding against Hawkins. This happened repeatedly. As a colleague recalled years later: "Most of the attorneys in the area . . . [believed that] he never

Figure 2.2. Virgil Hawkins speaking with supporters during a recess in his disciplinary hearing before the Florida Supreme Court, November 1983. Don Stainer, State Archives of Florida, *Florida Memory*, http://floridamemory.com/items/show/14116.

belonged in the profession in the first place [and that] he wasn't a very good attorney . . . so therefore what happened to him was exactly what he deserved."[64] Hawkins also could not afford secretarial help and was not adept at paperwork or keeping track of bills. While he was dealing with diabetes and high blood pressure, he faced his ultimate legal challenge. In 1985, after mishandling some financial paperwork and funds for a relative's Veterans Administration benefits, Hawkins was forced to resign from the Florida Bar. He would spend the rest of his life paying restitution.[65]

Fortunately, later honors came to Hawkins. The Florida chapter of the National Bar Association (the country's oldest organization for African American attorneys and judges) changed its name to the Virgil Hawkins Florida chapter in the 1980s. In 1983, Florida State University (FSU) law students petitioned the legislature to name the new FSU law library after Hawkins, and state senator Carrie Meek sponsored the necessary bill. When he was told of the petition and Meek's bill, Hawkins said that it was "the proudest day of [his] life."[66] However, when the financial accusations against Hawkins began to emerge in 1984, Meek agreed to withdraw her bill in exchange for establishment of the Virgil Hawkins Fellowships for African American law students at both UF and FSU. The scholarships not only helped law students but also allowed the state to save face and keep Hawkins' name off the library building. Many of the fellowship recipients, knowing nothing of Hawkins' history, thought he was a wealthy man who wanted to help African American law students.[67]

In later years, when Hawkins spoke to law classes, many students were amazed to hear his story. "They think it was always like it is now," he explained. "They think that when you're born, you're born in a posture of instant success."[68] Hawkins also found that students did not understand why they should be grateful to the "Uncle Toms" of the past. As he saw it, those Uncle Toms "were fighting but at the same time bowing and accommodating to the situation so that when the sun started shining, the black man could stand up like a palm tree. They were taking all that for their ancestry. . . . If they could take those lashes on the back, I could take the verbal lashes. Each of us has to do the best we can in our time."[69] Hawkins also talked of writing a book about his thirty-year battle to be an attorney. He kept files of yellowed newspaper clippings, planning to use them in a book about his triumphs, not his failures. A year before his death from kidney failure on February 11, 1988, Hawkins reviewed his eighty years and summarized his life: "I know what I did. I integrated schools in Florida. No one can take that away from me."[70]

Three months after Hawkins' death, and in an act unprecedented in U.S. history, the Florida Bar reinstated Hawkins' license posthumously. The following year, the legislature agreed to name UF's civil legal clinic after Hawkins. Now third-year law students, having received the education that Hawkins sought, represent indigent clients in his name. Two years later Hawkins was finally recognized in his hometown of Okahumpka. Near the three-year anniversary of his death, civil rights leaders and Hawkins' friends dedicated a seven-foot granite monument to him, honoring his integration of the UF law school.[71]

In 1999, Hawkins received further recognition, albeit circuitous. The FAMU law school, founded in 1950 only to keep Hawkins out of UF, had been closed in 1968. FAMU's law books were subsequently given to the new law school at FSU. Thirty-three years later, those books were designated as the "Virgil D. Hawkins Collection." Thus FSU students use books from a law school that was founded to circumvent a future lawyer's civil rights. Those books are housed in a building named, not for Hawkins, as FSU students had petitioned in 1983, but for Florida Supreme Court justice B. K. Roberts, who repeatedly opposed Hawkins' admission to UF in the 1950s. In 2001, in a final act of irony, the UF College of Law awarded a posthumous honorary degree to Virgil Hawkins,[72] the man who opposed the Johns Committee's assault on integration by thwarting the committee's barratry strategy and by integrating UF.

·

Fortunately, Hawkins lived long enough to enjoy his first honors. Perhaps he also saw a paradox: that he was both targeted and honored because of his desire to attend UF. Ultimately, the legacy of his legal battles outlasted the Johns Committee's reign of fear. In the end, Virgil Hawkins' dream trumped Charley Johns' ambition.

# 3

## Ruth Perry

The Librarian Raises Her Voice

Ruth Perry sat rigidly in the witness box, clenching her fists and facing the television cameras. Her strained expression reflected not only the tension of a possible jail sentence but also the escalating effects of three years of threats against her life, her reputation, and her career. A few feet away, her would-be assassins smirked and jostled one another. It was February 25, 1957, and members of Miami's White Citizens' Council were eager spectators for the Johns Committee's latest hearing. Council members had occupied the front rows of the courtroom since early morning. They were ready for a showdown, but so were Ruth Perry and the NAACP.[1] Perry was one of the local NAACP officials closely involved in the Miami chapter's fight against the committee. She served the organization as an activist, journalist, and witness; she also foiled the Johns Committee's strategy to portray the Florida NAACP as Communist influenced.

•

Fortunately, Perry's early years prepared her well for civil rights work in the South, for she described herself as "not strictly Northern or Southern in [her] outlook ... [but] a mixture of two viewpoints."[2] The granddaughter of a slaveholding Confederate officer who was with General Robert E. Lee at Appomattox, Perry grew up in both Ithaca, New York (home of Cornell University), and Williston, South Carolina, a town named for her father's upper-middle-class family. She spent her summers in Williston but attended elementary through high school in Ithaca, where schools and churches were integrated. Her father, Francis Marion Willis, was a successful dentist, and Perry grew up surrounded by educated people. Under her father's influence, Perry developed a great love for books and respect for a variety of ideas. Dr. Willis was also interested in politics, and the Willises were among the very few Democrats in Republican-dominated Ithaca. Thus Perry's childhood experience with divergent viewpoints provided good training for a future activist.[3]

Perry's later strength of character also emerged from her strong relationship with her father. She admired him, and he encouraged her strong work ethic and perseverance. In a letter written shortly after Perry graduated from Drexel University in Philadelphia with a degree in library science, and just before she began her first job at Cornell University, Dr. Willis praised her for becoming a well-educated woman. (She had previously earned a degree in English from Converse College in South Carolina.) He concluded his letter by predicting the moral courage that his daughter would demonstrate in the future, telling her, "Later in life you will learn that character is everything."[4]

Dr. Willis could not have been surprised when his daughter eventually married a soft-spoken, liberal man who admired Eleanor Roosevelt almost as much as Perry herself did. Walter Dean Perry, the son of an Ithaca family, was three years younger than his wife. By all accounts, theirs was a successful marriage, and Perry regarded him as her best friend. Although he did not attend college, Walter Perry was very well read. A professional horticulturist, he was also an environmentalist long before the term entered the English lexicon. In 1940, the Perrys' first and only child, Caroline, was born.[5]

In 1945, Perry and her family moved to Miami, and she began working for the Miami Beach Public Library as a cataloguer. In a very short time, she grew to love Florida and could not imagine living anywhere else. She and her husband shared their love of the state as well as their views on politics with their daughter. Perry believed that one of her duties as a parent was to create a better world for her daughter so that she could grow up free of prejudice. At Perry's dinner table, serious discussions were a regular occurrence, particularly if they focused on current events or the Miami NAACP. With the full support of her family, Perry had joined the local chapter because she was "interested in the Constitutional rights of everyone."[6] As she later explained to a reporter: "Rather than scatter my effort, I went into the NAACP to do what I could in one area. I feel very strongly that what I am doing (in the NAACP) I am doing for everyone."[7]

The Miami chapter, founded in 1935, was the last one chartered in Florida's major cities, partly because of the difficulty of enrolling white members. Although all branches were required to be biracial, by 1959 only 25 percent of the Miami's chapter's members were white, and many of those remained anonymous. The continued racist climate of the city in the 1940s and 1950s also made recruiting members difficult. Despite Miami's transplanted northerners and its tourist economy, the city had, as Perry saw it, "an appearance of more liberality and freedom than actually exist[ed]."[8]

Underneath Miami's cosmopolitan veneer ran a deep grain of racial violence for which the Ku Klux Klan (KKK) was primarily responsible. True to its post–Civil War history, the Klan had chapters throughout the South by the early 1950s, but rival independent organizations competed for members. The typical KKK member was someone from the lower socioeconomic strata for whom the organization functioned as a release mechanism for class insecurities and fears. The Klan's strength lay in its being an organized structure for violence, thus offering segregationists an alternative to legal methods for stopping integration. The KKK was most commonly known for bombing homes of NAACP members and burning crosses on their lawns. The Miami Klan had the distinction of counting the recently retired national Imperial Wizard among its members. The local Klan harassed African Americans who attempted to integrate new subdivisions, burning crosses and homes to intimidate potential homeowners and voters. Beginning in September of 1951, the KKK escalated its activities. A series of dynamite bombings destroyed parts of a newly integrated apartment complex known as Carver Village.[9] Three months later, and two hundred miles north, a bomb exploded under the bedroom of Harry T. Moore (the outspoken coordinator of the Florida NAACP) and his wife on Christmas night, eventually killing them both.[10]

Moore's assassination shocked many Floridians, particularly Perry, who had recently become the Miami NAACP secretary. Perry was "horror stricken that such things were happening in Florida and that killings like this would or could be tolerated by white citizens."[11] Just as his cousin's lynching was a turning point for Virgil Hawkins, so Harry T. Moore's death was for Perry. His assassination galvanized her into becoming even more active in the NAACP. Determined to help achieve "justice [and] equal rights under the law"[12] for everyone, she soon became a state officer for the Florida NAACP and a regular speaker and radio broadcaster for the Miami chapter. In short, she made the NAACP the focus of her activist energies for nearly twenty years.[13]

•

Her work for the Miami branch soon drew fire from local racists. On June 14, 1953—NAACP day in Miami—Perry began airing her Sunday afternoon broadcasts on Miami radio station WMBM, a white-owned station whose audience was exclusively African American. In her NAACP programs, Perry called for a total end to segregation as well as full equality for African Americans. She also denounced Klan violence and other forms of terrorism. Friends in her radio audience soon questioned such bold statements, asking her, "How have you got the nerve to say such things on the air? Suppose something happens to you?"[14] Her friends' concerns were not unfounded. A month before Perry began her radio show, Clarence McDaniels, a fellow broadcaster at WMBM, suddenly disappeared. Vice president of the Miami NAACP, McDaniels was fired upon by police (for supposedly stealing sod from a gas station) before escaping to New York. Despite the McDaniels incident, Perry took sensible precautions but told her friends: "I believe in some things so strongly that I will stand up for them, no matter what comes."[15]

Reprisals for her broadcasts came in a matter of months, first as anonymous phone calls and later as anonymous letters, which she described to her radio audience as "vilifying and malicious . . . stabbings in the dark . . . [that proved] that the writer [did] not have moral courage."[16] Segregationists objecting to her broadcasts often assumed that she was African American; one of them claimed that "practically everything you Negroes do is an imitation of the white race [because] you haven't been civilized long enough."[17] When one of her detractors wrote, "All you niggers better go back to Africa where you all belong,"[18] Perry told her listeners that she could only imagine how much angrier the writer would have been if he had known she was white. (Despite her broadcasts being aired to an African American audience, many of Perry's listeners would have known that she was white because WMBM's listening audience was entirely local and fairly small in the early 1950s.) She regarded such threats as proof of the

Figure 3.1. Ruth Perry at the Miami Beach Public Library, ca. 1955. Private Papers of Caroline Perry-Kilburg. Courtesy of Caroline Perry-Kilburg.

effectiveness of the Miami chapter's civil rights work and predicted that more intimidation tactics and threats of violence would follow.[19]

Perry was correct. Bomb threats were called into her home repeatedly during the mid-1950s, but, like Virgil Hawkins, she refused to be bullied. As she told the Fort Lauderdale chapter at its tenth anniversary celebration, "If you are afraid—afraid of what might happen to you—there is no room for you in the NAACP."[20] When one of her anonymous detractors called her a "half-breed and a crackpot" during her final broadcast in August of 1956, she remained undaunted and replied that she had no respect for those who wore hoods or refused to provide their names when slandering others.[21]

Perry maintained her poise on the air, secure in the knowledge that she had been instrumental in the growing membership and influence of the Miami chapter. By 1957, as both chapter and state secretary, Perry had watched the NAACP influence in the Miami area grow until the local branch was holding regular meetings at the Afro-American Life Insurance Company's offices. In addition, chapters organized in nearby Homestead, Liberty City, and Perrine worked with the Miami chapter during annual membership drives.[22]

In June 1956, the Miami branch further raised its profile by challenging Florida's segregation laws. In a single week, the chapter initiated two lawsuits to integrate the city's buses and schools. The driving force behind both suits was chapter president Father Theodore Gibson and chapter attorney Grattan Graves. Gibson was the African American rector of Christ Episcopal Church, a powerful congregation of eight hundred members, and Graves was involved in most of the major civil rights cases originating in Miami. The two men worked closely in several legal actions.[23]

The bus case began on June 7, 1956, when the Miami branch demanded an end to segregated buses and announced that they were considering a boycott. Fully aware of the number of African Americans riding the buses, the economic impact of the two-week-old bus boycott in Tallahassee, and the escalation of the Montgomery, Alabama, boycott, the Miami Transit Company found the threat troubling. Although the Miami branch eventually decided not to follow through with the boycott, in order to avoid violence, the chapter did continue with the lawsuit.[24] Six months later, the U.S. District Court ruled in favor of the NAACP. With a local victory in the bus suit, the Miami chapter grew even stronger. As Florida's NAACP field secretary, Robert Saunders, saw it in 1957, the Miami branch had almost 100 percent backing from local African Americans for the first time in the chapter's history.[25]

The chapter's school suit paralleled the bus case. In response to Florida's delay in implementing the 1954 *Brown v. Board of Education* decision,

Figure 3.2. NAACP chief counsel Thurgood Marshall (*second from left*) and Miami chapter attorney Grattan Graves (*far right*) discuss NAACP activities with Garth Reeves (*far left*), publisher of the *Miami Times* (which carried Ruth Perry's column), and attorney John D. Johnson. State Archives of Florida, *Florida Memory*, http://floridamemory.com/items/show/35926.

Miami NAACP president Gibson and five other parents filed suit on behalf of their children in federal court in June 1956 to end segregation in Dade County. Although NAACP chief counsel Thurgood Marshall corresponded with Perry about attorney's fees, her work on the case focused primarily on publicity and fundraising. As with the bus suit, Perry spoke to other NAACP chapters about the school case, urging members to support the action, not only through the NAACP but also through their churches and clubs. She was characteristically blunt in her appeals: "Our goal is this—to write off the word 'segregation' from Florida law. . . . If we want freedom, we can raise enough money here today or within a few days. Don't tell me you can't afford it."[26]

With two high-profile cases working their way through the courts, the Miami NAACP became one of the most aggressive branches in Florida.

The chapter provided much of the leadership for the state organization as well. At the state conference in October of 1956, all but one of the state officers for the coming year were from Miami, including Gibson and Perry, who were reelected as treasurer and secretary. Clearly, the Miami NAACP was central to the fight for integration in Florida.[27]

Shortly before her reelection, Perry launched her first criticism of the newly formed Johns Committee, characterizing it as the legislature's latest attempt to harass the NAACP. In one of her last broadcasts, she did add that her organization would try to cooperate with the committee as long as it had official sanction. Perry ended her broadcasts in the late summer of 1956 after the WMBM station manager told field secretary Robert Saunders that the White Citizens' Council was pressuring the station to drop Perry's show. The manager then refused to allow her to broadcast.[28]

Two months later, Perry took on a new assignment for the NAACP. She began writing a weekly column for the *Miami Times*, one of the oldest African American newspapers in Florida. Her column, Along Freedom's Road, provided a new forum for Perry, allowing her to reach an even larger audience and leave a more lasting impression. More forthright than her broadcasts, Perry's columns exposed racism by analyzing current events from an NAACP perspective, often quoting other NAACP officials and never hesitating to name racist organizations and politicians, whether national, state, or local.[29]

Consequently, the machinations of the Johns Committee were a pervasive theme for Perry. A portion of her first newspaper column addressed the committee's waste of tax dollars. Perry explained that, despite the NAACP's offer to cooperate with the committee, the legislature had still appropriated fifty thousand dollars to investigate the organization. Perry then suggested that the Johns Committee use the money to investigate the KKK instead. In another column, she described the Tallahassee bus boycott and told her readers that the committee was investigating the boycott as an example of NAACP agitation in Florida.[30]

In the months before the Miami hearings, Perry's criticism became increasingly harsh. She referred to the committee and the legislature as extremist and reactionary and noted that the pattern of the committee's Tallahassee hearings and its interrogation of Virgil Hawkins showed that the committee was trying to stop integration, defy federal law, and destroy the NAACP. Although she did not mention it in her columns, Perry also may have known that the committee ended its Tallahassee hearings by entering some of her NAACP correspondence into the record. Since Robert Saunders attended those hearings, it is highly unlikely that he would not have told Perry about the way the committee used her correspondence as a stepping stone to the upcoming Miami hearings. Thus, Perry wrote that the work of the Johns Committee was a hostile act and that its goals were a "foregone conclusion."[31] Several days before Perry herself testified in the Miami hearings, she told her readers that the NAACP "must resolve to stand courageously for what we believe or deny the present and turn back to the past, [which] would mean inevitable disaster."[32]

By the time Perry's words appeared in print, she had faced disaster of the worst kind. Only two days before she was scheduled to testify, she learned that she had been "marked for assassination"[33] by the White Citizens' Council (WCC). Violence was generally not associated with the WCC, a primarily middle-class group. The WCC appealed to white southerners who feared integration, blamed the NAACP's organizational strength for the *Brown* rulings, and thought a white organization could stop integration. Originating in Mississippi in 1954, the WCC had a maximum membership of two hundred fifty thousand two years later and included some politicians and elected officials. The WCC created the Citizens' Councils of America in 1956 in order to coordinate the councils in nine southern states, including Florida.[34]

The Citizens' Councils of America worked with allied groups as well, including the Florida Federation for Constitutional Government. Florida's WCCs found most support in north Florida's former plantation belt (from Marion County north) and in the central part of the state, where many of the organization's leaders lived. Unlike councils in Mississippi, Alabama, Louisiana, South Carolina, and Virginia, Florida's WCCs not only were small in membership but also remained on the edges of political power. Two of Florida's WCCs were also atypical in their use of violence. In one noteworthy case, the WCC of Daytona Beach later claimed credit, through the Klan, for the assassination of Harry T. Moore and his wife. In July 1956, six months before the Miami hearings, the WCC had circulated a flyer in Daytona Beach, stating that they would begin a "mild program of violence" to intimidate African Americans, "stopping only short of bombing their homes as we did at Mims [the home of Harry Moore] in 1951, through the old KKK."[35] The flyer, which also called for the destruction of NAACP records and the prosecution of its leaders, noted that this was a "step the legislature . . . [had] already taken," a clear reference to the Johns Committee.[36] (See appendix, document one.)

Two days before the Miami hearings, the Miami WCC failed in a plan to start race riots and kill Perry when chapter attorney Grattan Graves uncovered their plot. The plan was to begin with a cross burning, continue with bombings at two housing projects, and end with the assassination of five NAACP officials: Perry, Graves, and Gibson, as well as the current and former state presidents. Since Perry and Gibson were also state officers, the terrorist plan would have left the Florida NAACP with only one state officer (the vice president) and field secretary Saunders. Fortunately, Graves had paid an informant to infiltrate the WCC, so Graves, the police, and the media lay in wait for the terrorists. When they planted the cross, the police made their arrest. Meanwhile, Perry continued with her plans to testify.[37]

·

The Miami hearings began on February 25, 1957. As was customary in the 1950s, witnesses' home addresses were printed in the local newspaper. The committee subpoenaed all of the officers of the Miami NAACP, but most of the questioning was directed at Graves, as chapter attorney; Gibson, as chapter president; and Perry, as chapter secretary. First, the committee's chief counsel, Mark Hawes, tried unsuccessfully to get attorney Graves to admit that he had corresponded with Thurgood Marshall at the national office about the Dade County school integration suit. Hawes then called Gibson. The chapter president also refused to agree that the national office was directing branch offices to file integration cases. Clearly, the first phase of the committee's strategy—to show that the NAACP instigated and financed integration suits and thus was guilty of barratry—was not working any better than at the Tallahassee hearings. Hawes then shifted to phase two: to hunt for Communists in the Florida NAACP by demanding that the organization release its records. He asked Gibson who had the records of the Miami chapter. When Gibson replied "the secretary," Ruth Perry's moment in history began.[38]

As the official guardian of the chapter's membership lists and meeting minutes, Perry did not merely hold the files; her frequent use of them gave her extensive knowledge of their contents. Knowing much membership information from memory alone, she held a crucial position, particularly in relation to the Johns Committee's two-phase strategy to discredit the NAACP. It was one thing to establish that the organization had a role in integration suits; that was common knowledge. It was another matter entirely to show that the organization was Communist connected, and the committee could only hope to prove that connection by obtaining NAACP membership files, from either Gibson or Perry. Because she was secretary for both the state and local NAACP, she could protect—or reveal—the names of members for the entire state. As Gibson's testimony demonstrated, the future of the NAACP in Florida hung on Perry's testimony. Years later, Gibson insisted that "if members' names [had been] exposed . . . the NAACP would have been able to hold roll call in a telephone booth."[39]

The role of the NAACP secretary was also critical in eight other southern states, where one of the most common methods of attacking the NAACP was to demand that the association release its membership records. In Louisiana, a state injunction forced the organization to stop functioning. Even after some urban branches released their membership lists, the state badgered the association so much that rural chapters suspended activities for four years. Similarly in Alabama, a restraining order halted NAACP operations, and another court order required the organization to surrender membership lists and other records. When the NAACP refused to cooperate, it was fined ten thousand dollars, took its case through state and federal litigation, and was unable to function again in Alabama until 1964. In Florida, the demands for records were just beginning in 1957, and the NAACP secretary was not backing down.[40]

Less than two days after Graves and the police interrupted the assassination plan, Perry took the stand. While testifying, she faced not only the television cameras but also her would-be assassins, the men of the WCC: they sat only a few feet away from her. Leering and elbowing one another, they waited eagerly for her to break. She greatly disappointed them. When Hawes asked her about the location of the chapter's records, she told him that they were at the NAACP's national office in New York City. Hawes then altered his line of questioning, trying, as he had with Gibson, to get Perry to admit that the Dade County school integration suit was not entirely locally organized. She refused, although Hawes berated her repeatedly for not cooperating. He then lied, telling her that Gibson had already testified that the suit was not entirely locally inspired. Hawes was able to do this because witnesses were kept in a separate room, so Perry had not heard Gibson's testimony. Even after hearing this misinformation, Perry still refused to alter her testimony.[41]

Hawes also returned to the issue of the Miami branch's records. He asked that Perry request Graves (who was sitting next to her as her attorney) to get the records back from the national office. She agreed to do so, but it was clear from her and Graves' exchange that her request was a charade and that neither intended to return the records.[42]

The next part of Perry's testimony was particularly frustrating for the committee. First, two men on the committee reminded her of her record-keeping duties as secretary. Then, Perry explained that for several months she had sent no written reports to the national office, making only verbal reports. Also, she had notified members of meetings only via radio and newspaper, rather than mailing notices directly. Thus she had protected members' names and addresses even as she frequently published her home phone number in her column. Clearly, she had been protecting the NAACP for some time, probably soon after the Johns Committee was organized. When interrogated further about her lack of record keeping, Perry found a way to end the questioning. She simply referred to the investigations of the NAACP in Florida and other southern states as the reason for not sending in reports or having an election of new officers, thus implying what she had said more directly in her newspaper column: that the Florida legislature was trying to stop integration—even if it meant violating federal laws. Suddenly, the Johns Committee had no further questions for Ruth Perry.[43]

When Hawes recalled Graves to the stand, his testimony showed how much Perry was protecting the NAACP. He first explained that it was Thurgood Marshall's idea to send the records of all southeast Florida chapters to the association's national office. Graves added, however, that neither he nor Marshall had told Perry to stop keeping written records. She had done that on her own.[44] Whether it was because she was a woman or because she was a librarian, the committee had clearly underestimated Ruth Perry.

The Johns Committee ended the hearings by trying to save face. First, it passed a resolution condemning cross burning. Then it named Frederick John Kasper, an ardent segregationist, as a troublemaker. (Kasper, a hate monger from New Jersey, used Tennessee as a base of operations for his missions into racial trouble spots in the South and helped instigate race riots in 1956 during the integration of Clinton High School in Tennessee.) Then the committee concluded with a sales pitch, saying that the legislature should renew the committee's charter so that it could finish its work, which had been delayed by the refusal of national NAACP officials to return membership records.[45]

A week after the hearings ended, Perry told her readers how trying her experience as a witness had been. In her usual direct way, she said: "I have found out . . . that it is not an easy thing to appear in public and defend one's beliefs in an atmosphere of tenseness and strain."[46] Perry also described the suspenseful mood in the courtroom: the obvious desire of the committee to find detrimental information about the NAACP and the aggravation of the organization's members over the waste of tax money for such a hearing.[47]

Perry noted that her experience was an inspirational one as well, explaining that the unity of purpose and spirit among the NAACP witnesses "made it possible for all of [them] to do what [they] had to do."[48] The event reaffirmed her commitment to defy racism. That defiance was evident in the way that Perry ended her column, by doing what she had refused to do on the witness stand: name names. The men she named in her column were two dangerous Klansmen whom she described as "rabid segregationists."[49] (One of the men was the same Frederick John Kasper identified by the Johns Committee as a troublemaker.) However, she did not tell her readers that the other man was one of the Miami WCC members who had just been arrested for trying to assassinate her.[50]

Only two weeks after the Miami hearings, field secretary Robert Saunders was interrogated by the Johns Committee in Tallahassee. His response to the subpoena for NAACP records annoyed the committee: the only records he gave them were press releases and some general correspondence. Saunders also managed a slight gibe at Hawes for his treatment of Perry during the Miami hearings. First, Saunders told Hawes what he already knew: that Miami chapter officers had relinquished no records to the committee. Then Saunders further annoyed Hawes by reminding him that Perry was the one who had held the records that the committee had failed to obtain.[51]

Perry's columns and other news reports on the hearings had a positive effect on the Miami chapter. Robert Saunders noted that publicity from the hearings generated more interest in the NAACP from whites and African Americans. As he expressed it, the "Committee's only success was in saving itself [by being renewed and refunded for another legislative term]."[52] Indeed, the Miami branch had more success than the committee. Three months after the hearings concluded, the chapter's school suit reached another milestone when oral arguments in the case ended in the Circuit Court of Appeals. Later in the summer, Perry reported that segregationists anticipated that they would lose the suit and would then appeal to the U.S. Supreme Court, adding that such plans were part of the Dade County School Board's segregationist agenda to delay integration as long as possible. She also offered cautionary words for another group trying to delay integration—the Johns Committee—predicting that their intimidation tactics would fail again.[53]

When the legislature renewed the committee's mandate for two years and increased its budget, Perry pointed out the injustice of the situation: African Americans' tax dollars were helping to finance the very committee that worked to deprive them of their civil rights. In the fall, Perry was threatened again, but she addressed this issue in her column, saying people who are involved in making social change are often the recipients of such threats. Her opinion of her detractors was characteristically straightforward: "These [people] are the ones we hold in contempt."[54]

Perry also warned her readers that Florida could find itself in a situation similar to that of Arkansas, where federal troops were sent in to restore order in Little Rock. She blamed Florida's racial tension on politicians who incited conservatives' fears of integration and opposed the NAACP; she named Charley Johns in particular: "To politicians and state officials like Governor Faubus of Arkansas [and] Charley Johns of Florida, the NAACP is a red herring to use in political bombast or demagoguery."[55] A few months later, she noted the Johns Committee's increasingly familiar tactic of trying to show that the NAACP was the sole initiator and financier of integration suits in Florida. Perry reminded her readers that such tactics were not just a way to fight integration but a waste of their tax dollars as well.[56]

A few days later, in February of 1958, Perry was subpoenaed to appear before the committee at its second round of hearings in Miami. Perry's last column before the hearings focused on the Johns Committee. First, Perry reassured her readers that her repeat appearance provided "conclusive proof... that the NAACP [was] not only alive in Florida but [continued] to be effective. Why else would [they] be investigated?"[57] Then she added that the worst aspect of the committee's investigations was their institutionalized racism, "their use of legislatures and state legal machinery as their tools."[58] Her defiance was clear; NAACP officers were ready to defend their organization. The Johns Committee, though, was ready for a showdown. Both sides expressed particular interest in Perry's testimony. As eyewitness Robert Saunders explained, "[We knew that] the Committee had targeted Perry because she was a white civil rights activist who despised racial segregation. . . . She was a southern white woman who defied them."[59]

A different Johns Committee came to Miami in February of 1958. Although it had four new members, it had also prepared differently for the 1958 hearings. First, the committee still had the Texas attorney general's files from which Hawes had reconstructed many of the Florida NAACP records. Second, in true McCarthy-like fashion, it had collected many names: NAACP contributors, alleged racial and Communist agitators in Florida, names from national and Miami NAACP letterheads, records of NAACP-affiliated groups, and membership lists from the American Civil Liberties Union, Florida Council on Human Relations, Greater Miami Foundation for Civic Education, American Association of University Professors, League of Women Voters, and many other organizations. (See appendix, document two.) However, much of this information was collected by Johns Committee investigators and was inaccurate.[60]

The committee had also bolstered its anti-Communist credentials by taking the testimony of J. B. Matthews. A well-known member of the anti-Communist network, he had been the research director for the House Committee on Un-American Activities and Senator Joe McCarthy's assistant. Matthews accused the NAACP of being lenient toward Communists, as had government loyalty boards in the late 1940s. When examining both military and civilian employees, government interrogators, suspecting that Communists had infiltrated the NAACP, often raised the issue of a witness's membership in the association. The association's official position on Communism was straightforward: it was antithetical to the NAACP's goal of achieving full constitutional rights for African Americans, rights they never would have under Communism. The association also acted accordingly, excluding members of Communist organizations from a Washington, D.C., rally in 1950 and voting six months later at the NAACP convention to appoint a committee to remove Communists from its chapters. Later that year, the NAACP committee suspended the San Francisco branch's charter when it elected a known Communist to a leadership position. The association even used Harry T. Moore's assassination as a platform for proclaiming the NAACP's anti-Communism. Executive secretary Walter White characterized Moore as a hero who battled Communism, saying that his assassination had only furthered Communism and that "whoever did it rendered one of the greatest services to Joe Stalin that could have been rendered."[61]

The Johns Committee also became more blatant in its opposition to the NAACP. Although the committee's package of anti-barratry bills had failed to pass, the legislature did approve a bill requiring organizations whose activities tended to "destroy . . . peace, tranquility, and good order" to file their membership lists and financial reports with the secretary of state.[62] With the committee's powers expanded so that it could investigate subversive organizations, the Johns Committee could then focus the 1958 Miami hearings even more on its Communism strategy, rather than the barratry strategy.

Also, by 1958, the committee's chief counsel was one of the highest paid attorneys on the state payroll. Working only part time for the committee, Hawes' pay rate was still higher than that of most of the full-time assistant state attorneys general. He also continued his private practice in Tampa as a defense attorney. Hawes represented members of the Trafficante family, who were gambling syndicate bosses, as well as several people accused of theft.[63]

The 1957–59 Johns Committee differed from its predecessor in other ways as well. In the summer of 1957, Charley Johns chaired the committee for the first time, giving it the benefit of his political connections. Finally and most importantly, the committee also established a new operating rule, boldly stating that, in any duly called hearing, "*one* or more members will constitute a *quorum* [emphasis added]."[64] By July of 1957, Charley Johns had the option of being a committee of one.

When the hearings began in Miami in February of 1958, Johns was largely responsible for conducting them in an atmosphere of even greater tension than the previous year. In his opening statement, he first dismissed all of the witnesses to another room and then tried to prevent their attorneys from being present during all testimony. He failed; the attorneys remained in the hearing room.[65]

One of the first NAACP witnesses called was Graves, the chapter attorney. He refused to cooperate and was cited for contempt. On the second day of testimony, Ruth Perry, now chapter vice president, was the first NAACP witness called. The scene played out essentially the same as the previous year: once again Perry's would-be assassins (WCC members) were entrenched in the front rows of the courtroom.[66]

Facing them, and with TV cameras rolling, Perry testified. As she had done the year before, she refused to cooperate, objecting to most of chief counsel Mark Hawes' questions on the grounds of "pertinency." She then read a short statement saying that the committee's demands for NAACP records violated her civil liberties, based on both the First Amendment (free speech and association) and the Fourteenth Amendment (due process); thus the Johns Committee's demands were illegal. She added that the NAACP was neither violent nor Communist. When Hawes asked her if she was vice president of the Miami branch and secretary of the state conference, she refused to answer. He then berated her, insisting that he had the names of one hundred fifty Communists. Frustrated over his inability to obtain NAACP files, Hawes interrogated Perry about what she knew, based on her extensive knowledge and memory of state and local NAACP records. He repeatedly named people and asked if she knew them. Every time Hawes asked about someone, she refused to name names.[67]

Hawes' interrogation of Perry continued in this way for over an hour. He was very angry, as was the committee. Finally, committee member Representative Cliff Herrell, a Miamian who was acutely aware of his white constituency, lost his temper or, as Perry said later, "turned blue in the face and [appeared to be] having a fit."[68] Referring to Perry, he paced the floor and angrily asserted at her: "Any witness who appears before this Committee who refuses to give the help to this Committee and render a service to the state of Florida is not fit to be a citizen of the state of Florida"[69] (nor, he implied, of the United States). Herrell conflated Perry's refusal to name names with a lack of patriotism, a common tactic during the McCarthy years and the longer House Committee on Un-American Activities era. Under what one scholar has described as the House Committee's "Informer Principle,"[70] naming names was proof of patriotism while refusing to do so was proof of conspiracy. Thus uncooperative witnesses remained under suspicion and, at the very least, placed their careers in jeopardy.[71]

After some discussion about whether Perry should be allowed to respond to such character assassination, the Johns Committee decided to let her speak. With tears in her eyes, Perry simply said: "I would like to say that I have never been a member of the Communist Party and am not now and never intend to be. I am an American citizen. I believe in democracy and the Constitution of the United States."[72] When the committee cited her for contempt, the WCC members cheered from the front rows.[73]

After citing Perry, the Johns Committee adjourned for lunch. NAACP members rushed to get Perry out of the courthouse immediately, fearing for her well-being. Meanwhile, attorney Graves, Gibson, Robert Saunders, and Frank Reeves (counsel from the national office) met and planned how they would end the hearings. Gibson was very angry over the committee's treatment of Perry, saying, "They were painting her with all kinds of brushes. She was brave, and they abused her."[74] He was quite ready to break up the hearings, even if it meant being cited for contempt. Reeves and Graves then prepared a statement for Gibson to read.[75]

After the lunch recess, Graves first asked that the personal remarks made by committee members about Perry's character and integrity be expunged from the record. Charley Johns refused. Graves then persuaded Hawes to call Gibson next. He read a statement asserting that Herrell's criticism of Perry showed that the committee was not qualified to investigate any organization impartially, that he (Gibson) would not allow the committee to deprive him of his constitutional rights, and that he was not and had not been a Communist. He ended by saying that he refused to answer any questions because of Herrell's statement about Perry. Gibson then walked out on the committee as the audience applauded him. The committee cited him for contempt.[76]

The next NAACP witness, Vernell Albury, treasurer of the Miami chapter, also read a statement chastising the committee for its treatment of Perry. Albury called the committee a "star chamber"[77] and concluded that it had disqualified itself as objective. While the audience applauded, she too walked out. Albury was cited for contempt as well, and the hearings ended the next morning with the committee's attempt to appear impartial by passing a resolution to investigate the Klan and similar organizations.[78]

A few days after the very volatile 1958 Miami hearings ended, a *Miami Herald* reporter asked Perry what the results of the hearings would be. She replied: "There have been intimations [that] I'll lose my job."[79] Perry had worked for the Miami Beach Public Library for eight years. She went on to say that there were "rumblings" about her being fired and told the reporter, "If you print anything much, they might turn it into thunder. Anything's possible when people don't understand. Besides, I wonder if the damage hasn't already been done."[80]

There were people trying to do damage. Perry received an anonymous letter shortly after the *Herald* article appeared. The writer, who signed as "A Good American Citizen," said that he or she was sending a copy of the letter to both the mayor and city commissioner, hoping they would take action against Perry. The writer added: "I am going to ask the Mayor . . . to replace you in the position you now hold if you insist in [*sic*] protecting the undesirables in the NAACP."[81] Echoing Representative Herrell's castigation of Perry, this "Good American Citizen" also told Perry that she was not fit to be an American citizen much less to live in Florida. NAACP general counsel Robert Carter advised Perry that, if she were convicted of contempt, she could be suspended from her library job, would have to fight through the courts to get her job back, and could be unemployed for over a year. Carter also told her that he and everyone else at the national office were very proud of her testimony because "it took real courage."[82]

Ruth Perry devoted an entire column to her experiences as a witness before the Johns Committee, referring to February 27, 1958, as both the "hardest day [she] ever lived through, and . . . one of the most wonderful days [she] ever experienced."[83] She also said that she could not be in the hearing room when Gibson defended her and the NAACP but that she watched on television; only then did she allow herself to release fully the tears that she had wanted to shed earlier when she was on the witness stand. She added that Gibson's words and actions erased the pain of the indignity caused by the committee. Perry then concluded, characteristically, with these prophetic words: "There comes a time in each of our lives when we must make a stand for what we believe. If we don't, then what we are fighting for becomes a mockery. . . . All of us have faith that our stand will be justified."[84]

Perry saw her faith justified only after a series of legal battles. After the hearings, the Johns Committee and the NAACP were in and out of court many times over the contempt cases against Perry and her colleagues. In the meantime, Perry enjoyed announcing Virgil Hawkins' "long, long overdue victory" in the UF case and praised his courage in "opening the way for integration in higher education."[85] However, she also kept her readers informed about the committee's plans to reopen the Miami hearings in August of 1958. A few days before those hearings were scheduled to begin, she was able to celebrate a victory in her column: The NAACP had taken the contempt cases to the Florida Supreme Court, which issued a stay in July, forcing the committee to cancel its Miami hearings. Perry emphasized that the cancellation was a clear moral victory for the NAACP.[86]

By October, though, Perry's column reflected a shift in the NAACP's legal strategy. Frustrated with the Florida courts, where only delays could be achieved at best, the organization began to prepare a case for the U.S. Supreme Court. Perry asked her readers for financial help, stating clearly that the NAACP was fighting institutionalized racism: "Fighting prejudiced state legislatures and investigating committees is not done for nothing."[87] As the legal battles continued into 1959, Perry devoted an entire column to Charley Johns and his cronies, describing their behavior on racial issues as an excellent example of right-wing incompetence. She pointed out that the committee had not convicted any NAACP attorney of barratry, ended the battle for integration in Florida, or passed any legislation to stop NAACP activities in the state. However, Perry praised Governor LeRoy Collins. He was developing a reputation as a racial moderate who believed that defying federal authority would only hinder Florida from creating the stable environment needed for economic development. Perry noted that Collins had warned legislators not to pass repressive school segregation laws, especially ones that would close public schools. She concluded by lambasting Charley Johns' "pork chop clique," saying that they were holding Florida's future hostage through their "selfish sectionalism" and political games.[88]

No one was surprised when Ruth Perry was subpoenaed for the third time. However, by the time Miami chapter officers testified in November of 1959, Gibson had taken sole legal responsibility for the membership records that had been sent to association headquarters the previous year. The NAACP knew that the Johns Committee was really after Gibson: he was the one who broke up its 1958 hearings by walking out on the committee, and he was the only one of the six plaintiffs in the Dade County school integration suit to be subpoenaed by the committee.[89] Also, the NAACP's national office was planning its U.S. Supreme Court case with Gibson as the only plaintiff, so it was good strategy for him to take sole legal possession of the records. The November hearings were very brief, but the committee again wasted tax money and got no information from the NAACP. Robert Saunders recalled Perry testifying that she was no longer possessor of the records. Saunders also explained that Graves, according to NAACP plans, had instructed Perry to tell the committee that Gibson was now the legal possessor of the records. Her contempt citation was then dropped.[90]

If Johns and his committee thought that dropping her contempt citation would soften Perry's attitude toward them, they were wrong. She devoted her next column to the November hearings, describing the atmosphere in the hearing room as friendlier than in 1958 but also unprofessional: some Johns Committee members actually read newspapers while witnesses were testifying. Perry also followed the actions of the committee in her later columns. The next summer (1960), after several lunch counters in Miami were quietly integrated, Perry told her readers that the committee was rumored to be targeting sit-in demonstrators for investigation. Six months later, Perry reported with some annoyance that the committee was still talking about Communists in the NAACP.[91]

A year later, Perry could not conceal her joy when one Johns Committee member's reputation finally caught up with him. In 1962, state senator Cliff Herrell ran a close race for the U.S. House in Miami's newly created Third Congressional District against Claude Pepper. Herrell had been a state representative in 1957 and 1958 when the committee held the Miami hearings, and he was the one who had lost his temper and attacked Perry so blatantly, telling her and the press that she was "not fit to be a citizen of the state of Florida."[92] Four years later, Perry simply reminded her readers that they knew Senator Herrell very well—because of the hearings—and should vote accordingly.[93]

Two months later, Perry reported Herrell's defeat as a "vindication of the NAACP."[94] She added that, despite the *Miami Herald's* endorsement and his having been the favorite over Pepper and two other Democratic contenders (according to most newspapers), Herrell was mistaken to think that his Johns Committee reputation would not defeat him in Dade County. (Pepper also benefited from the Third District's many Jews and retired union members from the North as well as containing a significant portion of the city's African American voters.) Noting what a terrible experience the hearing had been for the Miami branch, Perry concluded by saying that Gibson, as he waited for the U.S. Supreme Court to hear his case, would be reassured by Herrell's defeat. Conditions behind what Perry called the "magnolia curtain" were improving.[95]

Perry took her last shot at the Johns Committee in one of her last columns. In 1963, she discussed the economic cost of prejudice. Perry first noted the millions of dollars required the previous year for federal troops and marshals to enroll and keep James Meredith at the University of Mississippi after the state's governor defied a U.S. Supreme Court order to admit Meredith. She then localized racism for her readers in much the same way as she had in her first newspaper column, by criticizing the committee's use of tax dollars. She added that the committee's funds might have been better spent on Florida's roads.[96] Perhaps this was even one last jab at Charley Johns, who campaigned from the seat of a road grader and was known for funding some road building that benefited himself and his friends in the construction industry.

Perry's later columns also recorded the developments in Gibson's case. She had known Gibson for many years and had worked with him in other civil rights groups; they were good friends. In fact, in the summer of 1960, when Gibson appeared before circuit judge May Walker in Tallahassee, Perry was there, not only as a friend but also as a witness and journalist. She told her readers which NAACP members were present, how the hearing was conducted in a dirty courtroom littered with Coke bottles and broken furniture, and how newspaper reporters talked and passed around a box of candy while witnesses were testifying. In 1961, when the Supreme Court granted Gibson a hearing, Perry celebrated by proudly reviewing the history of the case for her readers. Seven months later, she announced a fund-raiser for him. Clearly, Perry was proud to speak out on behalf of Gibson and the NAACP; as she said in one of her columns, she always considered it "a singular honor to belong to the NAACP and especially in the South."[97]

•

Whether one reads Perry's columns or her testimony, it is obvious that the voice of the activist is also the voice of the journalist. Above all, it is clear that hers was a courage empowered by conscience. Fortunately, Perry survived all of the attacks against her, from character assassination to physical assassination attempts, and was employed and promoted by the Miami Beach Public Library until her retirement.[98]

In 1963, the U.S. Supreme Court ruled in favor of Gibson and the NAACP in *Gibson v. Florida Legislative Investigation Committee*. That ruling not only prevented the Johns Committee from ever obtaining Florida NAACP records but also ensured the survival of the organization within the state. In Miami, the Gibson case helped to increase membership, which, according to Gibson himself, had declined briefly during the Johns Committee hearings. Once people knew that NAACP officers would risk going to jail to protect the membership lists, new members joined the organization.[99] Just as Perry had promised her readers, the Miami NAACP had prevailed.

As membership increased into the mid-1960s, Perry became less involved in chapter affairs. No one knows for certain why she became less active, but Perry's daughter offers the simplest and most plausible explanation: Perry had helped the chapter and her colleagues survive their most difficult years, and she felt that they—and the next generation of activists—had the necessary resources to continue the chapter's work. With a major legal victory and a growing membership list, she believed that the Miami chapter was out of danger. Perhaps Perry also realized that the civil rights movement was evolving, that the next generation was shifting the model of activism from the NAACP's litigation-based style to the militant approach of organizations such as the Student Nonviolent Coordinating Committee. In any case, as she said in her last column, "Five or six years in time make a great deal of difference in racial progress."[100] Florida's little McCarthyism was coming to an end.

The Johns Committee offered numerous excuses to the Florida legislature for the committee's failure to defeat the NAACP,[101] but the committee would never credit people like Ruth Perry and her foiling of the Johns Committee's Communism strategy. Still, her courage—as an activist, journalist, and witness—made the NAACP's legal victories possible and the committee's explanations to the legislature necessary. By the time the Johns Committee was making excuses, Ruth Perry had already made history.

# 4

## Sig Diettrich

The Geographer Draws the Line

Sig Diettrich could appreciate the desperation of his position but not its irony: that he—a devout Catholic—on the eve of St. Patrick's Day, 1959, knelt in a church dedicated to the Irish saint and argued with God. In an act of both faith and defiance, Diettrich insisted that his suicide would not be a sin because it was necessary. The middle-aged professor then returned to Floyd Hall on the UF campus for his afternoon class but first took what he hoped was a lethal dose of aspirin. After class, he went up to the third floor of the building, where he climbed into a window and stared down at the cold, rain-soaked sidewalk. He started to jump but stopped. He tried again, and for several "frightful minutes [his life] seemed to be hung on eternity."[1]

Finally, Diettrich returned to his department offices, where his staff noticed that he was acting strangely.[2] They did not know that the Johns Committee had just claimed another victim. Diettrich had been caught in the wide net of homophobia cast by the Johns Committee as it shifted from an attack on Communists and the NAACP to an assault on homosexuality; Diettrich never cooperated with the committee and was left with his integrity intact, but the Johns Committee continued to affect UF.

•

A hundred yards away from Diettrich's office, UF's Century Tower peacefully stood guard over his world that, until that day, had been the nearly idyllic product of many years of hard work. Sig (Sigismond) Diettrich had begun his academic career years earlier as an industrious student in Hungary. With bachelor's and master's degrees in economics from the University of Budapest, he immigrated to the United States in 1928 after receiving a fellowship to study at Clark University in Worcester, Massachusetts. Under the leadership of its third president, Wallace Atwood, a renowned professor of physical geography from Harvard, Clark founded the first graduate program for geography in the United States. Atwood would also be a mentor to Diettrich, who received his doctorate in economic geography in 1931.[3]

During one of Wallace Atwood's trips through the South, he convinced UF administrators that they needed a geography department. Atwood's elder son, Rollin, soon chaired the new geography program, and when a vacancy developed in 1931, he recruited Diettrich to teach economic geography. Diettrich brought his new bride, Iren, to Gainesville the following year.[4]

Like many nonnative Floridians, Diettrich came to love Florida very quickly. He also enjoyed teaching at UF and thought nothing of working on a research or teaching project until 2 or 3 a.m. A naturally gregarious and optimistic man, he made friends easily, both within UF and the larger Gainesville community. When his and Iren's only child, Rosemary, was born, he was delighted to be a father. Diettrich also became an active parishioner of St. Patrick's Catholic Church, even serving as choir director, with his wife as church organist. His interest in music also extended into the theater when he became a charter member and later president of both the Gainesville Community Playhouse and the Gainesville Music Association.[5]

Iren Diettrich did not adjust to Gainesville as quickly as her energetic husband. She must have missed the cosmopolitan atmosphere of Budapest, but she soon joined her husband in volunteer work for the city's community playhouse. Iren was glad that the theater season was during the fall and winter, when she felt restored by the cooler weather, because Florida's climate was her greatest concern. Coming from a city that was on the same latitude as Quebec, she found Florida's hot, humid summers extremely uncomfortable and annoying. After she contracted malaria in the early 1930s, her health was compromised. Diettrich himself remained healthy, energetic, and very busy at UF, teaching a new interdisciplinary course in the sciences. He also continued his work with the Gainesville

Community Playhouse. With classes and meetings during the day and play rehearsals at night, Diettrich admitted that, although he was having fun, he was hardly ever home. Despite her father's frequent absences, her mother's intermittent illnesses, and the Florida weather, Rosemary Diettrich thrived in Gainesville.[6]

In 1939, Diettrich tried unsuccessfully to leave UF. Although he had recently become a U.S. citizen, was happy at the university, and was very pleased with the circle of friends that he and Iren had made, she continued to struggle with bouts of malaria that left her weakened and with a recurrent nervous condition that doctors were unable to treat successfully. Added to Diettrich's concern was the fact that sending Iren again for a recuperative visit to Hungary was no longer an option because Hitler had occupied Austria and parts of Eastern Europe.[7]

Four years later, with the United States having entered World War II, UF was overwhelmed with seven hundred fifty new students for the Army War Training courses. Diettrich had to prepare the geography course for the war curriculum and train fourteen staff members. In 1943, Diettrich received a job offer from the Office of Strategic Services in Washington for temporary consulting work in its Europe-Africa division. UF president John Tigert, who was pleased that Diettrich's geography students in the Army War Training courses were evaluated as being among the best in the South, promoted Diettrich to acting chair of the Division of Geography and Geology and granted him six months' leave so that he could accept the job offer. Fortunately, the position allowed Iren, who had been ill again the previous year, to escape the Florida heat for the entire summer.[8]

Diettrich also found time to write and do research while in Washington. Thus he began to write about Florida's future in a series published by UF and known as *Economic Leaflets*. Each issue was comprised of several articles by UF faculty from various departments with an emphasis on business and government matters in Florida. Diettrich addressed such topics as population distribution, the state's change from a rural to an urban economy after the war, and Florida's role in the southern economy.[9]

When Diettrich returned to UF in late 1944, he began to plan for a postwar increase in students by hiring new faculty. By the fall of 1946, his division had expanded to five professors, and UF's enrollment was seven thousand students. His life at the university was busy and rewarding. At home, though, Iren's health problems persisted and were affecting the Diettrichs' marriage. Although they still loved each other very much, their physical intimacy declined, and, upon repeated advice from Iren's doctors, they ceased intimate relations for ten years. Diettrich, still a vigorous man during this time, turned to brief anonymous sexual encounters with men as an outlet and apparently never considered having an affair with another woman. As he explained: "[Iren was] the only woman I ever loved and cared to love. Our happy marriage was not a mirage but it was a true reality."[10] Later, when they attempted to resume marital relations, Diettrich found his abilities very limited.[11]

Despite his marital problems and additional administrative duties, Diettrich still pursued his scholarly interests, often presenting his research at national and regional conferences and publishing scholarly articles.[12] In the fall of 1958, his teaching and scholarly efforts were rewarded when he learned from the State Department that he had been awarded a Fulbright Fellowship, one of the highest honors a college professor or scholar can receive. Through the grant, he was to teach at the University of Dacca in East Pakistan for one year. A few weeks after receiving his Fulbright, Diettrich had more good news, this time from his daughter, who was now grown and married. Rosemary and her husband, Charles, had just had their first child, a daughter; Sig Diettrich was overjoyed to be a grandfather.[13]

•

While Diettrich was celebrating his first Fulbright and his first grandchild, Johns Committee investigators were peeping into toilet stalls in downtown Gainesville, trying to entrap gay professors.[14] From the committee's viewpoint, gay professors could be those who had actually been named as gay or had only been suspected of being gay. Sig Diettrich was one of the former, named by a colleague during the Johns Committee witch hunts at UF.[15] Those investigations reflected national fears about homosexuality during the cold war years.

Only a few days after Senator Joe McCarthy's famous Wheeling, West Virginia, speech, in which he insisted that the U.S. State Department was dominated by Communists, homosexuality became a more prominent cold war political issue. When Undersecretary of State John Peurifoy testified before a Senate committee in February 1950, he noted that most of the ninety-one State Department employees who were fired for "moral turpitude" were homosexual. Republicans then seized the opportunity to embarrass the Truman administration while congressional investigators offered three justifications for their witch hunts. First, investigators argued that gays were emotionally unstable people who could "have a corrosive effect upon . . . fellow employees."[16] Second, the witch hunters pointed out that since gays, like Communists, could not be recognized by their physical characteristics, gays could infiltrate government offices. Finally, investigators posited that gays and lesbians were more likely to be blackmailed by Communists and thus were not only greater security risks but also more apt to become subversives. As a result of such justifications, hundreds of gays and lesbians lost their federal jobs or were discharged from the military during the 1950s.[17]

Gays and lesbians were also seen as sinners who participated in immoral acts, according to the dominant Christian culture's interpretation of the Bible. Moreover, in the minds of most Americans, gays were predators who used children or young people to satisfy unnatural sexual appetites; like godless Communists, immoral gays and lesbians were corrupting America's future: its youth. Lesbian pulp fiction in the 1950s reflected this view and served as an object lesson for young women: because lesbians were depraved, any woman who flaunted social convention by loving another woman would ultimately be alone or suicidal.[18]

To the medical establishment, particularly psychiatrists and psychologists, homosexuality was a mental illness, and gays were deviants. President Eisenhower's 1952 executive order, which made gays ineligible for federal employment on the grounds of sexual perversion, reflected the medical and political view of gays as psychologically unstable subversives. The release of Alfred Kinsey's *Sexual Behavior in the Human Male* in 1948, followed by its companion volume on women in 1953, increased America's fears, particularly Kinsey's revelations that more than one-third of men and one-fifth of women surveyed had participated in homosexual activity. The homosexual menace must have seemed pervasive. The cold war view of homosexuality as an instrument for political subversion, a moral danger to children and to America's future, and a type of mental pathology were the dominant political, cultural, and psychological models of gays that most Americans, including the Johns Committee, endorsed.[19]

At the state level, homosexual acts, or "crimes against nature," were covered under Florida's sodomy laws. Although the statutes dated back to 1868, most Floridians would have still considered such laws relevant in the 1950s, given the negative view of gays in American society. The fact that Florida statutes also provided for prosecution of crimes against nature, whether they occurred in private *or* public, would not have troubled most Floridians. Reflecting their constituents' views of gays and lesbians, Florida's politicians also passed a sexual psychopath law in 1955, which provided for the institutionalization of a person convicted *or* accused of a sex crime. The 1957 legislature strengthened the law, requiring a suspect charged with any crime to be assessed for the possibility of committing sex crimes and for the need for institutionalization.[20]

The same legislative session also saw the renewal of the Johns Committee for another two years. The 1957–59 committee had four new members: Senator Randolph Hodges from Cedar Key, a businessman who had been in the Senate since 1952; newly elected senator Marion Knight, an attorney from Blountstown who had served in the House since 1953; Representative William O'Neill from Ocala, an attorney who had been in the House since 1955; and newly elected representative Ben Hill Griffin Jr., a wealthy citrus grower from Frostproof. Returning committee members in addition to Charley Johns, who was now chair, were Representatives Cliff Herrell from Miami Springs and J. B. Hopkins of Pensacola.[21]

The 1957–59 Johns Committee was still operating under the quorum rule established after the first Miami hearings in 1957: "At any duly called Committee hearing, *one* [emphasis added] or more members will constitute a quorum."[22] Thus Johns still had the option of acting as a one-man committee.

Soon after Johns took over as chair in July 1957, he sent his chief investigator, R. J. Strickland, "to investigate a matter in the Gainesville area"[23] for two weeks in August or September. By November, the press had also learned that the Johns Committee had held some clandestine meetings, but they could not determine who the committee's next target would be. Two months later, an internal committee memo about preparation for the upcoming NAACP hearings narrowed the target area. The January 1958 memo itemized groups of people about whom the committee planned to obtain records. At the top of this hit list were Sig Diettrich and his colleagues, that is, "college and university faculty members in Florida."[24] The membership rolls and the charters for the Florida chapters of the American Association of University Professors (AAUP), of which Diettrich was a member, were on the same list.[25]

By the late summer or fall of 1957, a pattern began to emerge. UF was a possibility as the Johns Committee's next target, but to what end? A later committee staff report on various investigations boldly stated: "This committee started its homosexual investigations *in 1957* [emphasis added]."[26] (See appendix, document three.) Allen Morris, clerk emeritus of the House of Representatives, connected UF and the time frame given in the staff report. A veteran observer of Florida politicians, Morris contended that, when Charley Johns' son, Jerome, was a student at UF, he told his father that there were gay professors at the university. Johns then sent chief investigator Strickland to Gainesville in the summer of 1957. Strickland himself contended that he went to UF initially to look for Communists but was also told about a problem with two gay professors. When the investigator informed Johns, he told Strickland to continue the inquiry to determine how much effect homosexuals had on students. Strickland insisted that he found a very strong influence by gay professors on students.[27]

Eminent political scientist J. Manning Dauer, who chaired the political science department at UF during the Johns Committee years, recalled that the committee was told during an NAACP hearing (most likely the Hawkins hearing in February 1957) that some UF professors were Communists. Dauer also said that the committee found no Communists but "stumbled into incidents of homosexuality, and they focused on that."[28] Dauer's statement is misleading, implying that the Johns Committee simply chose homosexuals because the committee could not find Communists at UF and gays were easy targets. However, based on the committee's staff report, the hunt for gays began during the committee's first full year of operations (1957) and thus predated the volatile 1958 NAACP hearings, despite what the committee told legislators. In its 1959 report to the legislature, the committee said that the UF investigations began because of complaints about gays and that the committee, "being otherwise stayed from pursuing its other investigations because of court orders [the Miami NAACP lawsuits stemming from the 1958 hearings], undertook an investigation concerning said complaints."[29]

Regardless of the committee's reasons for targeting UF, or the timing of its initial search for gays, by the summer of 1958 the Johns Committee was receiving outside help in its pursuit of college professors and gays. A Communism expert and former aide of Joe McCarthy, J. B. Matthews,[30] was sending the committee the records of professors connected with Florida colleges and universities. These professors were suspected Communists, according to Matthews. Two months later, Strickland received an offer of help from former Board of Control member R. H. Gore, who wanted to pay for an undercover agent to help find gays. Strickland, fearing that a separate inquiry might interfere with his investigation, voiced reluctance to work with Gore's agent. By this point, the search for gays took precedence over the hunt for Communists.

The committee also had help from the Board of Control itself. In September, the board met with the Johns Committee in Gainesville and gave the committee full support, even agreeing to the committee's request that the board have no involvement in the UF probe until it was finished and UF president J. Wayne Reitz had received the Johns Committee's report. Board chair James Love told the press of the agreement four months later, explaining that the board saw the investigation as a legislative matter. Governor LeRoy Collins said that he saw the investigation as a board matter.[31] In effect, the board and Collins had given the Johns Committee free rein at UF. Thus an investigation that had at some point been a search for Communists on campus became a hunt for gays.

Even with full board support, the Johns Committee still had to be circumspect in its early investigations at UF. The university was the alma mater of many of Florida's legislators; the members of the Johns Committee were aware that, if their investigations damaged the university, legislators would not look kindly on the committee or its funding. Also, the committee's enabling statute for the 1957–59 biennium gave the committee no authority to investigate professors for homosexuality. Finally, any publicity about the investigations would mean that the element of surprise, then in the Johns Committee's favor, would be lost. On the latter point, the committee actually benefited from Virgil Hawkins' attempt to integrate UF because reporters for the *Gainesville Sun* and UF's student newspaper, *The Alligator*, knew that George Starke, an African American veteran, had been accepted into the UF law school for the fall term of 1958.[32] Thus, the natural assumption was that the committee was investigating the racial climate at UF.

UF president Reitz knew that more extensive investigations were underway because the Johns Committee subpoenaed him twice in the summer of 1958. One subpoena requested all faculty records related to misconduct as well as all personnel and faculty records related to Communist or integrationist activities. The other subpoena was for all faculty applications and employment records. Two months later, when asked by a reporter if the Johns Committee was investigating faculty, both Reitz and his administrator in charge of faculty records refused to comment. Still, Wayne Reitz was no fool, nor was he a newcomer to UF. A native of Kansas, he had been UF's president for only three years but had taught agricultural economics for ten years at UF before serving as an administrator for another six years. He was the university's first president to be selected from its faculty. Reitz was also no stranger to political environments, having worked as an economist for the U.S. Department of Agriculture in Washington, D.C. His exposure to politicians must have helped him, not only in his difficult role in the UF investigations but also in his strained relationship with Johns, both of which centered on UF's dependence on funding from the legislature. Fearing that Johns could reduce UF's appropriations, Reitz cooperated fully with the Johns Committee. He also believed that, as a state administrator, he "had no alternative except to counsel . . . them [the UF employees who were fired or forced to resign] out of the university."[33] Thus Reitz played a major role in the UF investigations, second only to the Johns Committee and its staff.

Johns himself was not only a true power broker in the legislature, with influence over UF's funding, but also a meddler in the internal, day-to-day operations of the university. Reitz must have cringed every time he received a letter or phone call from Johns. The senator wrote frequently to Reitz, usually wanting jobs or promotions for friends as clerical staff, maintenance personnel, printers, or laborers. Reitz had been president less than a year when Johns asked him to intervene in a disagreement between the director of grounds and one of his employees, who was a friend of Johns. A few years later, Johns wrote to Reitz on behalf of a first-year law student whose poor grades had caused him to be put on probation, asking Reitz to "see if there . . . [was] a way to pull up [the young man's] grades."

Johns added that he was "deeply interested in seeing that [the student] receive[s] a law degree from the University of Florida."[34] Reitz referred the matter to the dean but reminded Johns that a student's grades were a result of his own "ability, motivation, and effort."[35] The most petty instance of Johns' interference at UF occurred several years later. He complained when UF stopped buying grits from his millionaire friend Cecil Webb, and told Reitz to "get [his] Purchasing Agent straightened out."[36] Johns then threatened to review all of UF's purchases. Reitz responded calmly, saying that the situation with Webb had been resolved and that surely Johns understood that the university could not say blatantly that they would buy all of their goods from any one company.[37]

By the fall of 1958, Johns had to explain his own committee's finances. Local reporters obtained expense records in the state comptroller's office, showing that committee staff had not only been in Gainesville for twenty-nine days in a two-month period but had also paid informants $165.00 during that time. Johns' only response was that his discussing the investigations would ruin the committee's efforts. Although the press could not give the reasons for the Johns Committee's investigations, UF's faculty and students soon deduced the true nature of the probe after numerous rumors were rampant about professors being taken from their classes by police and receiving late-night phone calls from R. J. Strickland, asking them to meet him at his motel.[38]

Remus J. Strickland was once described by a friend as having a "bull neck and a steel jaw and a cold stare that radiate[d] authority."[39] He had been a deputy under Leon County sheriff W. P. Joyce in the early 1950s but had been fired in 1953 by Joyce "for the good of the department."[40] Strickland insisted that he had resigned. He did resign from his next position with the state beverage department after only eighteen days because his supervisor found his investigative procedures questionable. Strickland then worked for Tallahassee chief of police Frank Stoutamire as head of the vice squad before joining the Johns Committee staff.[41]

As the committee's chief investigator, Strickland typically worked with the help of campus police, paid informants, and other investigators. By August, he also acknowledged that he had help from another investigator, the young, attractive John Tileston, who worked part time for both the campus police and the Alachua County sheriff's department.

Tileston acted as a decoy in the Thirsty Gator Bar, picking up men and bringing them back to Strickland's motel room, where Strickland would then confront them. One UF librarian, when entrapped by Tileston and Strickland, admitted that he had hoped to have sex with Tileston and that he (the librarian) could name other gay faculty and students. Still, he refused to do so, saying that he was "too much of a man to involve anyone else when it was unnecessary."[42]

In addition to the UF librarian, Art Copleston was also "too much of a man" to implicate others or to cooperate with the committee's investigators. A gay air force veteran attending UF on the G.I. bill, Copleston was stalked by Tileston for four years, beginning in Copleston's freshman year. Tileston often lurked outside Copleston's room, waited in the halls of his dorm, and sometimes followed him to class. During his junior year, Copleston returned to his dorm room one day to find that he suddenly had a new roommate. "Jim," an attractive, muscular young man, tried to seduce Copleston, who later learned that Jim, unable to afford college, was hired by the Johns Committee's staff to entrap Copleston. Despite the harassment from Jim, Tileston, and Strickland, Copleston never cooperated with the committee. Interrogated four times while at UF, he refused not only to admit his own homosexuality but also to name other gays. Despite a lack of cooperation from Copleston as well as the UF librarian, Strickland continued to watch the bars and found two gay professors through such surveillance.[43]

Strickland had also set up a successful sting operation at the Alachua County courthouse. His procedure for entrapping gay men was fairly simple. Strickland's assistant, most often Tileston, would approach a suspect. If he responded sexually, Strickland or another investigator was there to move in and confront the suspect. This process often resulted in Strickland's catching Alachua County residents as well as UF students and faculty, some of whom would then name gay professors or students.[44]

Surveillance and entrapment of this sort continued into December of 1958. Strickland's bathroom investigations were particularly productive on December 5, when he caught an English professor after he was approached by Tileston. Strickland elicited the names of one administrator and eight faculty in English, music, humanities, mathematics, and business from the English professor, who also named the "Head Professor, Geography," that is, Sig Diettrich. A week later and with the same method, Strickland nabbed a music professor who named at least two other UF faculty. Strickland was a busy man. In a two-week period alone, by having eight people under surveillance and interrogating ten more, he obtained the names of five suspected gays.[45]

Even with some recalcitrant suspects, Strickland's progress was enough to bring Johns himself to Gainesville a few weeks later, on January 5, 1959, to participate in the Johns Committee's five-day round of executive-session interrogations[46] by the committee's chief counsel, Mark Hawes, who was assisted by Strickland and the campus police. The presence of Johns, Strickland, and Hawes did not escape the notice of the local press, who reported that university officials had no comments on the committee's recent investigations, despite UF's police chief having been seen in conference with Johns and his staff that day. When questioned by a *Gainesville Sun* reporter about his closed-door meeting, Johns said that he would not be having a formal hearing. Still, the committee's new rule of one member equaling a quorum for a hearing allowed him to do so. Whether a formal hearing or not, the interrogations continued the next day, although without Johns. He told reporters that he was "a little sick at his stomach."[47]

Most likely many of those interrogated felt the same way. During that first full week of 1959, the Johns Committee questioned forty-two men, all suspected of being gay or knowing gays, including seven professors from music, humanities, speech, English, and business. The committee also interrogated thirteen UF students, including graduate students, and twelve of them named fellow students, faculty, and others. The committee later caught and questioned a number of men not connected with UF, including a minister, two insurance representatives, a medical technician, a trucker, and two chicken ranch owners. Most of the men were married. Half of them named professors or others as gay, and the other half said that they knew men who were gay but did not know their names or that they knew no gays.[48]

Before the committee could finish its interrogations and send its report to Reitz, a UF professor went to both Reitz and a *Tampa Tribune* reporter and told of Strickland and Hawes using "threats of physical harm in an attempt to wring an admission of irregular conduct"[49] from him when Johns left the room. The anonymous professor insisted that Johns either show proof of witnesses' guilt or clear them publicly. The professor also said that Hawes asked leading questions, implying that he had evidence of the professor's guilt, yet Hawes never produced any clear proof, only allusions to photos, statements, and surveillance.[50]

On Monday, January 19, one day before the *Tribune* reported the anonymous professor's complaint, the Johns Committee returned to Gainesville. Hawes, assisted by Johns, Representative William O'Neill from Ocala, Strickland, and campus police, questioned ten people about gays at UF, including one "expert," who was a sociology professor and marriage counselor. Excluding the expert witness, about half of the others named gay professors or other gay men. The witnesses included a nurse, a business professor, four public school teachers, and the chair of UF's division of geography and geology: Sig Diettrich.[51]

•

At 6 p.m. that evening, Diettrich received a call from one of the Johns Committee's staff, asking him to appear before the committee immediately. Diettrich complied but was kept waiting for approximately an hour before his interrogation began. As he had with other witnesses, Hawes tried to make himself and the committee appear benevolent by telling Diettrich that, although the committee was authorized to subpoena witnesses, they hoped to avoid doing so in order to prevent a public record and hearing that would generate publicity harmful to both UF and the people involved. He added that the committee had asked other people to testify without subpoena in executive sessions and asked if Diettrich would agree to do the same.[52]

After Diettrich agreed and was sworn in, Hawes began his intimidation tactics—at first less overtly—by establishing that Diettrich understood not only the nature of and penalty for perjury but also the felony status of a homosexual act in Florida. Hawes then explained that the Johns Committee was not conducting a criminal inquiry but a civil one, to ascertain the scope of homosexuality at UF as well as how to control or eliminate it. He also promised Diettrich that the committee would not release transcripts of cooperative witnesses to law enforcement. However, Hawes emphasized that the committee would not permit witnesses who did not make a full disclosure "to walk off with immunity."[53]

After establishing Diettrich's age, marital status, position as head of UF's geography department, number of years at UF, and salary, Hawes abruptly asked if Diettrich had committed any homosexual acts in Gainesville. After some pressure from Hawes, Diettrich admitted to engaging infrequently in mutual masturbation. His admission did not satisfy Hawes, who insisted that the committee was not probing into Diettrich's private life but merely doing their duty. Hawes then told Diettrich, "We didn't pull your name out of a hat and ask you to come out here; we have certain information concerning you, or we never would have called you out here."[54] After telling Diettrich that the men's restroom at the Alachua County courthouse had been under surveillance for some time, Hawes tried to get Diettrich to admit that he frequented that restroom, but Diettrich refused.[55]

From the outset of the interrogation, Diettrich's nervousness was evident as he often interrupted Hawes' explanations with a "yes" or "yes, sir" and reverted to the syntax and verb tenses of his native Hungarian, but Diettrich's agitation increased when Hawes asked who Diettrich's partners were. He insisted that his rare sexual encounters with men were spontaneous and anonymous, but Hawes persisted, telling Diettrich that many other witnesses had testified that they had seen him in the courthouse restroom. Despite further pressure from Hawes, Diettrich still would not give Hawes any names, insisting again that the encounters were anonymous. Hawes then tried to get Diettrich to admit that he had gone to the courthouse for sexual purposes, but again Diettrich refused. Hawes persisted, first telling Diettrich again that many witnesses had said that they had seen him there and then naming one of the witnesses, a UF professor. Even when given the identity of a professor who had named him, Diettrich declined the opportunity for revenge. He still refused to name anyone, even the colleague who had named him.[56]

Hawes then switched his line of questioning to the restroom at the UF library, and Diettrich admitted that he had had sexual experiences there. After pressuring Diettrich for the intimate details, Hawes again asked for names, but Diettrich still insisted that the encounters were anonymous. Hawes then asked if Diettrich had been in the library restroom much more than in the courthouse facility. Diettrich objected to this query, feeling desperate and trapped, characterizing it as a "When did you stop beating your wife" type of question. Hawes, ignoring Diettrich's point, responded:

"I'm not going to ask you whether you beat your wife or not."[57] Diettrich then insisted that whatever he answered would be wrong and added that he had not only reduced the number of his sexual experiences but had also succeeded several times in talking himself and his partner out of having sex.[58]

Hawes clearly was not interested in Diettrich's efforts to control his behavior, nor was Hawes content to question Diettrich only about his brief encounters with men. The Johns Committee's chief inquisitor then pressured Diettrich for details about his relationship with his wife of twenty-seven years, trying repeatedly to humiliate and break him. Diettrich refused to give Hawes any detailed information about his wife and insisted that she was not the cause of his problem. He added that they still loved each other very much but that he was "sort of weak now."[59] Although Diettrich's meaning was clear, Hawes demanded details, forcing Diettrich to elaborate on his impotence. Diettrich then added: "We are down here to the rock bottom of a man's inner life."[60]

The Johns Committee had not interrogated Ruth Perry "down to the rock bottom" of her life. They had presented her refusal to name names as a failure of patriotism (allowing Representative Herrell to pronounce her as "not fit to be a citizen of Florida"),[61] but the committee interrogated Diettrich differently. His inquisition was more personal. The committee's attempts to convince him to name names became what one scholar has called a "degradation ceremony."[62] Given the number of names that the committee had obtained prior to interrogating Diettrich, eliciting names from him was repetitious at the least.[63] Also, did having the names of gays help the committee write relevant legislation, one of the Johns Committee's ostensible goals? Clearly not, since names were not mentioned in bills drawn up by the committee or in the meeting minutes of the advisory board of medical, educational, and law enforcement experts who assisted the committee in writing such legislation. The Johns Committee's interrogation of Diettrich was almost ceremonial, an attempt to break and shame him as a sexual outcast. In fact, near the end of Diettrich's inquisition, Hawes specifically asked Diettrich *not* to give the names of men in photos shown to him but only to indicate whether he had had any sexual contact with them.[64] Clearly, the committee already had the men's names.

Despite being vigorously coerced and deeply humiliated for an hour and a half, Sig Diettrich never gave the Johns Committee any names. The last witness for the day, he was excused at 9 p.m. After the session ended officially, he asked his inquisitors what he should do then. Hawes explained that Senator Johns had made no decisions at that point but that Diettrich should tell no one about the interrogation and should "act normally as ever."[65] Johns had, in fact, already written to Reitz the same day, telling him that the committee would be giving him some evidence very soon. In a six-month period, the Johns Committee and its investigators had interrogated more than seventy-five people; more than 60 percent of them gave the committee names of supposed gays, including Diettrich's name. Diettrich named no one.[66]

Diettrich returned home, believing his "life's work was in shambles."[67] He also thought that anyone who read the transcript of his interrogation would be left with the worst possible view of him because he "was guilty of breaking conventions."[68] As he explained to a friend, "I carried my secret I thought well-concealed, feeling my own private little hell whenever I yielded."[69]

The day after Diettrich's interrogation, UF's chapter of the American Association of University Professors (AAUP) began to take action, sending a meeting notice to its members, which included Diettrich. The meeting, to be held a week later, was to discuss retaining counsel for faculty as well as ongoing efforts to amend UF's constitutional provision for tenure and dismissal procedures. A letter from the chapter's executive committee was part of the meeting notice; it warned members that professors' civil rights were being violated. Of course, the warning came too late for Diettrich and others. The Johns Committee also obtained a copy of the letter and included it in the transcripts of its interrogations the next day. At the meeting a week later, a senior professor from the law faculty was available to advise faculty about their civil rights. AAUP members then voted to investigate the Johns Committee for exceeding its authority and trying to discredit UF for "personal political gain."[70] Members also authorized their executive committee to present the results of their investigation to the press.[71]

After the January 27 meeting, chapter records are contradictory on the extent of the chapter's attempts to fight the Johns Committee. Chapter president Winston Ehrmann reported that the UF chapter issued a public statement of protest, met with Reitz and other administrators, made reports to the national office, and wrote to and visited public leaders throughout Florida. However, the chapter's newsletter reported that a new committee on legislative activities was formed because of "developments of this year [in 1959] in respect to . . . *potential* threats to academic freedom" [emphasis added], yet in the committee's later, undated report, the Johns Committee was never mentioned.[72]

Meanwhile, Diettrich tried to implement the Johns Committee's advice to act as if nothing had happened. He waited, never knowing when the final blow would come. He jumped every time the phone rang. He also threw himself completely into his teaching and administrative duties. Spurred on by the depth of the impending catastrophe, Diettrich relished teaching more than ever, giving what he considered the best lectures of his life. Still waiting for a call from President Reitz, Diettrich began to collect what he hoped was a lethal dose of aspirin.[73]

Nearly a month passed after his interrogation. Then the Johns Committee gave Reitz its report on Valentine's Day. Two days later, Johns issued a press release, saying that the committee had given the UF administration and the Board of Control testimony, evidence, and a report for use in taking appropriate action. Reitz and board chair James Love both promised to take whatever actions were needed after studying the report.[74]

Another month passed; spring was beginning. On Monday morning, March 16, Dean Ralph Page called Diettrich, saying that Reitz wanted to meet with them that afternoon. Though preoccupied, Diettrich met with Page to discuss the reappointment of renowned cartographer Erwin Raisz as distinguished research professor. After lunch, Diettrich went to Reitz' office where he and Page waited uncomfortably. The president soon joined them and began by saying, "Sig, this is a most serious and to me most unpleasant task."[75] Diettrich answered in a hollow voice, "Yes, I know."[76] Reitz was so courteous and gentle that Diettrich actually felt sorry for him because he was in the position of having to ask for the resignation of a friend. At the end of the twenty-minute meeting, Dean Page, though deeply stunned and perplexed, put his arm around Diettrich, telling him that he still cared about him very much.[77]

Diettrich, deeply touched by Page's reaction, left campus and turned to his priest, Father Thomas Gross, who realized that his parishioner was nearly out of his mind with grief and wisely allowed him to rave for an hour. Diettrich then went into the sanctuary, disputing with God that suicide was necessary for him and thus not a sin.[78]

He soon returned to campus for his afternoon class but first took eighty-five aspirin. In class, he talked with his students about the "creed of geography, [realizing that] to them it may not have made much sense"[79] but that it did to him. After class, he went up to the third floor of Floyd Hall and into the study hall, where he shooed a colleague out of the room, climbed into the window, and then stared down at the hard, damp sidewalk, starting to jump. He later explained to a colleague: "I could not jump. I tried it once more. . . . The aspirin started to act. It dulled my senses."[80] Diettrich walked downstairs to his office, looking very distressed and causing his staff much concern, but he told them he had a headache. His secretary gave him two aspirin, and he took them.[81]

By then, Diettrich was perspiring profusely, so he went home, where Iren, wondering what was wrong, asked him directly why he seemed so nervous. He finally told her that he had lost his job, knowing how hurt she would be by the news. Diettrich called Father Gross before falling into a stupor, having told no one about the megadose of aspirin. Gross came and counseled Iren. After he left, she retreated to Rosemary's room for the night, and Diettrich went to bed.[82]

In the darkness, fear enveloped him. He tried to call out for help but could make no sound as he felt his feet, then legs growing numb. When the phone rang, he answered it but could hear nothing. The caller was Father Gross; he was on his way. Still unable to hear, Diettrich later reeled into the living room, where Iren was talking to the priest. By this time, Diettrich felt "half-way out of [his] wits . . . [and] blurted out that [he] had taken enough aspirin to kill a cow"[83] before passing out in a chair. When he awoke, Iren was holding him and trying to boost his spirits, and his doctor had arrived to give him an emetic, which quickly emptied the contents of his stomach. The doctor gave Diettrich a sedative, and he soon fell asleep.[84]

The next morning, he awoke to see Father Gross, who had to slap him awake. Gross had told Harwood and Olive Dolbeare, two of the Diettrichs' closest friends, what had happened and how grave the Diettrichs' situation was. The Dolbeares sprang into action immediately and had a plan also: to take the Diettrichs to south Florida for several days to relax, starting the following day. Later, Diettrich's friend and colleague Erwin Raisz came over and gave Diettrich a pep talk, promising various kinds of help.[85]

The next morning, one of the forced resignations became public when the *Gainesville Sun* reported that English professor James E. Congleton had resigned after twenty-two years at UF. Although the newspaper gave poor health as the reason, university records later listed him, Diettrich, and others as being terminated.[86] After reading about Congleton's resignation over morning coffee, Diettrich went to campus for his last staff meeting, feeling like the "little Caesar of a department head for the last time."[87] All of his staff greeted him with sadness but also with great affection. After giving his keys to a colleague, Diettrich took one last tour of the department that he had built, his life's work, and then left campus.[88]

The Diettrichs and the Dolbeares left Gainesville in a driving rain, with Diettrich comforted somewhat by his rapidly improving hearing. The four friends found lodging near Punta Gorda on the Peace River and stayed for three days. Initially, Diettrich struggled with the problem of how to tell his daughter about his forced resignation, until Olive Dolbeare suggested that they call Father Joe Curtin in Richmond, Virginia. He had married Rosemary and her husband, Charles, and had christened their baby, Elizabeth Anne. Diettrich called Curtin, who graciously offered to break the news to Rosemary and invited Diettrich to spend some time with him in Virginia. Rosemary then called and was very encouraging, telling her father that she, Charles, and the baby were coming to Gainesville soon for a week's visit. As she talked while holding the baby, Diettrich was able to hear his grandchild's voice for the first time. His spirits lifted immediately.[89]

While the Diettrichs and Dolbeares were in Punta Gorda, Reitz finished studying the Johns Committee's report and told the press that "where valid evidence exists, we have taken and are taking appropriate action."[90] Although the press speculated that ten to one hundred fifty people could be accused of misconduct, Reitz did not indicate the number of people involved or the specific actions that he was taking. He added that he would have a press release when university responses were complete but would not give the names of those involved or what action was taken against them.[91]

The day after returning from Punta Gorda, Diettrich realized that only one of his professional obligations was still unresolved: *The Atlas of Florida*. He had been working to finish the text of his latest project when he was forced to resign. Erwin Raisz had petitioned UF's Academic Council (an advisory committee of faculty and administrators) to allow Diettrich to work in the Florida room of the library to complete his work, an arrangement that would cost UF no money. The council met, and in a display of administrative pique, rejected Raisz' petition.[92]

The same day, Diettrich also received good and bad news about his UF pension: although it was unaffected by his forced resignation, he could not draw it for another two years. He would have his Fulbright funds for the next year but no money after that. Thus he and Iren decided that he would go to Pakistan alone to save money and she would stay in Gainesville to rent out Diettrich's study and Rosemary's room as a source of income. As the Diettrichs were planning how they would survive financially, Charley Johns assessed the situation at the university and praised Reitz for "cleaning up" UF.[93]

One week after being forced to resign and considering suicide, Diettrich's major concern was Iren, who had withdrawn from almost everyone, pulled the curtains of their home, and refused to answer the door or the phone. Although her refusal to answer the phone was understandable, given the number of unpleasant calls the Diettrichs received, it pained Diettrich even more to know that he had wounded the one woman he loved. He believed their marriage had been a happy one, despite their physical problems, and that his occasional sexual encounters with men were like being possessed by an outside force.[94]

Three days later, the Diettrichs' spirits were lifted tremendously by the arrival of their daughter and her family for a week's visit on their way to south Florida. Diettrich was overjoyed to see his daughter and her family and to meet his three-month-old granddaughter for the first time.[95] In a few weeks, Iren improved further. Having taught classical piano for many years, she resumed teaching, and all of her students returned when they learned that she was not going to Pakistan. This boosted her morale considerably and brightened the couple's financial outlook as well.[96]

Just as the Diettrichs were on a stable, upward path, the full impact of the Johns Committee witch hunt hit the front page of the *Gainesville Sun*. Reitz announced that fourteen UF employees, some academic and some not, had been dismissed. The records of the fourteen had also been marked accordingly, but no names were released. Fortunately, Rosemary and her family paid another visit on their return from south Florida, so the Diettrichs' spirits were lifted again.[97]

Diettrich soon wrote to some of his friends and colleagues, although not in great detail, about the reasons for his resignation. He wrote simply that he had not abided by some conventions or that UF was the subject of a witch hunt which caught him and other people in its web. However, he wrote very openly to Ray Crist, his closest friend and colleague, who was on research leave in France. Crist and his wife, Hilda, were essentially part of Diettrich's family. They were Rosemary's godparents, and she referred to them as "Uncle Ray" and "Aunt Hilda." Diettrich revealed more of his Johns Committee ordeal, though not the prurient details, to Crist than anyone else other than Father Gross. Diettrich was very concerned about how his colleagues would react to his resignation, but the overwhelming majority stood by him. Appropriately, the first to write was Ray Crist in France, emphasizing that his great respect for Diettrich, both personally and professionally, was undiminished and that he and his wife would always be Diettrich's admirers and friends. Similar messages came from other colleagues and even from his students.[98]

Father Joe Curtin in Virginia offered a different kind of help: an invitation to spend a few days at his religious enclave. Diettrich accepted, and his stay proved therapeutic.[99] Curtin, who taught at a Catholic high school, asked Diettrich to talk to three classes about Florida. It was the first time he had taught since the day of his resignation and, other than time spent with his daughter and her family, the first time he had felt joy.[100] Diettrich also experienced a psychological turning point after a few days in Virginia. Curtin helped Diettrich to see that his pride in not telling his friends or family about any of his problems with work, money, or personal challenges created a wall between him and others that stopped him from being emotionally intimate with anyone.[101]

During his few weeks in Gainesville before leaving for Pakistan, Diettrich was able to do some further work at home on *The Atlas of Florida*. He also enjoyed several dinners with his and Iren's friends. A few days before his departure, he returned to the new student center, where one of his doctoral students hosted a farewell party for his former professor.[102]

As Diettrich prepared to leave for Pakistan, the Johns Committee's additional impact on UF began. The committee decided to make its files on public employees' homosexual conduct available to their superiors and to give employers the committee's "substantiated facts"[103] on homosexual conduct by any person. The Johns Committee also finalized its report to the 1959 legislature, listing certain "facts" discovered by the committee, such as: highly educated people were more likely to be gay; homosexuality was a result of environment rather than genetics; gays, particularly teachers, were excellent recruiters of youth (and thus adept at inducing them to become teachers);[104] a good investigator could find proof of homosexual conduct at any school, using only photos of school personnel; and the Johns Committee's investigations resulted in the dismissal of fifteen people at UF and a number of public school teachers and other state employees. The committee's legislative program included loss of state pension for employees dismissed on morals charges and a centralized state records system of public school personnel. Requiring state employees to be fingerprinted and to have a current photo on file were the final elements in the committee's recommended legislation.[105]

Although unaware of the committee's legislative recommendations, UF students soon protested two other bills sponsored by Johns and a fellow Pork Chopper. One bill would have permitted the firing of any employee in public education who favored integration. The other bill would have allowed the banning of any university textbook that was not patriotic enough. Students, indignant about both bills and the Johns Committee's investigation of their university, collected more than two thousand signatures on a petition and organized a campus protest. During the protest, an electrical blackout prompted a panty raid that quickly became political. Shouts of "We want Johns"[106] soon led to students throwing rocks at campus police and setting fire to trash dumpsters and other university property. After two arrests followed by expulsions and several hospitalizations, the protests ended. Neither bill passed.[107]

Meanwhile in Pakistan, Sig Diettrich joined a thriving geography department at Dacca. The department also had graduate courses and an honors program, serving more than one hundred students a year. As his fellowship was nearing its end, Diettrich received another honor. His work in Pakistan had been so successful that he was reappointed as a Fulbright fellow for another year. This meant not only that he would be teaching at the University of Dacca until the summer of 1961 but also that the Diettrichs were now financially secure, since he could begin to collect his pension in the same year.[108]

Even as Diettrich completed his second year in Pakistan, Reitz continued to deal with interference by the Johns Committee. In the fall of 1961, the committee told Reitz that it had received complaints about female students being asked for dates by African American janitors. The committee wanted Reitz to stop employing African American men in women's dorms immediately. The committee also planned to inform the Board of Control that UF was hiring too many out-of-state residents. (Perhaps the word had already spread through Florida's higher education networks that UF was still being harassed by the committee.) In addition to African American janitors and employees from out of state, Reitz also had to manage further interference from the Johns Committee about gays at UF. Late in the same year, he received a form letter from Johns, also sent to other state university presidents, asking for an explanation of UF's policies for dealing with homosexuality. Reitz simply replied that, for faculty or staff about whom clear evidence of gay activity was found, UF's policy was prompt dismissal, a report in the personnel record, and a release of that information to potential employers. The Board of Control expanded UF's policies, requiring all state universities to screen employees as to "ideology and moral conduct" as well.[109]

No one in authority screened the Johns Committee's moral conduct. Soon the committee's short-term effects on UF were evident. According to professors who actually lived through UF's little McCarthyism, the university lost twenty to twenty-five faculty because of the committee's investigations. Two professors even recalled that, soon after the committee gave its findings to Reitz and the Board of Control, the results (including a list of names) were well known. "Every week they fired an additional professor on that list, and all the firings happened in alphabetical order."[110] Although the Johns Committee's 1959 report to the legislature noted fifteen professors fired while Reitz' correspondence and the *Gainesville Sun* gave fourteen, university archives list as few as ten people terminated in 1959.

Those professors' years of service to UF ranged from a minimum of eighteen months to Diettrich's twenty-seven years, which was the maximum.[111]

The higher number of terminations recalled by UF professors would also include those who, after being interrogated by the Johns Committee, resigned preemptively because they feared that they would be asked to resign. Also among the terminations would be employees who were never interrogated but chose to leave UF rather than work in an atmosphere in which civil liberties were not protected. Furthermore, professors who left UF during 1958 or 1959 could be suspected of hiding some transgression. Even those who remained at UF and were never approached or questioned by the Johns Committee were demoralized by the witch hunts. Lillian Seaburg, a librarian who served the university for twenty-five years, explained that the committee put the entire university's morale at an all-time low: "Of course they started with communism and then they took the [charge of] homosexual [sic] finally to get the people [they wanted in trouble]. You were afraid to even have a friend of your own sex.... The Johns Committee really did tear us up.[insertions in original]"[112] Dr. Thomas A. E. Hart, a professor of English and humanities during the 1940s and 1950s, lost two or three colleagues during the witch hunt, describing them as "fine people ... [whom he] admired immensely."[113]

Of course, the UF purges occurred when the American public viewed homosexuals as, at the very least, mentally ill and sexual predators, if not security risks or criminals. Also, during this time, some gay teachers' certificates were revoked without a hearing, despite a requirement by Florida law that teachers accused of moral turpitude must be allowed formal hearings before the State Board of Education. For professors who actually asked for a hearing, the charges alone were enough to raise suspicion, smearing their reputations and thereby forcing them to resign, whether the charges were true or not.[114]

Inaccurate newspaper articles about UF students were another short-term effect of the committee's investigations. The *Miami Herald* announced that the Johns Committee's report mentioned five hundred students as being involved in the investigations. The *Herald* then implied that those students were gay or engaged in clandestine activities. President Reitz labeled the *Herald*'s articles as false and explained that the figure of five hundred was an estimate based on national statistics and was never intended to apply to an individual university. He emphasized that homosexuality was not unique to UF. The *Herald* refused to retract its articles. Reitz also tried to convince the editors of the *Gainesville Sun* to limit their coverage of the Johns Committee's report on UF, arguing that such publicity would harm the university. The *Sun* refused.[115]

The Johns Committee's records also reflect the long-term effects of their witch hunt at UF. The committee collected background material on seventeen suspected gay professors (along with a few integrationists and suspected Communists), creating an information packet on each educator. Among these professors were the following: two Fulbright scholars; three widely published authors; five graduates of highly esteemed institutions (Harvard, the University of Chicago, the Juilliard School of Music, the University of North Carolina, and Columbia University); and three professors who had taught at Princeton, the University of Michigan, or Johns Hopkins. These records show not only how much the Johns Committee overstepped its authority but also what highly credentialed professors UF had hired. The same records also raise never-to-be answered questions: What high degree of teaching and research excellence might UF have reached much sooner if the committee had stayed out of Gainesville? How much faculty recruiting momentum was lost in the 1960s because of bad publicity created by the Johns Committee investigations in the late 1950s?[116]

Of course, Charley Johns insisted that the investigations were warranted: "I don't get no [*sic*] love out of hurting people. But that situation in Gainesville, my Lord have mercy, I never saw anything like it in my life. If we saved one boy from being made homosexual, it was justified."[117] Nine months after the great purge at UF, Johns also sympathized with Reitz for his "having to do all of the dirty work [of meeting with] those professors, whom we exposed, whom you had known for years and [whom you had] to fire." Johns added that "when the cards were down, . . . [Reitz was] not lacking."[118]

•

Charley Johns felt no sympathy for Sigismond Diettrich. Fortunately, he did not need it. By the time Diettrich finished his second year in Pakistan, he was eligible to draw his UF pension and could retire with a modest but comfortable income. He returned to Gainesville and to Iren. One of the Diettrichs' greatest joys during those years was their daughter and grandchildren. Rosemary had remarried, returned to Florida, and had a son, Michael. Diettrich also remained active in his church and in his community as well. The Diettrichs established the Foundation for the Promotion of Music, an organization that still works locally to assist young musicians, sponsor musical events, and offer scholarships.[119]

Had he been allowed to remain at UF, Diettrich most likely would have produced additional and more extensive scholarly works. However, in one regard, he did write a comprehensive work: *The Atlas of Florida*, published in 1964. UF did not allow him to finish the book, even though he was its original author, nor did he receive full credit for the work he did on the project. Although *The Atlas* became a quite profitable publication for the University of Florida Press,[120] there is no evidence that Diettrich or his family ever received any revenue from *The Atlas* before or after his death from cancer in May 1987.[121]

Above all, Sig Diettrich was a survivor. Within weeks of being forced to resign from UF, he had put his life in order and prepared for his work in Pakistan. When he returned to Gainesville, the Johns Committee purge was still very much on the minds of his neighbors, but Diettrich did not allow the witch hunt to dominate his life. In refusing to name names or to act like a victim, he became a witch hunter's ultimate nemesis: a person of courage empowered by conscience. Never having cooperated with the committee, Diettrich was still an honorable man, while the committee's disgraceful acts affected UF for years. Clearly, the Johns Committee took Sig Diettrich's job—not his integrity.

# 5

## G. G. Mock

Surrounded by Fear, Empowered by Love

Fear was not a new experience for G. G. Mock. However, she had always been able to defy her fears—until now; for the first time in her life, Mock was "scared of something [she] couldn't fight."[1] She could not fight a police officer, particularly one who hated lesbians as much as George Walker did. Having a lesbian sister had done nothing to diminish Walker's homophobia but rather had exacerbated it. When Mock sympathized with Walker's sister after he had beaten her and left her with two black eyes, the Tampa policeman then focused his anger on Mock.[2]

Walker had also propositioned Mock and her ex-girlfriend, Hazel Storey, insisting that they go out with him. Their consistent refusals continued to enrage him. By the summer of 1958, he began to threaten them, telling Mock he would "get even with . . . [them], that either [they] had better go out with him or get out of town."[3] The threats soon escalated. Walker told them that he would frame them if they did not leave Tampa. Having very little money and no other resources, the women were desperate. They decided that, if they could manage to get enough money, Storey would flee to Texas and Mock to New York City. At this point, they were propositioned by another policeman: if they would "put on a [sex] show"[4] for him and his girlfriend at Mock and Storey's apartment, he would pay them very well. Feeling that they had no other options, the two women reluctantly agreed. On June 13, 1958, soon after the "show" began, Walker and seven other officers burst into the women's apartment with guns drawn. They supposedly acted on a tip from an anonymous woman who would later testify against Mock and Storey. The policemen shackled Mock and Storey—in the nude—and arrested them for a crime against nature.[5] The worst was yet to come for Mock; the Johns Committee's assault on gays and lesbians, particularly teachers, was just beginning. Gay and lesbian bars were at the center of the attack, especially in Tampa, and G. G. Mock was harassed by the committee both before and during her years in prison.

•

As discussed in chapter 4, crimes against nature were covered under state laws and carried a maximum penalty of twenty years in prison.[6] Local politicians also legislated against gays in the 1950s. In Miami, a 1954 city ordinance prohibited bar owners not only from employing gays or lesbians but also from selling them liquor or allowing them in the bars. Although not always enforced, such ordinances gave police significant latitude in pursuing gays and lesbians. Two years later, police benefited further from an expanded definition of disorderly conduct that included not giving an acceptable account of oneself and using profanity. Another type of ordinance often used against lesbians was based on dress and forbade anyone, whether in public or private, from appearing in clothes customarily worn by the opposite sex. Some of these local ordinances remained on the books for almost twenty years in places such as Miami and Tampa.[7]

Tampa also had at least one lesbian bar by the 1950s. It drew patrons from as far away as Jacksonville and Gainesville because those cities had no lesbian bars at the time. Even during the Johns Committee's gay witch hunts in Gainesville, UF students continued to drive to Tampa and patronize gay and lesbian bars. For those students, the Tampa bars, which were already weekend escapes from the heterosexual world, became a respite from the tensions created by the Johns Committee as well. Such public places were also important for young and working-class lesbians like Mock and Storey who sometimes lacked homes in which to host private parties and had very few places to socialize. Along with softball teams, the bars became an important institution within lesbian culture.[8]

Such establishments were the only public places where lesbians were free to be themselves. They could make friends, find lovers, and experience a lesbian culture with its own social customs. One of the most prominent mores of that culture in the 1950s, and a staple of lesbian bar culture, was the butch/femme dynamic. These roles had become more apparent

Figure 5.1. Lesbian party, ca. 1950s, Tampa. Rex Maniscalco Collection of Bobby Smith Photographs and Other Materials, Special Collections Department, Tampa Library, University of South Florida, Tampa. By permission of the Special Collections Department, University of South Florida, Tampa.

during the 1940s, when work in war factories required women to wear trousers. Once such clothing became acceptable attire for women, butch and femme styles of dress, as well as behavior, became more distinct. For working-class butches, the lesbian bars offered the additional benefit of being the only place where they were expected to dress according to the butch role, that is, in trousers. In taking on the traditional masculine role seen in heterosexual couples, butches not only dressed in typical male clothing but might also work in such blue-collar fields as auto mechanics or carpentry. Femmes, of course, wore traditional female attire and often held such working-class positions as waitresses or factory workers. Lesbians were expected to choose one role or the other, and lesbian bar culture strongly reinforced such roles.[9]

Most middle-class lesbians of the 1950s, though, were uncomfortable with the butch/femme roles displayed in the bar culture. Like upper-class lesbians whose social position (and family-controlled inheritances) required them to function in wider circles, middle-class lesbians were not frequent bar patrons. As professional women (teachers, librarians, and social and government workers), adhering to butch/femme roles would have meant risking exposure when they most wanted to be accepted or at least tolerated by heterosexuals. These professional women followed "a mode of behavior and dress acceptable to society,"[10] a stated goal of the Daughters of Bilitis (DOB), a pioneer lesbian organization founded by middle-class lesbians. Dressing with what the DOB described as "sufficient, though never excessive femininity"[11] (for example, skirted suits and low heels) was as important to the middle-class lesbian culture as the butch/femme dress code was for working-class lesbians.[12]

Inevitably there was a clash between the two cultures. Middle-class lesbians believed that they had hardly anything in common with most bar patrons and often blamed the more overt working-class butches and their femmes for lesbians' outcast status in society. However, such criticism ignored the significance of the bars. First, bars provided employment for some lesbians and gays; both Mock and Storey worked as bartenders in several lounges in the Tampa area. Second, by providing a place for lesbians to congregate and form networks, the bars helped lesbians to create a sense of group identity. By using such opposing terms as "good lesbians" and "bar dykes," middle-class lesbians detached themselves from the most accessible, group-conscious women in lesbian society.[13]

A variety of dangers inherent in the bars also kept many middle and upper-class lesbians away. First, the bars strongly encouraged women to drink, since patrons usually were not allowed to remain in the bars without drinking. Bar employees sometimes even pushed drinks to keep the bars financially viable. For working-class lesbians in low-paying, dead-end jobs, drinking in the bars was often a relief valve of sorts and sometimes one of a few pleasures available to them. Thus alcoholism was more frequent among bar patrons. Second, lesbian bars were often located in dangerous neighborhoods. The possible illegality of doing business with "sexual perverts" fostered Mafia investment and control, which usually meant establishments in poorer, industrial neighborhoods. Lesbian bar patrons had to frequent dangerous areas of a city at night and risk being abused or attacked. A third danger in the bars was police harassment in the form of entrapment and raids.[14] Undercover agents would frequent the bars, hoping to trick or pressure patrons into revealing their sexuality or giving out names of other lesbians. Police raids often occurred because the bar owners had been delinquent in paying for police protection or because an incumbent in a local election needed to "get tough on crime." Some raids were simply random acts. Often referred to as "jump raids,"[15] they were intended to intimidate lesbians and disrupt their social networks. In any case, police methods during a raid could be brutal and included the use of police dogs and strip searches accompanied by various forms of sexual harassment. If arrested, lesbians would often find that their names were in the local newspaper, or their employers had been informed of their arrests, or both.[16]

Typical of jump raids of the time was a series of eleven raids in Miami in August 1954. Sheriff Tom Kelly, with the help of forty-four deputies, arrested fifty-three people and jailed eighteen on the pretext of checking for venereal disease. On the same night, a raid on the 22nd Street beach, a well-known gay gathering place, netted thirty-five arrests. The catalyst for the raids was the murder of a gay man, which local newspapers then used as a reason to call for an investigation of sexual perversion in Miami.[17]

Not to be outdone, Charley Johns, with only two months left as acting governor, touted his own contribution to the battle against the "perverts" in Miami. Shortly after the beach and bar raids, Johns released an open letter to Miami mayor Abe Aronovitz, announcing that he (Johns) had appointed Miami attorney Morey Rayman to "coordinate Miami's campaign against perverts."[18] However, the Miami police chief noted that, if he ran all gays and lesbians out of the city, "members of some of the best families would lead the parade."[19]

Two years later, in a volatile Dade County sheriff's race, incumbent Tom Kelly, who had led the large jump raid in 1954, was accused of "frequent homosexual acts"[20] by his opponent. It appeared that, in Miami, it was becoming difficult to distinguish the witch-hunters from the witches. The *Miami News* also contributed to the drama with an exposé series on gay and lesbian bars, publishing owners' names, home addresses, and photos of their homes, along with stories on the "homosexual menace" and children. Police soon conducted more jump raids in bars and on the notorious 22nd Street beach, followed by surveillance of private homes. Police officials later shared surveillance findings with the Johns Committee.[21]

In the spring of 1957, a different legislative committee, the Senate Committee to Investigate State Tuberculosis Hospitals, authorized a gay witch hunt in Tampa. Local officials easily accommodated the committee, having already begun a crackdown on gays and lesbians. As in Miami, the "campaign against perverts" was initiated after the murder of a gay man who, like the Miami victim, had been lured to a deserted area by young men posing as gay and then been beaten and robbed.[22] Although the Southwest Florida Tuberculosis Hospital investigation netted only three homosexual employees, one of them named the dean of boys at a local high school as gay. The Hillsborough County sheriff's department then began to investigate the public schools, as well as the University of Tampa (UT), for gay and lesbian teachers. At UT, investigators found suspected gay professors who had allegedly recommended gay teachers for jobs.[23]

The possibility of gay professors recommending gay graduates for teaching jobs particularly interested the Johns Committee. In February 1959, only two weeks after interrogating Sig Diettrich at UF, Mark Hawes interviewed a deputy in the Hillsborough County sheriff's department who had worked on the investigations of both the hospital and the Hillsborough County schools in 1957. He had used a contact in the personnel department for Hillsborough County schools to provide leads and then used informants and conducted surveillance in gay and lesbian bars, most likely the same ones where Mock and Storey worked and socialized. After collecting names, the deputy questioned some teachers, using polygraph tests. The deputy explained that some professors at UT wrote letters of recommendation for public school teaching jobs for their former students, knowing that they were gay. He added that gay professors in the physical education departments at FSU and UF had done the same.[24]

The Johns Committee included much of the deputy's information in its 1959 report to the legislature, in which the committee focused more on the results of the UF investigation and the problem of homosexuality than on the committee's failure to destroy the Florida NAACP or stop integration in Florida. Playing on legislators' fears, the committee reported that some gay teachers were "recruiting teen-age students into homosexual practices."[25] The legislature promptly renewed the Johns Committee's

Figure 5.2. Senator Charley Johns talking with B. R. Tilley (*left*), president of St. Johns River Junior College, and A. E. Mikell (*right*), superintendent of Levy County schools, about plans to screen teacher applicants for homosexuality. State Archives of Florida, *Florida Memory*, http://floridamemory.com/items/show/42894.

mandate for two more years, increased committee funding, and expanded its powers to include examining state agencies for gays and lesbians.[26]

During Hawes' interview of the Hillsborough County deputy, Hawes asked what advice the deputy had for the Johns Committee staff, based on his investigations in 1957, and the deputy noted: "The hardest that I found to break is the females. They go right to the bitter end before they finally give up, and they were the roughest that we had."[27] In the Tampa area, the deputy most likely found some of those hard-to-break women at bars like Jimmie White's and Fungi's. In the summer of 1957, while the Tampa school system was being investigated for gay and lesbian teachers, Fungi's was raided, and one woman was arrested because of her masculine attire.[28] A police detective told her, "If you're a woman, you ought to dress like one."[29] Local police also used such charges as disorderly conduct or vagrancy, which were frequently handled in municipal courts. (Because they did not involve the right to a jury trial or much judicial oversight, such charges were excellent tools for police harassment.) The vice squad also recorded the tag numbers on cars in the bars' parking lots. Detectives on the Tampa vice squad believed that the Miami raids had driven many gays and lesbians to Tampa. One detective even told a reporter, "[Tampa] is their headquarters now."[30] In June of 1957, the city's Board of Representatives had responded by calling for a crackdown on gays and lesbians as well as a city ordinance against "perverts."[31]

During this time, raids were considered particularly successful if gay or lesbian teachers were found in the bars or if investigators obtained names of gay or lesbian teachers from bar patrons or employees. The raid on Fungi's was soon followed by a raid on the Knotty Pine Bar, which was frequented more by gay men than lesbians, but fifteen people were arrested there and later released. The raid was supposedly in response to complaints from neighborhood residents. However, the Knotty Pine was surrounded by parking lots, a brewery, a garage, and a few minor businesses that were not open at night. After the Tampa vice squad had conducted a number of bar raids in the city, lesbians and gays would shift to bars in the St. Petersburg area for a time. St. Petersburg police sometimes found lesbians difficult to manage. Like the Tampa sheriff's deputy who believed that lesbians were the most difficult to break, a police detective in St. Petersburg expressed a similar opinion to a reporter, explaining that lesbians were dangerous and adding: "It's not like arresting the little old lady. They'll go round and round with you."[32] After a few rounds with St. Petersburg police, gays and lesbians would shift back to Tampa when police activity "cooled off" there.[33]

The largest lesbian bar in Florida did not escape the 1957 raids in Tampa. Jimmie White's Tavern was also one of the oldest lesbian bars in the city but was typical in its configuration: two rooms, one with a bar, pool table, and booths, and the other with a second bar and a dance floor. Jimmie White's was sometimes referred to as the La Concha Bar or Cucujo's, the latter a reference to its owner Jo. According to a local reporter, the bar's managers ran it "with a firm hand, often concealing switchblade knives in the pockets of their trousers."[34] Control was necessary because some of the bar's customers were rowdy, hard-drinking women. On July 12, 1957,

Figure 5.3. Couples dancing at Jimmie White's Tavern, ca. 1950s. Rex Maniscalco Collection of Bobby Smith Photographs and Other Materials, Special Collections Department, Tampa Library, University of South Florida, Tampa. By permission of the Special Collections Department, University of South Florida, Tampa.

eight members of the Tampa vice squad raided Jimmie White's and arrested twelve women for dressing in a "mannish" fashion. The officers also interrogated two women bartenders wearing men's clothing but did not arrest them. When the bar's owner objected to the arrests, a police captain told her that orders for the raid "came from the top"[35] and confidently predicted that the police's "war on perverts" would end lesbian and gay activity in Tampa. The twelve women were interrogated, fingerprinted, photographed, and put on general investigation but not charged. The police captain admitted that the women would be released if they had no criminal records. He also said that his vice squad would pursue the women in order to "run them out of town."[36] Unfortunately, Jimmie White's Tavern offered an additional incentive to police and later to Johns Committee investigators: G. G. Mock, one of its bartenders, was dating a lesbian teacher.[37]

Mock tended bar at both Jimmie White's and Fungi's in the 1950s, as did Hazel Storey. Despite being lovers in the past, the two women were now platonic roommates and were dating other women. Although not Tampa natives, both women had lived in the city since early childhood and had attended Hillsborough County schools. Storey left school after the eighth grade, married, had two daughters, and divorced her husband about 1951. She soon married again, but her children were put in the Texas Baptist Home for Children in 1954, and she left her second husband the following year. Storey began going to gay and lesbian bars in Tampa with her second husband. One of those bars was Fungi's, where she noticed the lesbians there, although she knew nothing about gays or lesbians at the time. However, after being married twice, she had come to realize that she "didn't care anything about men."[38] She found sex with neither of her husbands to be satisfactory. In 1955, at age twenty-four, she left her second husband and began living with Mock, who was twenty-five. Storey had never lived with another woman before.[39]

After high school, Mock's mother had given her daughter three choices: get a job, go to college, or get married. Choosing what she thought was the easiest option, Mock married at age nineteen but divorced four years later after having a daughter. Knowing she lacked the financial stability that her young daughter needed, Mock agreed to let her daughter live with her father and saw the child during summers and holidays. Mock held a number of jobs during her mid-twenties. She worked for the Yellow Cab Company and bartended at Fungi's and Jimmie White's, which were both located on Grand Central Avenue. Storey tended bar at the same places as well as working at the Echo and Circus lounges in Sarasota. The two women rented an apartment on Howard Avenue, not far from Jimmie White's.[40]

Unfortunately, they came in contact with lecherous heterosexuals and corrupt public officials. Heterosexual men came into the bars frequently, usually intoxicated, and tried to pursue one of their ultimate fantasies: sex with a lesbian. About a year before meeting Storey, Mock had noticed a Tampa municipal judge soliciting women at the bars. He would ask them to perform lesbian sex acts for him, and he often chose women who were in trouble with the law. If they acquiesced to his sexual propositions, they would find that their cases had been dropped or their charges reduced.[41]

Later the same judge solicited Storey at Fungi's while she was working, laying a hundred-dollar bill on the bar and propositioning her for mutual oral sex. After Storey "told him what he could do with the $100,"[42] the judge left. A bar maid who had overheard the exchange between Storey and the judge criticized Storey for refusing him and asked Storey if she knew who he was. Storey said that she "didn't care who he was. [She] didn't like the way he was talking."[43] After that, the judge would patronize the bars where Storey worked and would always arrive very inebriated. He would try to fondle other women in the bar, offering money openly to get someone to leave with him.[44]

Storey was later brought before the same judge when she was arrested for "B drinking" (a common practice among women who frequent bars and get free drinks by flirting with bar patrons). She had just started singing with a band that was performing in one of the lesbian bars, but she had not yet obtained a work card, a requirement for bar workers in Tampa. A policeman who made frequent arrests in the gay and lesbian bars jailed her for not having a work card. Although the bar manager arranged for Storey's bail immediately, she was charged with B drinking, with no mention of the work card. However, the judge gave her a light fine because, according to the bail bondsman, the judge wanted Storey to procure women for him. They were to work at stag parties where friends of the judge gambled. Some of the men were from Miami, and two others were owners of the Echo Lounge, where Storey worked. One of the owners was an ex–chief of police, and he and his business partner profited from the gambling. Storey led the judge to believe that she would find women for the stag party but then left town in order to avoid him.[45]

While some public officials were making heterosexual advances toward women, others were making homosexual advances toward men. A former Tampa police clerk who had assisted the vice squad as a decoy was often approached by gay men, among them a Tampa policeman. The clerk turned most of the men's names over to the vice squad but withheld a "few of the bigger names . . . because [he] was just plain scared that [he] was getting into something that [he] couldn't handle."[46]

Starting around 1956, Mock and Storey were repeatedly propositioned by policemen for oral sex and to perform lesbian sex acts for them. When Mock and Storey refused, the policemen would sometimes threaten the women. Mock was also asked to perform at sex shows, which, according to her, were attended by the police, the mayor of Tampa, and the FBI. The shows were run by a woman named Monica and her husband and held in clubs and other locations with an audience of about one hundred people. The shows included strip acts and gay or lesbian sexual performances. At about the same time, Storey was also approached for oral sex by an attorney who was a public official. He often took several women at a time to a motel. Storey refused him but knew a woman who had been with him regularly.[47]

Mock and Storey continued to witness the hypocritical pursuit of lesbians and gays by corrupt public servants. Working as bartenders, Mock and Storey had watched the July 12, 1957, raid at Jimmie White's in which police arrested twelve women and later held them for questioning. Mock and Storey were interrogated themselves during the raid but not arrested. However, one of the twelve women was a friend of Mock and Storey's. Mock called her attorney, who said to her: "If there happened to be any school teachers mixed up in that thing . . . it was going to be too . . . hot for . . . [me] to handle."[48] He advised her to wait, telling her that, if none of the twelve was a teacher, then Mock had nothing to worry about. All the women were released in about twelve hours; there were no teachers in that group.[49]

It was about this time that George Walker began to sexually harass Mock and Storey. They had befriended his lesbian sister, allowing her to stay at their apartment after Walker had beaten her. Although his sister left town, Walker threatened to retaliate if Mock and Storey did not go out with him. The two roommates also began to see more gays and lesbians being jailed for vagrancy and other charges. Unlike Storey, who had been imprisoned briefly, Mock had never been in jail and feared having a police record as well as the incarceration itself.[50]

In June 1958, when Walker and his fellow officers arrested Mock and Storey in their apartment for a crime against nature, they had no money to hire a lawyer. Fortunately, Mock's sister paid an attorney five hundred dollars to represent Mock. While she spent six weeks in jail awaiting trial, Johns Committee investigators (having unofficially shifted their focus to gays in Tampa) interrogated her. The committee wanted names of gay and lesbian teachers. The investigators especially wanted the name of the teacher that Mock was dating and told her that she would go to prison for twenty years if she did not give up the woman's name. Despite the threat of a twenty-year sentence, Mock refused to give the Johns Committee her girlfriend's name.[51]

Shortly before the day of Mock's trial, police told her lawyer not to appear in court; he didn't. Mock was then given a twenty-year sentence by a verbally abusive judge. He later altered the sentence to five years and then three. Except for a traffic accident, Mock had never been in trouble with law enforcement before. Storey was also sentenced to three years in prison.[52]

•

The women were transferred to Lowell State Prison near Ocala on July 28 to serve their sentences. At Lowell, Mock was a very well-behaved prisoner and was soon put on the honor system as a trustee. She was also given a job she liked: working on the prison grounds, driving a tractor. The job allowed her to be outside most of the time, and she found the work easy.[53]

About a year later, with the Johns Committee's hunt for lesbians and gays now having official sanction, R. J. Strickland focused on the Tampa area and was particularly interested in Hillsborough and Pinellas county teachers. In August of 1959, he went to Lowell Prison and spent two days questioning thirteen women prisoners, including Mock and Storey, about lesbians and gays.[54] The majority of the women had not been sent to Lowell because of a homosexuality conviction; most (eight of the thirteen) were imprisoned for some form of stealing: grand larceny, robbery, or forgery. One was incarcerated on a drug charge. The remaining four women, including Mock and Storey, were convicted of a crime against nature, and their sentences ranged from three years each for Mock and Storey to five years for another inmate. About half of the women interrogated, including Mock and Storey, were admitted lesbians; the rest said they were heterosexual. The women ranged in age from seventeen to forty-four, and most were from the Tampa area.[55]

The entire focus of Strickland's interrogations at Lowell was to obtain information about lesbians and gays, particularly teachers, preferably in the Tampa/St. Petersburg area. Strickland would have had some experience with places frequented by gays and lesbians, having spent significant time hunting for gays in Gainesville with Officer Tileston and implementing sting operations at the Alachua County courthouse and local motels. However, the Tampa area initially would have been less familiar territory for Strickland since the large urban area had gay and lesbian bars as opposed to only restaurants or certain areas merely frequented by lesbians and gays in Gainesville. Thus, by the summer of 1959, with the gay purge at UF completed and the Johns Committee's investigative powers extended by the legislature, Strickland was building his database on gays and lesbians in the Tampa area.[56]

Strickland's interrogation of Mock was the first and the longest, followed by Storey's. Strickland specifically asked Mock and Storey about "homosexual hangouts in Tampa."[57] Mock gave him the names of places known to be lesbian or gay bars, such as Jimmie White's, the Knotty Pine, and the Belfry in St. Petersburg, while Storey named Fungi's in Tampa as well as the Echo and Circus lounges in Sarasota. When he asked in which neighborhoods gays and lesbians tended to live, Storey told him about Hyde Park, an older neighborhood near downtown Tampa.[58]

Of course, Strickland's ultimate goal was to convince Mock and Storey to give him the names of as many gay and lesbian teachers as possible. However, Mock told him that she only knew of three lesbian teachers, two from Lakeland and one that had left teaching, and that they had told her they were lesbians and had patronized Jimmie White's bar very often. She added that she only knew their nicknames or first names, although both were physical education teachers and one was married to a marine. Such information would have already been available to Strickland, since the women had already outed themselves to a number of people and had frequently patronized bars that investigators would have had under surveillance.[59]

When Strickland asked if she knew any more teachers, Mock then played dumb. She told him: "No, sir. That's all the teachers I knew. They were too smart for me. I never like to talk to a smart person."[60] (One wonders if Mock considered Strickland a "smart person.") Of course, Mock's statement blatantly contradicted the fact that, at the time of her arrest, she was dating a teacher. Whether Strickland did not know that Mock's girlfriend was a teacher or was diverted by Mock's having been arrested with Storey is unclear. However, Mock apparently did outsmart him by playing the role of the uninformed female because he did not pursue that line of questioning.[61]

Instead he returned to her previous statement about the three "out" lesbian teachers. When he asked again if she knew of any other places that the teachers might have frequented, she told him that they had left town. Although Mock did name a male teacher about whom there had been rumors, she also told Strickland that the man was quite old and long since retired. Thus she named teachers who were beyond the reach of investigators. Mock also mentioned a woman who was a dean at Hillsborough High School, but Mock made it clear to Strickland that she had no reason to believe the dean was a lesbian. In fact, Mock used this as an example of how a rumor can be started or passed on by children.[62]

Despite or perhaps because of obtaining very little information on lesbian or gay teachers in the Tampa area, Strickland also asked Mock for the names of other gays and lesbians. Again Mock named lesbians who were "out," in this case because they had participated in sex shows for public officials and law enforcement. She also gave Strickland the name of George Walker's lesbian sister, whose name would most likely have been known to law enforcement, given her brother's position and his intense homophobia. When Strickland asked about lesbians in Jacksonville, Mock said that she only knew nicknames, except for one woman who performed in clubs in Jacksonville and Miami and who had already cooperated with police.[63]

Strickland then interrogated Storey.[64] She also provided little help in his hunt for lesbian and gay teachers, giving him the first names of several lesbian teachers who had outed themselves to a number of people and who frequently patronized gay or lesbian bars, including Fungi's. These women were most likely the same three whose nicknames (or first names) Mock had given to Strickland. Storey also found a different way to refuse Strickland. When he asked her if she had heard any of the other inmates talking about any lesbian teachers at the Florida Industrial School for Girls (a state-run reformatory in Ocala), Storey reminded him: "Well, that involves another inmate,"[65] that is, hearsay. Strickland quickly dropped that line of questioning. When he asked Storey about other lesbians and gays, she gave him the names of women who had had sex with police officers or a public official and the first names of the two women from Lakeland that Mock had told him about. Storey gave him the name of one lesbian, but she would have been beyond his reach because she had moved to New York City. Storey also said that any other gays or lesbians that she knew would be too afraid to talk to him. Near the end of her interrogation, when Strickland asked for names of lesbian or gay personnel at the Southwest Tuberculosis Hospital, Storey gave him the nickname of one lesbian who was a nurse but at a different hospital.[66]

Strickland seemed particularly interested in why Storey was a lesbian. However, he showed no such interest in Mock. Perhaps the origins of Storey's sexuality were of greater interest to him because she had been married twice and had children. He was also familiar with the meanings of the terms "butch" and "femme," as used in lesbian and gay culture, employing those terms during his interrogation of Mock. So, he would have invariably seen Storey as femme and wondered what had caused her to forsake heterosexuality. He first asked her how long she had been a lesbian. Her answer (four years) was the same amount of time that she had been living with Mock. Strickland then asked why she had become a lesbian, if it was "acquired through association and environment."[67] He may have been surprised when she told him that her husband took her to Fungi's the first time and that, although she knew nothing about lesbians beforehand, she did know before she went to Fungi's that she "didn't care anything about men."[68] When Strickland asked if sex with either of her husbands was satisfying, she said no. When he asked if she found satisfaction after becoming a lesbian, Storey said, "not really,"[69] but explained that the fear of being caught by law enforcement as well as doing something that was contrary both to how she had been raised and how she had been taught to interpret the Bible had been very depressing for her. Strickland concluded his inquiry into Storey's psyche by asking if she played the part of butch or femme; she replied that she was "femme."[70]

Having had little success in obtaining the names of lesbian and gay teachers from Mock or Storey, Strickland also pressured some of the other inmates during the rest of his interrogations. He had few results. When one inmate, who had recently come out as a lesbian, said that she knew very few lesbians or gays, Strickland reminded her that she was under oath and quoted the definition of perjury from the Florida Statutes. Asking her about her sexual history, Strickland continued to pressure her until she gave him the names of three people who could give him more information on gay and lesbian teachers.[71]

After getting the names of about a dozen lesbians and four gay men in Tampa, but no teachers, from the next inmate, Strickland encountered opposition from a heterosexual inmate, whose husband was in Raiford prison on a conviction for lewd and lascivious conduct with an underage girl. After the inmate failed to give him any information, Strickland ended the interrogation in a strange way, insisting that lewd and lascivious conduct was a homosexual charge, despite the husband's being involved with a young girl.[72] Clearly, Johns Committee investigators were interested in only one type of sexual behavior, and their definition of homosexuality changed with the results of the interrogation and the mood of the interrogator.

After obtaining names of over a dozen lesbians, one gay man, and two gay policemen, but still no teachers, from the next inmate, Strickland finally secured the names of a few teachers who may have had sex with their female students. However, the teachers were not employed in the Tampa area, and Strickland did not get their names from Mock or Storey but rather from other inmates that he questioned about the Florida Industrial School for Girls in Ocala. The majority of the women that Strickland interrogated (excluding Mock and Storey) had been sent to the Ocala school when they were young. Following the theory previously advanced by investigators—that young people were more likely to be converted to homosexuality if they were recruited before they were in their late teens or early twenties—Strickland asked about lesbian sexual activity at the school, particularly lesbian teachers. One young inmate from Tampa had spent eighteen months at the Ocala school, starting at age sixteen. She named a teacher, Yvonne Brown, as a sexual partner and said another student had had sex with the same teacher.[73] Brown, who had taught at four Florida high schools, denied having sex with any of her students and pointed out that her accusers were delinquent, impressionable children. Another inmate who had been at the Ocala school for over two years, Betsy Hall, had been sentenced to five years for a crime against nature and was an admitted lesbian. In addition to Brown, Hall, who was only twenty, named two other teachers and two students as lesbian. She also named a teacher who was fired for approaching a student sexually.[74]

Hall's interrogation was one of Strickland's longest and most productive, for she not only named teachers but, after repeated pressure from Strickland, made a likely connection to Mock and Storey. Hall admitted knowing the bartender at Jimmie White's, most likely a direct reference to Mock or Storey. She also told Strickland that the same bartender was a lesbian, but when he asked her how she knew, Hall balked, saying that she did not want to discuss other people. After Strickland asked the same questions repeatedly, Hall eventually explained that she knew because they went to the same parties and then gave him the names of some of the other partygoers. She eventually named many lesbians and gay men in the Tampa area, including her current partner and a city judge. Near the end of the interrogation, when Strickland asked again if she could think of anyone who knew about gay or lesbian teachers in the Tampa area, she named the bartender at Jimmie White's once more, most likely another direct reference to Mock and Storey: "As I said before, _____ [name blacked out] knows everybody that comes and goes in Jimmy [sic] White's. She knows everybody that comes in there to pick up everybody else. . . . And she would probably know more than anybody else, her and _____ " [name blacked out].[75]

R. J. Strickland probably considered his two days at Lowell to be successful. Ten days later in a letter to Charley Johns, Strickland was upbeat, saying that he had obtained significant information about several teachers. He had also added to his database on other gays and lesbians in the Tampa area, even obtaining full names in some cases. However, practically none of his success could be attributed to Mock or Storey. They had given him the names of places frequented by gays and lesbians in Tampa, but that was information easily obtained from the Tampa vice squad. Mock and Storey only gave Strickland names of lesbians or gays who had either outed themselves or who frequented bars that were under surveillance. Also, Mock and Storey gave Strickland names of lesbians or gays who were beyond the reach of investigators. Finally, Mock played dumb rather than name her girlfriend or any other teachers, and Storey caught Strickland's attempt to use hearsay as reliable information. Mock and Storey, treated so badly by public officials and men in law enforcement, retaliated in the only way available to them: by not cooperating with one of their abusers' colleagues. In 1959, blatantly defying the Johns Committee's chief investigator at Lowell Prison was not an option for Mock and Storey.[76]

Mock did openly defy other Johns Committee investigators while at Lowell and did so during her most vulnerable time there: at her parole hearings. Each time Mock was eligible for parole, the Johns Committee sent an investigator and a typist to the parole hearing to interrogate her. Just as they had done in Tampa, Johns Committee investigators demanded that she give up the names of gay and lesbian teachers, including the name of her girlfriend. The investigators warned her that she would not be paroled unless she gave them names. Mock still refused to cooperate with the Johns Committee; she never gave them the name of her girlfriend. Mock also paid the price for defying the committee: despite being a model prisoner and a trustee, Mock did not receive a parole until very close to the end of her three-year sentence. However, Storey was released in a short time, despite giving the committee no information. Mock believed that Storey was released early because the committee was really interested in Mock herself. As she explained, the Johns Committee "was really after me. She [Storey] just got caught up in it."[77]

•

Mock was eventually paroled near the end of her three-year sentence. She returned to Tampa, where the Johns Committee's hunt for gay and lesbian teachers was shifting into an investigation of the University of South Florida (USF). Mock worked with her father in his landscaping business for several months, but, once her parole ended, she moved to Miami. She lived there for about fifteen years, working for a large printing company. She enjoyed the work, made more money than she would have in Tampa, and was later promoted to foreman. While in Miami, Mock and some of her coworkers were arrested one evening at Miami's notorious gay beach at 22nd Street. The police called her boss, and he asked: "Are you telling me this because you want me to post bail?" The police officer replied, "No, we just wanted you to know that you have lesbian employees." The boss, now aggravated with the police, responded, "I don't care if they're lesbians; they're reliable workers."[78]

Mock moved back to Tampa in the mid-1970s. Having been much more involved in her daughter's life in the years after leaving Lowell, Mock was proud of the woman that her daughter had become. Mock was particularly delighted when her first grandchild was born in 1976. She settled in Tampa, bought a print shop, the Village Printer, and later purchased a home in a neighborhood near USF.[79]

After Lowell, Mock had lost contact with Storey, who also returned to Tampa. About twenty years later, Storey called Mock abruptly with some surprising information. Storey had found the woman who had not only given police the anonymous tip that had led to their arrest but also had testified against them in 1958. Storey wanted Mock to go to the woman's home and beat her up. Mock refused, saying, "Leave it alone; that's in the past."[80] Soon after, Storey was shot and killed. So far as Mock knows, Storey's murder still remains unsolved.[81]

In the mid-1980s, Mock continued her work as a printer and donated printing time and supplies to Tampa's growing lesbian community. She was the first printer for *Womyn's Words*, which is based in Tampa and is Florida's longest-running lesbian publication. This newsletter was a lifeline for the Tampa women's community in the 1980s before the rise of the Internet. Mock later sold her first printing business and bought another, Print Pad, before retiring.[82]

In the mid-1990s, Mock finally met the "love of her life."[83] She and Linda Bothwell were together for eleven years before Bothwell's untimely death in 2006. Other than Mock herself, Bothwell may very well have been the first person to recognize the significance of Mock's defiance of the Johns Committee. After learning the full story of Mock's struggles against the committee, Bothwell insisted that the story "needed to be told."[84] In 1995, she published a brief account of her partner's encounter with the Johns Committee in *Stonewall*, a local gay publication in Tampa.[85]

Bothwell must have understood that Mock lived under multiple layers of fear in the late 1950s. Working in gay and lesbian bars in Tampa, she was at the center of the committee's early attacks on gays and was harassed by the Johns Committee, both before and during her years in prison. As discussed in chapter 4, the prevailing political, cultural, and medical models of gays and lesbians as subversive, predatory, and mentally ill were enough in themselves to create a climate of fear. State laws with a penalty of twenty years' imprisonment for a crime against nature; city ordinances fueling surveillance, bar raids, and arrests; and local campaigns against so-called perverts further heightened gay and lesbian anxieties. The Johns Committee not only capitalized on this existing climate of fear but also raised it to a new level through its witch hunts at UF and in the Tampa area. Thus fear was not a new experience for G. G. Mock, even when she refused to cooperate with the Johns Committee, and her decision to defy the committee still resonates today. One can draw a larger historical meaning from Mock's defiance because it enabled her love for her girlfriend to survive, even in the Johns Committee's toxic climate of fear in the late 1950s. For years, Mock (like most gays and lesbians) had lived in fear because of whom she loved, even though not many love relationships could survive living that way.[86] Then, by refusing to give the committee her girlfriend's name, Mock showed that lesbian love was stronger than the cumulative fears induced by a state-sponsored witch hunt.

# 6

## Margaret Fisher and Her University of South Florida Colleagues

### Intellectuals versus Inquisitors

Margaret Fisher was not afraid; she was apprehensive. As director of student personnel, she knew that the Johns Committee's trip in May 1962 to the University of South Florida (USF) "was not a friendly visit."[1] An experienced educator, she was also familiar with attacks like the Johns Committee's on books, teachers, and schools, so she thought, "How do we play this one?"[2] Fisher and her colleagues chose to defend USF's vision and policies against the committee's assault on liberal teaching and academic freedom; she and her colleagues also dealt with the aftermath of the investigation as the Johns Committee was coming to an end.

Fisher was not satisfied just to prepare for the investigation; she also wanted to alter the tone of the committee's hearings to make them less of an adversarial, clandestine operation. She was particularly concerned about university counselors and student confidentiality issues, so she consulted with local attorney Ed Cutler, who was on retainer to USF's chapter of the American Association of University Professors (AAUP). He first explained that Florida law was vague in the area of student confidentiality. Cutler then offered what Fisher considered to be the most concise, complimentary advice she had ever received from an attorney: "Obfuscate; exercise your talents."[3] Clearly, Cutler had no doubts about Fisher's abilities to frustrate the committee.

·

Margaret Fisher had been raised with confidence in her abilities. As she later explained, hers was "a family in which every woman [was] supposed to be *somebody*" [emphasis in original].[4] In 1939, she graduated summa cum laude from the University of Texas with a bachelor's degree in liberal arts, the first interdisciplinary degree program of its type in the United States, and earned a master's degree in religious education, also summa cum laude, from Columbia University two years later.[5]

After working for the YWCA in management positions, Fisher earned a doctorate in the philosophical foundations of education from Columbia University in 1953. Soon after, she became director of student affairs at the University of Buffalo and taught social work courses there, beginning a lifelong pattern of holding dual appointments. In 1955, she accepted another dual position at Mills College, a private women's college in Oakland, California. Active in a variety of professional organizations, she began to publish widely on a number of topics in education. In 1958, Fisher accepted a position as dean of student affairs and assistant to the president at Hampton Institute, a private, historically black college in Virginia. A year later, when the president resigned, Fisher promised well-known anthropologist Margaret Mead, who was on Hampton's board, that she (Fisher) would remain to help with the new administration's transition. However, when her annual contract was suddenly terminated by the outgoing administration, she again looked for a dual position, telling Mead, "I will be an administrator if I can also teach."[6]

Soon after writing to Margaret Mead, Fisher published her first book. Coauthored with Jeanne Noble, *College Education as Personal Development* would be used as a textbook for college orientation classes, including those at USF. Fisher first heard about the new university through her networks in higher education. Then a friend from her graduate school days at Columbia, who had recently arrived at USF, asked her to come to Tampa for an interview. That friend was Russell Cooper, dean of liberal arts, whom she had known for many years. However, USF's interdisciplinary approach to education and the university's plan to link student affairs with instruction were the main reasons that she agreed to an interview. After declining an offer from the U.S. Office of Education, Fisher came to USF in September of 1960 as the director of women's activities. Soon after her arrival, Fisher's job title and responsibilities changed suddenly when her counterpart, the newly appointed director of men's activities, died suddenly. She then became director of student activities.[7]

As she had elsewhere, Fisher accepted a dual appointment, part instructional and part administrative. She managed to continue her scholarly work as well, publishing articles in several professional journals and presenting her research at a variety of professional conferences.[8] The instructional portion of her workload included teaching courses in human behavior and introductory psychology and teaching a senior seminar. Fisher was eager to begin creating new interdisciplinary curricula and programs. She wrote to friends, telling them that USF would be different from other universities, built on the "most advanced and carefully considered plans and values in American education . . . [with a] very solid liberal arts foundation with lots of interdisciplinary work."[9] Fortunately, Fisher's view of the new university fit very well with President John Allen's vision for USF.

•

As Allen told the local press, "We have an opportunity for something new and great here. We are not bound to the past by any traditions. . . . There are no fences, no boundaries holding us and limiting our search for knowledge or our methods of teaching knowledge."[10] By the time the Board of Control (which oversaw the state university system) chose Allen as USF's first president, Allen had acquired almost thirty years of experience in higher education. He had taught astronomy at Colgate University before serving as the director of the Division of Education for the State of New York. Prior to taking the position at USF in June 1957, Allen had been executive vice president at UF, a position from which Charley Johns had tried to have Allen fired while secretly offering the UF presidency to Wayne Reitz. However, Allen remained UF's acting president until Reitz was hired; two years later, Allen accepted the USF position.[11]

Allen's vision for USF's innovative approach to learning came not only from himself but also from his faculty and administrators. His first academic hire, librarian Elliott Hardaway, reflected Allen's focus on academics and learning. Hardaway came from UF and was soon as busy planning for USF as its new president was. Allen found that having a strong faculty and an able administration was not going to be a problem. Professors and administrators throughout the United States were drawn to the concept of a new university and the opportunity to create using a "clean canvas."[12] Faculty, in particular, developed a strong esprit de corps since they all had come to USF from good positions elsewhere in well-known universities. However, they had also come to a new institution that had no established reputation. Thus, as Allen's wife, Grace, recalled, all professors knew that "their careers were on the line. So, everybody worked very hard to make ... [USF] go. And it did."[13]

Among John Allen's early administrative hires was Sidney French, a chemistry professor and former dean of liberal arts at Colgate University and Rollins College. Dean French would lead the College of Basic Studies and later become USF's first vice president for academic affairs. After hiring French, Allen gave his new dean the major task of articulating the philosophy and blueprint for USF's academic programs, that is, the vision for the new university. French, Allen, and other administrators decided to set a strong intellectual tone for their new university: academic work would have a value in and of itself, and opposing ideas would be explored openly by a faculty who would be allowed "free inquiry."[14] USF's first catalogue reflected that decision. *Accent on Learning* was the title of the catalogue and soon became an unofficial motto for the university. Written primarily by French, the catalogue made it clear that USF would be a university that focused on intellectual development, not a place to train only for a job or to build up credits. *Accent on Learning* even cautioned students who disliked intellectual challenges or who expected to spend their college years socializing to "think twice" before applying to USF.[15]

"Accent on Learning" was more than a catalogue title or motto; it was a mission statement. This concept was the first of two major policies for academics. "Accent on Learning" sought to balance general and specialized education so that all students took interdisciplinary courses in basic studies and in their majors. This policy also emphasized teaching. All faculty taught basic-studies courses as well as the beginning curricula in various majors. More importantly, administrators emphasized teaching by doing it themselves; even Allen taught astronomy and basic-studies classes during USF's early years.[16]

The other major policy for USF's academic programs was a concept known as the All-University approach, designed to create a holistic com-

Figure 6.1. USF's opening convocation, September 1960. State Archives of Florida, *Florida Memory*, http://floridamemory.com/items/show/42365.

munity of scholars. Under this approach, USF did not have traditional academic departments but rather programs organized around degree sequences that were interdisciplinary. Thus, faculty were often borrowed to teach in different programs, which helped to connect general, liberal arts, and professional studies for students and to reinforce USF's focus on interdisciplinary methods. The best example of the All-University concept was the All-University book, which was chosen each term by a faculty-student committee and was to be read and discussed by all members of the university. One debate-discussion on the book was held each term with both the university and the community attending. The hope was that the debates would give the entire university community common ground, not only for discussion but also for the kind of cultural and social connections normally found at much older institutions.[17] For the local community, "Accent on Learning" and the All-University approach first bore fruit on September 26, 1960, when faculty marched in academic procession at USF's first convocation and students went to class immediately after. USF had officially opened.[18]

•

Although many people in the Tampa area and elsewhere in the state were pleased to see the university open, some legislators had opposed the establishment of USF. The most adamant opponents, including some members of the conservative, segregationist Pork Chop Gang from north Florida, feared that a fourth state university could jeopardize the importance of the other three institutions. Although all members of the 1961–63 Johns Committee had voted to create USF, the Johns Committee first began to intrude upon the university in January 1961, when the committee began to collect copies of letters of recommendation for USF's faculty applicants. Although the actual purpose of such data collection is unclear, it demonstrates the committee's desire to encroach upon USF's hiring practices.[19]

USF was vulnerable not only to legislative intrusion but also to problems encountered by all urban universities. Because it was not a residential university, the influence of family and the local community was constant. Also, as commuters, USF students had less time for the type of student activities that foster a residential university's sense of community. As a new university, USF faced the additional limitations of having no established traditions and no upper-division students or alumni to pass on those traditions. Many of the students were also the first in their families to go to college and thus were less intellectually sophisticated in regard to new or controversial ideas than children of college graduates. Finally, USF faced the possibility of being seen as inferior in quality because it competed with Florida's more established universities. All of these factors contributed to USF's vulnerability.[20]

Unaware of most of these limitations, the Tampa community welcomed USF's arrival, but, by the summer of 1961, some local citizens began to question the university's leadership and teaching methods. When Jane Tarr Smith's son Skipper began to bring home textbooks that she found questionable, she read them and soon decided that they were antireligious and emphasized sex and evolution. She and three other parents met with Dean French, as well as with two deans subordinate to him, in September of 1961. Smith later told the Johns Committee that the deans explained to the parents that the reading material was chosen to broaden students' experiences and viewpoints, and French called the parents a pressure group and said that they were witch hunting. However, Dean French recalled that no one called the parents a pressure group or witch-hunters. Feeling there was nothing to be gained by more meetings, most of the parents did nothing for several months.[21]

Only two months after the parents' meeting with French, a member of the Johns Committee was calling for an investigation of USF, but not because of the university's choice of reading material. Representative George Stallings from Jacksonville sent Johns a news clipping about a USF professor who had praised the university for integrating peacefully. Stallings was unequivocal: "I hope that our Committee will be able to do something about this bird and his big mouth."[22] A week later Johns told Stallings that investigator Strickland would "see what he . . . [could] find out about . . . [the] integrationist professor."[23]

Six months after her meeting with Dean French, Smith sent a letter to

Figure 6.2. Jane Tarr Smith, a USF critic; Johns Committee attorney Mark Hawes; Johns Committee member Representative William O'Neill; and Senator Charley Johns, chair of the committee, 1963. State Archives of Florida, *Florida Memory*, http://floridamemory. com/items/show/42895.

about one hundred local people, announcing a meeting in her home for April 9, 1962. She invited newspaper editors and a number of prominent citizens, including Tampa mayor Julian Lane. At the meeting, one issue discussed was whether the Smith group should go to Allen, the Board of Control, or the Johns Committee about (as Smith described it) the "daily problem of extreme liberal, atheistic teaching"[24] at USF. Although all agreed that they did not want to harm USF, 80 percent of the citizens voted to contact the Johns Committee. Mayor Lane then volunteered to call his friend Charley Johns and followed up with a letter, telling Johns: "If we [referring presumably to Lane and the parents/citizens from the Smith meeting] do not get the action we are seeking, we will request your committee to handle the investigation for us."[25] He also enclosed a list of names and addresses of citizens willing to help the Johns Committee.[26]

The day after Lane wrote to Charley Johns, the committee's chief counsel, Mark Hawes, met with Thomas Wenner, a disgruntled adjunct professor from USF. His written critique of USF, titled "The University of South Florida, Going Soft on Communism," accused university administrators of condoning Communist sympathizers and allowing pro-Soviet textbooks. Three days later, Allen asked for Wenner's resignation. Wenner then met again with a Johns Committee investigator, naming numerous USF staff members as gay, starting with Allen himself and including Margaret Fisher, other administrators, librarians, and faculty. Having collected such questionable information, as well as complaints from parents and Representative Stallings, the Johns Committee began to organize an investigation of USF that included all of the committee's former areas of attack (integration, Communism, and homosexuality) to varying degrees, as well as a major assault on liberal teaching and academic freedom.[27]

Johns was chair of the committee during the 1961–63 biennium and thus presided over the USF investigation. As chair for the 1957–59 biennium, he had directed the volatile 1958 NAACP hearings in Miami when Representative Cliff Herrell of Miami had castigated Ruth Perry for her beliefs and told her that she was not fit to be a citizen.[28] As the Starke senator prepared to preside over another Johns Committee hearing, he was supported by a committee that had only one charter member: himself. The 1961–63 committee contained four new members, Representative Stallings of Jacksonville, Senator Ed Fraser of Macclenny, Senator

Houston Roberts of Live Oak, and Representative Richard Mitchell of Tallahassee. The other two members, Representative Ben Hill Griffin of Frostproof and Representative William O'Neill of Ocala, had served since 1957. As usual, the Johns Committee was dominated by Pork Choppers and North Florida legislators. As they had since 1956, Johns Committee members and staff continued to have legislative immunity. Thus they were not required, even under subpoena, to answer questions about the committee's work or function.[29]

By April 18, 1962, the Johns Committee supporters in Tampa had organized into an "inner group" that included Smith and Wenner.[30] The group planned meetings with Johns Committee staff and emphasized, in a memo marked "Strictly Confidential," that additional members must be selected carefully for their "ability to make good witnesses."[31] The memo also noted that Johns would like to get to Tampa to begin investigating soon and that Hawes was "anxious to make sure he had the 'evidence.'"[32] Apparently not content to be simply a member of the inner group, Wenner decided that exposing the Johns Committee's covert inquiry would accelerate the investigation. He revealed the investigation to the *St. Petersburg Times*, which published his story on May 17.[33]

Soon after the story appeared, Donald Harkness, president of the university's AAUP chapter, called a meeting because faculty told him that university police were interrupting classes in order to bring students in for questioning by R. J. Strickland. This tactic was quite familiar to those who had been UF professors during the Johns Committee investigation in Gainesville. After much discussion, AAUP members agreed to cooperate with the Johns Committee under the following conditions: that the investigation be open and on campus; that faculty be interrogated only on legitimate issues; that witnesses receive a copy of their recorded testimony; that no testimony be made public; and that witnesses have legal representation. For a fee of two hundred fifty dollars, the chapter also kept attorney Cutler on retainer for a year. Unbeknown to his faculty and staff (other than chapter president Harkness), Allen paid almost half of the retainer fee but insisted that Harkness tell no one.[34]

People interrogated by Johns Committee staff during the first phase of the investigation in early May did not have the protections requested by the AAUP. Most of these early interrogations were done at a Tampa motel, and most of those questioned were underage students. Typically, they were asked about administrators and professors suspected of being gay or Communist and about liberal professors whom the students believed were antireligious, used inappropriate language or reading materials, or discussed sexual matters too openly.[35]

President Allen first learned about the motel interrogations on May 15 from Donald Harkness and other AAUP chapter representatives. Of course, Allen knew that he could not stop a committee created by the legislature, but he decided that he would demand that the Johns Committee do its questioning on campus and in the open. He understood better than most people the threat that loomed over his university because he had not forgotten the committee's UF investigation in 1958–59 when he was vice president there. Thus, Allen was faced with the dual task of protecting USF from an investigation that could destroy the vulnerable new university while still presenting his staff as people with nothing to fear or conceal.[36]

On May 21, Allen addressed an assembly of faculty, staff, and students, announcing that he had invited the committee to move its headquarters onto the campus. He explained that the interrogations would not be open to the public and that witnesses could have a tape recorder, a witness of their own, or an attorney during their interrogations. Allen concluded by emphasizing that the people who started the investigation were responsible for proving any wrongdoing, not, he said, "any one of us."[37]

Two days later, the second phase of the investigation began as the Johns Committee held hearings on campus. Conducted during final exam week, the hearings were very disruptive for students and faculty. Of course, the committee would have preferred to continue the interrogations at their motel. As Strickland said later, "[On campus] word gets out in a hurry. . . . It was no way to run an investigation. . . . We did not want to go to the university."[38] Margaret Fisher was proud of Allen for demanding that the committee become "guests" of USF. As she expressed it, "We made them do it on our territory [and] not in somebody's little motel."[39] The campus hearings lasted nine days. The committee interrogated twenty-eight witnesses, including six students, the rest being faculty and staff. Several administrators were questioned, including the deans of student activities, academic affairs, liberal arts, and the College of Basic Studies, as well as

President Allen. Faculty from the social sciences, languages, literature, and fine arts were also interrogated. Four witnesses of special interest to the committee were recalled to testify a second time, among them Margaret Fisher, now director of student personnel.[40]

Fisher's first impression of Johns Committee members was that they did not understand the vision that she and her colleagues had created for USF. As she recalled, the committee showed very "little comprehension of the mission which the University had undertaken and its special, unique place in the whole state system and in the whole system of higher education, generally, in the United States."[41] For example, the dual-appointment system, one of the greatest inducements for Fisher to come to USF, puzzled the committee. As Fisher recalled: "They couldn't understand how administrators could possibly teach. There was very little understanding of what universities were about, the fact that it is a very different kind of institution from a business enterprise or a legislature."[42] Fisher and her colleagues soon realized that, since the Johns Committee did not understand USF, its vision, or its policies, the university would have to teach the committee. USF faculty and administrators approached the hearings as if they were preparing for a credentials review by an accrediting agency. Four of Fisher's administrative colleagues, whose interrogations preceded hers, would be particularly instructive about USF's vision and policies: Robert Warner and Deans Cooper, French, and Howard Johnshoy.[43]

•

Robert Warner was the first to testify when the campus hearings began on May 23, 1962. Like Fisher, he had accepted a dual appointment. A former Fulbright Fellow, he held degrees from Harvard and Yale. Warner chaired and taught The American Idea course, an interdisciplinary, two-term, sophomore-level course that included political science, history, sociology, and economics. The Johns Committee was particularly interested in the reading materials used for this course and took great issue with J. D. Salinger's *Nine Stories*, a collection of stories used in several courses, including freshman English. Johns (who chaired the hearings) was very blunt about his assessment of Salinger, asking Warner if USF couldn't find anything better than "this trash for the students to read."[44] Warner explained that, if Johns had studied the book with one of USF's excellent professors, he would not rate the work as trash. The committee was also annoyed because the Salinger collection was chosen as an All-University book to be read and discussed by students, faculty, staff, and parents. Johns concluded Warner's testimony by telling him that, before serving on the Johns Committee, he (Johns) did not know that homosexuals even existed. (This was certainly a lie, since, as acting governor, Johns had appointed an attorney to oversee Miami's "campaign against perverts" in 1954.) Johns also accused Warner of corrupting students through his liberal approach to teaching, saying: "You teach all this kind of stuff to our children, warping their minds. I am 57 years old, and when I read this stuff it stimulates me. What does it do to these teenage children?"[45] Before Warner could reply, Hawes dismissed him.[46]

The committee asked Dean French about reading materials as well. A former dean at Colgate University and Rollins College, he told the committee that a university and its faculty must decide on reading material and cannot function if various groups dictate what books it uses. French's explanation was in reference to his possibly having described the Smith group as a "pressure group" when he met with them.[47]

The Johns Committee then questioned administrators and faculty about USF's vision. Central to that vision was the principle of academic freedom, which the committee addressed repeatedly in the campus hearings. Invariably, the committee saw the issue from the standpoint of USF's responsibility to the public and frequently asked witnesses if USF should be concerned with its public image. Howard Johnshoy, dean of student affairs, was a former dean at Ball State College, and, like Margaret Fisher and many of his colleagues, he had been drawn to USF by the excitement of starting a new university. Although he agreed that USF should be interested in its public image, he quickly added that USF's concern with its image was epitomized in its motto, "Accent on Learning." He explained that the best universities are free to explore opposing viewpoints, allowing their students to learn from a wide spectrum of ideas.[48]

The committee raised the more difficult question of religion and academic freedom during its interrogation of Dean French. When asked if a university should cause students to question their religious beliefs, French was very clear, saying that all universities should cause students to question all of life's issues, including religion, but that professors should not proselytize. When Hawes tried to ask if a professor converting students violated the separation of church and state, French interrupted him, saying: "I would like to put on the record that I don't think this is appropriate questioning in terms of the Committee's investigation," adding that he would continue to answer any questions, once that statement was in the record.[49] The committee then asked if there were any atheist faculty at USF. French replied that he did not know, since state institutions do not have the right to ask people that question.[50]

As with Johnshoy, the committee asked Russell Cooper, dean of liberal arts, about a concern for USF's public image. A political scientist and former dean at the University of Minnesota, he taught The American Idea course and was on the All-University book committee. Cooper addressed the political aspect of academic freedom, saying that when politicians try to tell university professors how to teach, the politicians damage the university's integrity. He added that such interference is "a perversion which is likely to lose the accreditation of the university,"[51] which USF was trying to achieve at the time. Having served for fifteen years in the North Central Association of Colleges and Schools, the northern branch of the same agency that would be determining USF's accreditation, Cooper spoke with authority on such issues. The Johns Committee did not pursue the accreditation issue further.[52]

Consistent with their previous investigations in Tampa and at UF, the greatest area of interest to the Johns Committee was gays and lesbians. The committee was particularly interested in USF's policies and protocol for responding to reports of gay or lesbian employees approaching students and rigorously pursued an incident involving a student and Professor John Caldwell.[53] The committee then briefly asked Dean Johnshoy if Professor Caldwell had reported a student complaint about Professor Wayne Hugoboom's alleged homosexual conduct; Johnshoy had received none. Hawes then quickly concluded Johnshoy's interrogation, saying that the committee had "an important witness" scheduled next.[54]

That witness was Margaret Fisher, and Hawes asked her if Caldwell had reported the same complaint to her. To the Johns Committee's dismay, Fisher was very adept at answering questions in a circuitous way. After first explaining that Caldwell had reported problems of that sort on two previous occasions, Fisher hesitated when Hawes asked if Caldwell had reported to her about a complaint made to him by a student, Michael Winn. Fisher said that she was restricted by professional ethics from violating student confidentiality and doubted if she could even say if Winn was a student with whom she had met. The Johns Committee then decided that, if she felt she would be betraying confidentiality, she did not have to answer questions of that type.[55]

Hawes then told Fisher that he was holding an eight-page statement made by Winn (who had left USF and was living in Winter Park, Florida) in which he described a homosexual incident with a USF employee.[56] Hawes then insisted that Fisher would not be betraying Winn's confidentiality, since he had already told Johns Committee investigators about both the incident and his reporting it to Caldwell. Fisher disagreed. Warming up her obfuscation skills, she said that she was bound to confidentiality, regardless of what the student said to other people. However, she did then tell Hawes that Caldwell had reported a complaint to her, made by Winn, and that Caldwell told her that he had also reported it to the appropriate dean.[57]

Hawes then left the Caldwell-Winn complaint temporarily and asked her how she handled such complaints generally. He probably regretted that question, for Fisher talked at great length about her office's counseling methods and added that USF needed a psychiatrist to help her staff deal with homosexual incidents, making a rather bald bid to the legislators present for an increased budget for USF.[58]

Hawes then returned to the Caldwell-Winn incident, asking if she had met with Winn. Fisher said they were now getting close to the type of question that she could not answer because of confidentiality issues but did say that the usual procedure was followed with Winn. Fisher added that she never knew whom Winn had accused, that Caldwell reported that side of the incident to his dean while she worked with Winn.[59]

Hawes asked Fisher if she felt obligated to report the incident to a higher administrator, even if she did not know the identity of the accused man. It was at this point that Fisher's obfuscation skills truly began to flourish. She talked at great length about USF's chains of command, counseling goals and techniques, and the need to have the student and professor involved handled by two different people so that both sides might face their responsibilities. In such cases, she added, she would rather not know the identity of the faculty member because of her counseling relationship with the student. When Hawes voiced surprise at her not wanting to know, Fisher continued to obfuscate, elaborating on the student personnel and academic chains of command. When Hawes asked where the system broke down, resulting in no investigation being made of this incident, Fisher then talked again at length, telling him it was not her responsibility to investigate employees but that having funding for additional staff in the medical area, that is, a psychiatrist, would be useful.[60]

At this point, Fisher's ability to frustrate the committee was taking effect because Charley Johns interrupted, telling her: "You have been talking kind of in generalities. I would like us to, let's get to the point."[61] Fisher then obliged him by talking in circles again, this time on the definitions of homosexual relationships versus homosexual acts.[62]

Hawes returned again to the issue of no investigation being made of the Caldwell-Winn incident. Fisher told him the system broke down only at the point where "there was a reluctance on the part of the student to give the information necessary" and that "USF was doing as well as it could with the limitations [she had] outlined."[63] The committee became increasingly frustrated near the end of Fisher's two-and-one-half-hour interrogation, and Johns told her that he and his colleagues had received the message that USF needed more money.[64]

However, Fisher was recalled the next day, after having reviewed her files on Winn. She explained that she did not connect him with the Caldwell incident until shortly before he left USF for academic reasons. She added that she made no follow-up on the incident because of the potential counseling relationship with the student and because she believed Caldwell was following up on the university employee side of the issue.[65]

Concerns about gays, particularly the Caldwell-Winn incident, were still a frequent theme during President Allen's six-hour interrogation. When Hawes asked Allen if he knew about the incident, he said that he had only learned of it that day, shortly before coming in to testify. Hawes then distorted Fisher's testimony, telling Allen that she had not wanted to know the identity of the accused faculty member, but Hawes did not add that Fisher did so in order to protect Winn's confidentiality. Allen then calmly assured the committee that USF would pursue the incident. He also had the last word on the Caldwell-Winn incident, reminding the committee that USF would continue to follow the basic judicial principle of presumed innocence.[66]

Hawes next questioned Allen about D. F. Fleming, a well-known political science scholar from Vanderbilt University. In February 1962, he had accepted a part-time teaching position offered by Allen. In the meantime, Fleming had caught the Johns Committee's attention as a potential Communist sympathizer, based mostly on reviews of his writings and somewhat on testimony of one former student and one Vanderbilt administrator. Allen told the Johns Committee that he had received a letter from the House Committee on Un-American Activities stating that they had no record of Fleming being a Communist sympathizer. However, the Fleming affair and the question of academic freedom would later return to haunt Allen and USF.[67]

Fortunately, Allen's concept of academic freedom meshed well with that of his administrators. However, Hawes soon drew Allen onto the slippery slope of the separation of church and state versus academic freedom by asking him if it was proper for a state institution to cause students to question their religious beliefs. Allen first patiently explained that such questioning is a common pattern for college students and added that USF—even before it opened—had invited churches to establish centers on campus to provide students with religious advisors. After Hawes repeatedly asked the same question about the separation of church and state versus academic freedom, Allen finally told him quite bluntly: "Well, I don't want to be goaded by your words because you are trying to put words in my mouth."[68]

As Allen's patience wore thin near the end of his six-hour interrogation, Hawes' aggressiveness escalated. When Hawes asked if Allen read all of the books on the All-University reading list and was told no, Hawes described Allen as being "derelict in [his] duties." Allen cleverly replied: "I don't teach all of the classes either."[69] Hawes then turned to the issue of the notorious J. D. Salinger's short stories, which Charley Johns had described as "trash." After Hawes told Allen how many times various profane words were used in one story and asked for his reaction, Allen expertly quoted the U.S. Supreme Court's definition of obscenity from *Roth v. United States*, to make the point that any book must be studied in its entirety before its merits or flaws can be analyzed. Hawes then concluded the interrogation and, with it, the campus hearings.[70]

As she had during the hearings, Fisher continued her work as an administrator and professor after the Johns Committee left campus. Unfortunately, she lost one of her favorite colleagues as a result of the investigation. Dean Howard Johnshoy, a man whom Fisher described as very intelligent and enjoyable to work with, resigned his position as dean of students in protest over the committee's invasion of USF.[71] However, amid the great amount of anguish caused by the Johns Committee, Fisher found positive elements. She believed that the solidarity between faculty and students was enhanced considerably because many students testified voluntarily, voicing their "support of the university and its programs."[72]

Another positive element was the creative coping skills of President Allen's wife, Grace. During and for a time after the campus hearings, Grace Allen worried about the stress that the committee and the hearings had inflicted upon her husband and, in turn, on her. Then, during a visit to their new home, which was in the final stages of construction, she discovered numerous nail heads protruding from the home's paneling. She immediately grabbed a hammer, approached the first recalcitrant nail head, and shouted, "Charley Johns!"[73] Allen then brought her hammer down with a combination of relish and rage. She continued her work for several minutes and returned to the house often, enjoying the therapeutic value of the senator's name when combined with a violent blow from her hammer.[74]

Unaware of the therapeutic value of his name, Charley Johns spoke briefly with reporters on the last day of the campus hearings, telling them that the committee had found very few problems at USF. The next day, Johns issued a retraction, saying that the committee had been investigating USF since April 10 (1962) because of major complaints against the university and some of its employees. He went on to explain the committee's agreement with the Board of Control, namely that the committee would release the hearing transcripts only to the board and would not comment on any details of the investigation "*before* the Board . . . [had] the opportunity to act [emphasis added]."[75] As arranged, the Johns Committee soon delivered twenty-five hundred pages of testimony, bound in twelve volumes, to the Board of Control, which met in July and appointed a three-man special committee to study the transcripts and issue a report to the board.[76]

Meanwhile, the Johns Committee worked on its own report to the board about the USF investigation, completing the report by mid-August. On August 24, while President Allen was in Europe on vacation and while most faculty were off campus before the beginning of fall term, Johns gave the committee's report to the Board of Control, the Board of Education, and to the press simultaneously. Reneging on his earlier promise not to publish any specific information until the Board of Control had a chance to take action, he gave the entire text of the report to the *Tampa Tribune* on condition that they publish all of it. In printing the report, the *Tribune* did not black out names of professors accused of improprieties. Also, there were excerpts from witnesses' testimonies, all given in executive session— not in a public hearing—a format used ostensibly, according to Johns himself, to protect witnesses. In one move, Johns had violated his agreement with the board, broken the confidentiality of the executive sessions, and undone months of work by Allen and his faculty and administrators to prevent harmful publicity for USF.[77]

The report charged that USF was (1) lenient toward Communism, (2) had liberal professors who assigned antireligious and vulgar or profane readings to their classes, and (3) had four gay professors. Under the first charge, the committee repeated accusations against D. F. Fleming that were raised during Allen's interrogation, still referring to Fleming as a "Soviet apologist."[78] Before the report was completed, Hawes had told Allen that he (Hawes) had been wrong about Fleming and that the professor had never been listed as a Communist. However, the Johns Committee's report was not corrected.[79]

On the second charge, the committee returned to J. D. Salinger's work as an example of profane and vulgar language and noted forty-five examples of such language in one short story. The report also distorted testimony, saying that President Allen believed that only a literary critic could decide upon appropriate reading materials, when, in fact, Allen had said that one should not judge literary passages out of context.[80]

The report addressed the gay issue last, stating first that the committee had "devoted but little of its time and efforts to homosexuality"[81] during the investigation, despite the committee's interrogating more witnesses about this issue than any other during the campus hearings. The committee was critical of Fisher's role in the Caldwell-Winn incident in particular, implying that she violated Winn's confidentiality by telling Dean Johnshoy that a faculty member was involved, even though she did not give him the professor's name. The report also did not mention that Fisher did not know the name of the professor. The committee also criticized Fisher for saying that USF lacked sufficient information from Winn to investigate. However, when the committee included that additional material from Winn himself in the report, it did not add that Fisher had never had access to such information.[82]

Florida's media quickly responded to the report. Several newspapers (including the *St. Petersburg Times, Tampa Times, Daytona Beach Evening News*, and *Gainesville Sun*) ran editorials attacking the Johns Committee and supporting USF. The *St. Petersburg Times* strongly recommended that the public treat the committee's report with the disdain it deserved. In an August 30 broadcast, WLCY of Tampa/St. Petersburg blamed the Johns Committee for not keeping its report to the Board of Control confidential, while on the same day WLOF in Orlando called the committee's "one-sided prosecutor's indictment" un-American.[83]

•

Because Allen was in Europe when the Johns Committee report was published, Dean Russell Cooper was the first administrator to deal with the aftermath of the report. He issued a news release in response to the report. Stunned at the report being made public, Cooper focused on Charley Johns, saying that if he had meant for the investigation to help USF, the publication of the report had done the opposite because it used only negative information on USF. Margaret Fisher told reporters that Johns' publishing the report was simply shocking, later adding that she and her colleagues were "terribly disgusted about the ordeal that the Committee put us through."[84] When Allen returned from Europe, he issued a press release, agreeing with both Cooper's and Fisher's assessments. Allen also revealed that he had received the report three days after it was given to the press. His copy also came with a cover letter noting that the report was confidential because it dealt with hearings transacted in executive session.[85]

A few days after Allen's statement was released, Margaret Fisher wrote to him, praising his effective leadership under such trying circumstances. However, Fisher soon demonstrated her own leadership skills, working off campus with the American Association of University Women (AAUW), a professional organization that took a proactive stance against the Johns Committee. Although she had been a member of the AAUW at the national level for years, Fisher joined the local branch only a few days after testifying before the Johns Committee. She then met with a local AAUW panel that was studying the damage done by the committee and assisted a statewide AAUW committee with a large petition drive and letter-writing campaign. Thus, Fisher served on two different AAUW panels that fought the Johns Committee, giving her both local and state perspectives.[86]

The AAUW took a unique approach to fighting the Johns Committee: they "investigated the investigators."[87] After the release of the Johns Committee report, the Florida AAUW launched an investigation of academic freedom at all of the state's universities and concluded that the committee's investigations had violated not only its mandate but also citizens' rights and academic freedom, while threatening USF's accreditation as well. The Florida AAUW then formally petitioned the legislature to abolish the Johns Committee and to audit its use of funds. Looking back on her work with the AAUW, Fisher proudly explained: "It was the women who really moved in on the Johns Committee, [and the AAUW] came out with fire in their eyes."[88]

In August 1962, President Allen, under the pressure of mounting publicity generated by the committee's report, took what appeared to be the last step to resolve the Caldwell-Winn incident and suspended John Caldwell, despite faculty opposition. Allen decided to allow Caldwell to finish out the 1962–63 academic year but would not rehire him, a compromise that pleased no one: Caldwell, USF faculty, or Charley Johns, who told reporters that Caldwell was hung over when the Johns Committee interrogated him. Caldwell resigned in September 1962, taking a job as a producer for a theater in Virginia.[89]

In October, shortly after Caldwell resigned, the Board of Control issued a set of directives to the state universities, including a requirement that all discussions of religion in the classroom were to be limited. Of course, university faculty saw this directive as a violation of academic freedom, an issue that also surfaced when the board discussed a complaint against USF English professor Sheldon Grebstein, an eminent scholar who had assigned an essay to which Jane Smith's daughter objected. Although the board called for Grebstein's immediate resignation, Allen suspended Grebstein temporarily but asked faculty to investigate the matter. Their investigation lasted two months as they tried to deal with both the facts and the politics of the case. Fisher aptly described faculty frustration: "[We are] sitting up late at night with ice packs trying to figure out . . . this [case], and to figure out how we can get the politicians off the hook."[90] The faculty committee recommended reinstatement of Grebstein.[91]

As news of the Grebstein case spread, support for USF began to pour in from around the state. Professors and administrators from UF and FSU, as well as two private colleges (Florida Southern College and Jacksonville University), wrote letters of support to Allen, condemning not only Grebstein's forced suspension but also the Johns Committee's witch hunt and the board's overall attack on academic freedom. Soon, Florida's college professors began to rebel further. USF's AAUP chapter called on other Florida chapters to consider the Grebstein suspension an infringement on their rights, and the UF chapter quickly announced its support.[92]

FSU's faculty senate asked the board to protect university professors from the Johns Committee, but it was Professor Michael Kasha's statement to the press that generated headlines. One of FSU's nationally known scientists and head of the university's Institute of Molecular Biophysics, Kasha announced that he and his colleagues were considering leaving FSU because the board's directives were a threat to Florida's universities and their future. Kasha shrewdly chose to make his announcement to a homecoming crowd of well-connected alumni who then threw their support behind him and the rest of FSU's faculty. Five days after Kasha's announcement, the Board of Control met in Jacksonville, reconsidered its directives, and soon approved a new academic freedom policy created by Kasha and other professors.[93]

Meanwhile, at UF's homecoming, students vigorously lampooned Charley Johns in a well-received skit. Dressed as a villain in a black cloak and hat, a student portrayed Johns and sang bold new lyrics to the tune of "I'm in Love with a Wonderful Guy":

. . .

Down dirty back alleys
To student pep rallies
Through classrooms and hallways I'll go
Then faculty lounges
To seek out the scrounges
That lurk there and think I don't know.

. . .

By God, I will chase them,
Hate and disgrace them
'Cause I'm such a wonderful guy.[94]

Incensed not by the homecoming skit but rather by the successful rebellion of Florida's faculty—and with media criticism mounting—Charley Johns responded. He tried to have both the Johns Committee report on USF and the Grebstein case materials printed in the *Senate Journal*. Fortunately, Johns' colleagues voted down his request because of the financial cost. The Grebstein case was finally settled in November, when Allen, in defiance of the board, reinstated Grebstein with censure for poor judgment. Allen's decision, a compromise hammered out in a late-night meeting between him and the board, pleased no one, including Allen himself. The board and the Johns Committee wanted Grebstein fired; Fisher and the faculty committee believed that the evidence and the need for academic freedom called for full reinstatement. Allen chose a middle course, trying to save one professor's job (and perhaps Allen's as well), and ultimately alienated many of his faculty. Grebstein refused Allen's terms and left Tampa. Unfortunately, the Grebstein case affected faculty recruiting. USF's director of educational resources told Allen, after a recruiting trip to Ohio and Michigan, that candidates were being advised to stay away from USF because of the board's failure to protect the university and because of the Johns Committee's violation of academic freedom.[95]

Meanwhile, the committee became embroiled in a sting operation that backfired and led to other setbacks. Early in 1963, the committee attempted to silence one of its main critics, Robert Delaney, a reporter for the *Orlando Sentinel*, who covered the news from Tallahassee. Knowing Delaney was a reformed alcoholic, committee investigators arranged for him to meet Janet Lee by "chance" at a local bowling alley. An attractive woman, Lee told Delaney that she had a drinking problem. Delaney, as part of his twelve-step program, offered to help; she suggested that they talk in her motel room. Unknown to Delaney, Strickland had booked two adjoining rooms at the motel and had a photographer and police standing by. Lee invited Delaney into her room, wearing a half-open robe. As he sat on the edge of the bed talking, she pulled his head down into her lap. The photographer snapped incriminating photos, and Delaney was arrested for committing an unnatural sex act. When the press revealed that Strickland had booked the rooms and had allowed Lee to leave town, the committee was embarrassed and on the defensive.[96]

A few weeks later, the Johns Committee suffered another defeat when the William Neal case was resolved in favor of the plaintiff. The teaching certificates of Neal and two other Pinellas County teachers had been revoked by the Board of Education in 1961 after the board allowed Strickland to conduct hearings on its behalf. The Florida Supreme Court ruled that the committee's 1959 enabling statute did not give it the authority to investigate moral turpitude cases and that the board had not adhered to established procedures, either in allowing Strickland to act on its behalf or in using his testimony as the only evidence for revocation. The court added that the 1959 statute also did not give the Johns Committee authority to search for gays and lesbians or to subpoena them for hearings. A month later, the U.S. Supreme Court ruled against the committee in the NAACP's *Gibson* case. Citing the First and Fourteenth Amendments, the Court said that the Johns Committee had tried to punish Ruth Perry for her political beliefs and that the committee had failed to show any connection between the NAACP and subversive activity in Florida. Thus the committee's demands for NAACP records were unconstitutional.[97]

Still smarting from the *Gibson* ruling, in April of 1963 Hawes presented a report on USF to the legislature, Governor Farris Bryant, his cabinet, and the press in an invitation-only session in the Senate chamber. His report contained the same information as the Johns Committee's report, released in August of the previous year, but with some additional space devoted to Hawes' defense of the committee's methods during the USF investigation. There was no written transcript of Hawes' report, but Strickland had set up a tape recorder at the Senate podium so that the committee (and no one else) would have a record. However, a member of the Hillsborough County delegation had also managed to get a recording and turned it over to President Allen to use in preparing his response to Hawes. A few days later, Allen addressed a joint session of the legislature, reviewing and debunking the Johns Committee's charges of Communism, homosexuality, anti-Christianity, and vulgarity in teaching materials. He also defended academic freedom, telling legislators: "A college is not engaged in making ideas safe for students. It is engaged in making students safe for ideas."[98]

A few months later, after an abundance of negative publicity generated by the Johns Committee's activities, the legislature decided that the committee needed a reorganization. Several legislators (and other critics) also

Figure 6.3. Mark Hawes, April 1963, reporting to a joint legislative session on the USF investigation and defending the committee's methods. *Left to right*: Representative Richard Mitchell, House speaker Mallory Horne, Senate president Wilson Carraway (*behind Hawes*), Senator Charley Johns, Senator Houston Roberts, Representative George Stallings, and Representative Ben Hill Griffin. All seated men are Johns Committee members, except Horne and Carraway. State Archives of Florida, *Florida Memory*, http://floridamemory.com/items/show/42900.

Figure 6.4. USF president John Allen, April 1963, speaking to a joint legislative session and defending USF after Hawes' report to the legislature. Seated in the foreground is Senator Tom Whitaker of Tampa, and on the far side is Senate president Wilson Carraway. Frank Noel, State Archives of Florida, *Florida Memory*, http://floridamemory.com/items/show/42366.

pointed out that the committee had yet to produce a legislative program, as required by its mandate. In August 1963, Representative Richard Mitchell replaced Johns as chair, and both Hawes and Strickland resigned. John Evans, who had worked for the *St. Petersburg Times* and a Tampa television station, as well as directing Governor Bryant's Center for Cold War Education, was hired as the committee's staff director. His public relations skills would be severely tested the following year.[99]

In January 1964, the committee voted to publish its report, "Homosexuality and Citizenship in Florida." Because of its garish purple cover, the report quickly became known as the Purple Pamphlet. The first page featured a photo of two men, naked from the waist up, engaged in an embrace and kissing. This photo was followed by another, showing a teenage boy bound by ropes and wearing only a thong. Purporting to be a study to allow "state administrators and personnel directors" to learn the "nature and manifestation" of homosexuality, the pamphlet discussed gays and lesbians and proposed solutions to the "homosexual problem."[100] The appendix included Florida's sex crime laws, a glossary, and a bibliography. The state seal was on the back cover. The glossary in particular elicited surprise, including such entries as "dreamboat: a term used to characterize an unusually attractive homosexual."[101] Girls and women who used the term "dreamboat" in the 1950s and 1960s to describe attractive males would have been baffled by the Johns Committee's definition. Other awkward terms were "seafood: homosexuals in the Navy" and "crushed fruit: a homosexual who tries to deny he is a homosexual."[102] Not surprisingly, the Purple Pamphlet generated a firestorm of negative publicity for the committee. Many saw the pamphlet as pornography, including State Attorney Richard Gerstein in Miami. He warned the committee to stop distributing "obscene and pornographic" material.[103] The media soon agreed with Gerstein, asking why tax dollars were used to publish such material. One positive result of the Purple Pamphlet was the establishment of the first Mattachine Society chapter in Miami in 1964. The national president of the society published an open letter to the Johns Committee in the *Mattachine Review*, criticizing the pamphlet for its poor research, unjustified recommendations, emotional bias, and irresponsible opinions.[104]

While the Johns Committee was dealing with the negative publicity generated by the Purple Pamphlet, USF was facing another investigation, this time by the AAUP. The D. F. Fleming affair had returned to occupy both Allen and the AAUP. Although he had defended the professor during the campus hearings, Allen later rescinded his job offer to Fleming, notifying him that additional information from Vanderbilt had caused Allen to withdraw the offer. Fleming then asked the AAUP to investigate. The organization published its findings in the *AAUP Bulletin* in the spring of 1964, concluding that, whether the board forced Allen to withdraw Fleming's job offer or not, both Allen and the board were responsible for Fleming's dismissal. The AAUP added that the board and Allen were also delinquent in not protecting USF's academic integrity from the "forces of ignorance, prejudice, and repression," that is, the Johns Committee.[105]

When USF became the first public university in the state to be censured by the AAUP, Allen made light of the censure and said it would not

Figure 6.5. January 29, 1964, Johns Committee meeting, during which members voted to publish the Purple Pamphlet. Committee members, front to back: Representative C. W. "Bill" Young, Senator Charley Johns, Representative Leo Jones, Representative Richard Mitchell (chair), Senator Robert Williams, Representative George Stallings, and Senator William Owens. Standing at right is committee attorney Leo Foster. State Archives of Florida, *Florida Memory*, http://floridamemory. com/items/show/42898.

hurt USF. Most faculty disagreed. One professor explained: "It wasn't the censure that threw us—everybody was more or less resigned to the inevitability of that—it was the president's reaction.... [H]e pooh-poohed the censure by saying 'We're in good company.' Now people here feel we're not only claiming innocence but making no effort to get off the [censure] list, and, as a result, what little faith the faculty had regained in the president has been destroyed again, maybe for good."[106] Allen's arrogant reaction to the censure is puzzling. His willingness to compromise during the Grebstein affair contradicts his dogmatic underestimation of the censure. In any case, even if Allen downplayed the significance of the censure in an attempt to reduce the impact on USF, he cheapened his relationship with his faculty in the process.

Surprisingly, the executive director of the Board of Control told a few faculty informally that Allen should just get the USF Foundation to pay Fleming for his lost salary. Allen did not attempt such a move, perhaps because he believed the foundation would not agree. A few weeks after the AAUP report was published, a Johns Committee staff memo described the report as "offer[ing] an interesting insight into the thinking of [the AAUP] ... and present[ing] some conclusions of dubious value."[107] Unfortunately, USF's censure was not removed until the spring of 1968.[108]

Even though some legislators had not anticipated the AAUP censure, Charley Johns had another surprise in store for his colleagues when, five months later, he resigned from his own committee. Johns' resignation was soon followed by those of the new staff director, chief investigator, and secretary and by another committee member, Senator Robert Williams. With these resignations, and with chair Richard Mitchell fighting cancer and unable to be involved fully in committee activities, the committee was ineffective.[109]

As Florida's little McCarthyism was ending, USF continued to work to repair the damage done by the committee. The investigation had not only compromised the university's reputation but also created a breach between its president and faculty, particularly after Allen's response to the AAUP censure. Some professors had to leave, and other people were not permitted to speak on campus. USF began to focus more on textbook selection and handling of parents' complaints. Fortunately, by 1965 USF's enrollment had doubled.[110]

While USF was growing, the Johns Committee finally ceased to exist. On July 1, 1965, its enabling statute expired, and its records were sealed under a provision that they would not be opened until 2028, when Charley Johns would have been 123 years old. The committee's members and staff also destroyed many of its documents before the remaining files were closed. Had it not been for the persistence of two USF graduate students, the Johns Committee records might still be sealed. Bonnie Stark, writing her master's thesis in the mid-1980s, was the first to attempt to get the records unsealed. Although she did not succeed, a decade later James Schnur worked with his local legislators, Professor Steven Lawson at USF, the media, and others to unseal the records. After Floridians passed a constitutional amendment to open public records, the Senate secretary opened the files (which contain thirty thousand pages of documents) but first had the names of witnesses and the committee's victims blacked out. On July 1, 1993, exactly twenty-eight years after the Johns Committee expired, its records were revealed.[111]

Opening the files elicited many excuses from former committee members. Charley Johns died three years before the records were unsealed, but C. W. "Bill" Young, one of the last committee members, insisted that he was not aware of the committee's pursuit of lesbians and gay men. William O'Neill, who was on the committee for six years, said that he did not recall much about the committee. Cliff Herrell from Miami said, "As I recall, there wasn't much investigation of the NAACP."[112] R. J. Strickland, when asked about his actions as chief investigator, offered a more creative excuse: "I'm bound by secrecy to the Committee by sworn affidavit. As far as I know, I'm still legally bound."[113]

•

While former Johns Committee members and staff were busy making excuses, Margaret Fisher continued as before. Under her dual appointment at USF, she taught a variety of courses in the humanities and social sciences and became dean of women in 1962. In that position, she frequently focused on women's issues and saw to it that USF hosted conferences on careers and continuing education for women.[114]

By the late 1960s, USF had changed. The university and President Allen dealt with such larger issues as opposition to the Vietnam War, the civil rights movement, and students' demands for a greater role in university affairs. Faculty also challenged Allen over the dissolution of the interdisciplinary, All-University approach to higher education and the emergence of separate departments and colleges. Weary of all the dissension, Allen resigned in 1970 and was succeeded by Cecil Mackey in 1971. As Fisher explained, "Mackey wanted USF to look like other universities,"[115] so he dismantled USF's approach to higher education. He eliminated a major, All-University element, the senior seminar; fired the dean of liberal arts; and closed the College of Basic Studies by making it part of the College of Liberal Arts. Fisher believed that Mackey's "coming in and taking the [Colleges] apart" was a mistake that led to a time of "compartmentalized curriculum."[116] By the mid-1970s, USF became a traditional institution rather than the avant-garde university that Allen, Fisher, and their colleagues had envisioned.[117] "Accent on Learning" became more motto than mission statement.

In 1975, after fifteen years at USF, Margaret Fisher retired as assistant to the vice president for student affairs. However, she continued to function in dual roles, working as a research consultant for the U.S. Department of Education and teaching in USF's Open University program. On her ninetieth birthday, the USF Alumni Association honored her with a special luncheon to recognize her "significant role in shaping the University and the lives of countless students."[118]

Looking back on USF's battle with the Johns Committee, Fisher insisted that she and her colleagues were not heroes. She viewed the fight against the committee as just another instance of having to respond to ill-informed critics. Still, Fisher and her colleagues defended the university's vision and policies against the committee's assault on liberal teaching and academic freedom. When the investigation concluded and while the Johns Committee was coming to an end, Fisher and her colleagues were left to deal with the aftermath, knowing that they had not just answered their inquisitors but had educated them as well.[119]

# 7

## Conclusion

Majorities of One

Johns Committee members trafficked in fear. Skilled in appealing to colleagues' and constituents' anxieties about integration, Communism, homosexuality, liberal teaching, and academic freedom, the committee perpetuated Florida's version of McCarthyism for nine years by brokering fear into power. In the minds of many conservative Americans during the cold war, those fears were intertwined. First, to many segregationists who had followed Senator McCarthy's Communist witch hunts, integration was a Communist plot, or, as Charley Johns told Floridians, "There's no doubt that Communist people are behind all of this racial agitation."[1] Also, segregationists warned that integrated schools would lead to biracial marriage, which was a form of racial perversion just as homosexuality was a form of sexual perversion. Additionally, opponents of integration insisted that liberal, atheist teachers and their subversive reading materials caused young people to question traditional moral, religious, and sexual standards and then to become racial agitators, Communists, or homosexuals. In the minds of those on the right wing, academic freedom was a way for teachers and professors to avoid responsibility for their influence on students. Finally, conservatives linked Communism and homosexuality in American political culture: while leftist professors polluted young people's minds, homosexuals defiled the bodies of America's youth. Right-wing partisans emphasized that neither Communists nor homosexuals could be distinguished by their physical features and thus could easily infiltrate government. Conservatives also saw homosexuals as more likely to be blackmailed, making them susceptible to Communist influence. Right-wing partisans argued that both Communists and homosexuals were more loyal to their passions (one political, the other sexual) than to their country, and both were godless or immoral. Thus, the Johns Committee and its staff were able to exploit the cold war anxieties of the 1950s until the committee's demise in 1965.[2]

•

One might ask why Florida's little McCarthyism thrived when McCarthy's influence had begun to wane nationally, or why the Johns Committee continued to flourish even after the House Committee on Un-American Activities was in decline. The answer is twofold. First, as one scholar has explained, anxieties about integration, Communism, homosexuality, and liberal teaching (as well as their being intertwined) still resonated with conservative Americans in the late 1950s and on into the 1960s. This allowed the Johns Committee to "reap . . . from what McCarthy and others had sown."[3] Another answer is the committee's use of universities and schools as a place for fighting Communists, homosexuals, and the demands of liberal teachers for academic freedom. (Of course, southern schools were already a battleground over integration.) The Johns Committee's additional use of schools was, in turn, reinforced by popular fears that integrated schools, as a Communist plot, would lead to racial and sexual perversion while liberal teaching caused America's youth to question traditional values.[4] Fortunately, some citizens in Florida refused to yield to these popular fears.

By the time the Johns Committee released the Purple Pamphlet in 1964, Virgil Hawkins was attending the New England School of Law, and Ruth Perry was seeing the first effect of the *Gibson* case in Miami: more people were joining the local chapter because NAACP officers had protected the membership lists. Meanwhile, UF had published *The Atlas of Florida*, for which Sig Diettrich did significant work but received minimal credit. G. G. Mock had moved to Miami, where she was happily working for a large printing company and making more money than she could have in Tampa. While the Florida legislature debated the Johns Committee's fate in the spring of 1965, Margaret Fisher, now dean of women at USF, was working with the Governor's Commission on the Status of Women and hosting conferences at USF on careers for women.[5] A few months later, the groundswell of opposition to the Johns Committee peaked, and the committee ceased to exist.

Of course, the momentum against the committee really began in February 1957 when Virgil Hawkins became the first person to defy the committee. After that, it was a very slow but steady building of individual resistance by witnesses that helped to create a gathering momentum of opposition. Once the media, the American Association of University Women, and others joined in, a domino effect began to take over. By 1965, the growing success of the civil rights movement and the public relations damage done by the committee (especially with the Purple Pamphlet) further increased the momentum against the Johns Committee. Florida, attempting to attract more tourists and new businesses, could not afford to have a public image as a state dominated by racist, meddling legislators. Thus, committee adversaries eventually created a preponderance of opposition that really began as "one man with courage . . . [who eventually made] a majority."[6]

From Henry David Thoreau's viewpoint, "any man more right than his neighbors [also] constitute[d] a majority of one."[7] Citing his opposition to slavery and to the Mexican-American War as a landgrab favoring Southern slaveholders, Thoreau chose not to pay his poll taxes. He spent one night in jail before an anonymous donor paid the delinquent taxes needed to release Thoreau, and he published "Civil Disobedience" in 1849. His essay reminded nineteenth-century Americans of one of their country's founding principles: that government's powers are derived from the consent of the governed.[8] "Civil Disobedience" also became a primer for citizens who refuse to relegate their conscience to their government.

Ida B. Wells was such a citizen, insisting that she "would rather go down in history as one lone Negro who dared to tell the government that it had done a dastardly thing than to save [her] skin by taking back what [she] said."[9] Wells' lifelong campaign against racial lynching began in 1892 with editorials in her Memphis newspaper denouncing the lynching of three of her friends. Terrorists then looted and burned her newspaper office and threatened to hang her. Undaunted, she shifted her antilynching campaign to Chicago and began working for federal antilynching legislation. Her investigative journalism documented lynching in three pamphlets published from 1892 to 1900. Eventually, her efforts began to change public opinion so that, by the 1920s, African American and white organizations would name lynching as a national crime. Unfortunately, the NAACP, which Wells helped to found, and other civil rights organizations never succeeded in persuading Congress to pass antilynching legislation.[10]

Alice Paul had an assertive nature similar to Wells, and, after working with the militant British suffrage movement, she returned to the United States in 1910 and convinced the National American Woman Suffrage Association (NAWSA) to allow her to lobby Congress to pass a federal suffrage amendment. Then she and some of her more militant colleagues planned the successful 1913 suffrage march in Washington, D.C., which generated nationwide publicity for the movement. After conflicts with NAWSA over strategy and tactics, Paul's group became the National Woman's Party (NWP). While nonviolently picketing President Woodrow Wilson at the White House, Paul and other NWP members were attacked, beaten, shot at, and dragged along the sidewalk. As the picketing continued, many of the women were imprisoned, beaten, and hung by their wrists. Along with other NWP leaders, Paul was also sent to a psychiatric ward, deprived of sleep, put into solitary confinement, and forcefed many times. Eventually, she succeeded; the Nineteenth Amendment was finally ratified in 1920.[11]

Like Paul, Ella Baker was a proponent of such direct civil-action tactics as picketing and mass arrests. Mentoring generations of activists, Baker often worked behind the scenes during the civil rights movement. In the 1930s and early 1940s, she was an NAACP field organizer and developed a network of southern activists who became part of the base of the civil rights movement. In 1957, she helped establish the Southern Christian Leadership Conference (SCLC), bringing the young Martin Luther King Jr. into the organization while chairing a voter registration drive. In February 1960, when African American students organized a sit-in at a lunch counter in Greensboro, North Carolina, she left the SCLC to assist in the student sit-in movement and helped establish the Student Nonviolent Coordinating Committee (SNCC), which used Baker's concept of group-centered leadership to develop an autonomous role for the organization within the civil rights movement. Baker was a SNCC advisor until the mid-1960s, when she moved to New York City, but she continued to work for human rights until her death in 1986.[12]

Like Ella Baker, Virgil Hawkins was nothing if not persistent.[13] His dream of attending UF and becoming an attorney was with him from his preteen years, and it never left him. From his days attending court with his father, through the lynching of a young cousin, on through Hawkins' years at Edward Waters College and Lincoln University, through his years of teaching, and finally as public relations director at Bethune-Cookman College, he persevered. When he was rejected by UF in 1949, his dream took on a new dimension: the lawsuit that would make him famous in Florida. Just as he had persisted with his goal, so he continued with his suit to enter UF's law school, despite death threats, hate mail, an attempt to fire him, and financial harassment by the IRS. When he won his case in the U.S. Supreme Court in March 1956, he could not have known that the Florida legislature would soon create a new threat to his dream: the Johns Committee.[14]

Horace Hill, Hawkins' attorney, once compared his client to a pit bull. The simile was particularly appropriate in regard to Hawkins' confrontations with the Johns Committee. The more Mark Hawes tried to get Virgil Hawkins to admit that his lawsuit to become an attorney was controlled by the NAACP, the more opportunities Hawes gave Hawkins to show his potential as a lawyer. Hawkins met Hawes' relentless repetition with either simple denials or with emphatic, confident repetitions of his own: "For the fourth time, no sir. . . . No, no. That's the NAACP again, isn't it? No, No!"[15] Hawkins also found flaws in Hawes' interrogation, reminding him that he should be asking Hawkins about his reasons for wanting to attend UF, not Hawkins' reasons as relayed by third parties. Finally, Hawkins showed a lawyer-like ability to parse words when he insisted that "passing the hat" at speaking engagements constituted his personally paying his attorney.[16]

By the time the *Hawkins* case was finally resolved in June 1958, it had taken nine years and been the subject of four Florida Supreme Court decisions, three U.S. Supreme Court rulings, and three federal reviews. Despite the opposition of the State of Florida and the Johns Committee, the *Hawkins* case integrated UF graduate schools when, under the federal court ruling, Hawkins chose not to reapply to UF so that other African Americans could be admitted immediately.[17]

Although the case ended, Hawkins' perseverance continued when he earned his law degree and was admitted to the Florida Bar sixty years after his boyhood dream began. He also persisted even after achieving his goal. Opening a law office at the age of seventy, he practiced law for seven years before being put on probation for serious legal errors. Other attorneys in historically racist Lake County then tried to undermine his practice by sending him bogus clients. Hawkins also mishandled some paperwork and funds for a relative's Veterans Administration benefits and was forced to resign from the Florida Bar at the age of seventy-nine. Still, history was on his side. He was particularly delighted when the Florida legislature established the Virgil Hawkins Fellowships for African American law students at UF and FSU. Shortly before his death, he described his place in history with his characteristic tenacity: "I know what I did. I integrated schools in Florida. No one can take that away from me."[18]

Even though Ruth Perry joined the NAACP because she wanted to help achieve "justice ... [and] equal rights under the law"[19] for everyone, the blatant injustice of Harry T. Moore's assassination galvanized her into a greater role in the NAACP as an officer, broadcaster, and journalist. Justice—and the lack of it for African Americans—was a recurrent theme in her broadcasts and columns. Some of Perry's first broadcasts were about the 1954 *Brown* decision, which she said essentially came down to a "simple question of right and justice."[20] Her newspaper columns also reflected a desire for justice and a deep respect for the Constitution, which she described as the very embodiment of democracy. Perry's respect for justice and the Constitution was not mere lip service. She risked her life, her freedom, and her career during the Johns Committee witch hunts because, as she said in her parting words to the committee, she "believe[d] in democracy and the Constitution."[21]

Her protection of NAACP membership lists and other records was also grounded in simple justice and the law of the land. By preventing the Johns Committee from obtaining NAACP records, she hoped to protect members and the organization from false accusations of Communism. Also, by ending her record keeping soon after the committee was formed, she denied the committee any additional information with which to fight integration, believing (as she told the committee) that the Florida legislature was trying to stop integration even if that meant defying federal law.[22]

Sig Diettrich would most likely have agreed with President Kennedy that "a man does what he must—in spite of personal consequences, in spite of obstacles and dangers and pressures."[23] Whether it was in his role as a professor (both in the regular curriculum and later in the War Training courses), as a geographical consultant, as an administrator, or as a scholar, Diettrich worked hard and did his best, both in his profession and for UF. His being awarded a Fulbright Fellowship is certainly evidence of his conscientiousness.

Although Diettrich's integrity and sense of honor were evident before the Johns Committee came to Gainesville, those qualities were not really tested until 1959, when Mark Hawes grilled Diettrich for several hours. Although Hawes used several tactics to convince Diettrich to name gays at UF, Diettrich did not cooperate. Appealing to Diettrich's desire to protect UF was a particularly hypocritical ploy since the investigation itself was harming the university. Hawes also employed coercion, his most commonly used tactic, threatening Diettrich with twenty years in prison and with outing him. Hawes next discovered that appealing to Diettrich's sense of revenge would not work, even when Hawes told Diettrich who had named him. Repeated humiliation did not work, either. This must have been the most difficult part of the interrogation for Diettrich. He was most vulnerable emotionally in regard to questions about his wife simply because he loved her so much. Appropriately enough, Diettrich was also the most adamant when he was the most vulnerable, refusing to give Hawes any detailed information about his wife and insisting that she was not the cause of his problem. Hawes timed his final humiliating question to follow the questions about Diettrich's wife, eventually forcing him to admit his sexual impotence. This caused him to describe the interrogation as the "rock bottom of . . . [his] life," but still he named no one.[24] Diettrich left the Johns Committee's motel room at 9 p.m., honor intact.

The issue of honor raises a question in regard to Diettrich. Can he be considered honorable in other ways if he was unfaithful in marriage? To answer this question, one must examine Diettrich's actions within the circumstances of his marriage. First is the medical fact of Iren Diettrich's illness after she came to Florida. She contracted malaria in the early 1930s, before a vaccine was available, and thus suffered intermittent bouts with the disease for twenty to thirty years. Upon her doctor's advice, starting in about 1949, the Diettrichs stopped having intimate relations.[25] Thus,

Diettrich had not had sexual relations with his wife for ten years at the time of his interrogation.

When Iren's doctor told the Diettrichs to abstain, Diettrich would most likely have assumed that their period of abstinence would have to be indefinite, perhaps even permanent. Lacking a sexual outlet, he turned to brief sexual encounters with men. Such contact, while not a total solution to his problem, did offer certain benefits. First, the encounters relieved his sexual frustration, or, as he said: "It merely relieves your tensions; there's no emotion involved."[26] Second, because these encounters lacked feelings, he may have felt that he was at least being emotionally faithful. Third, such release and lack of emotion also offered what must have been a major benefit to Diettrich: a way to avoid having an affair with another woman and being blatantly unfaithful. Finally, Diettrich may not have seen these encounters as a great threat to his marriage, certainly not as much as an affair with a woman would have been in his eyes.

Diettrich's sense of honor also refused to allow him to live as a victim. Within weeks of being forced to resign from his job of almost twenty-eight years, he had put his financial life in order, prepared for his Fulbright work in Pakistan, and planned future writing projects. After Diettrich returned to Gainesville, he and his wife also established the Foundation for the Promotion of Music. To this day, the foundation continues to offer UF scholarships to young musicians.[27]

Whereas Ruth Perry's striving for justice was directed more toward a community (African Americans) and a cause (constitutional rights for all), G. G. Mock's efforts were primarily person-to-person actions, much as Sig Diettrich's refusals to name individuals were a manifestation of his sense of honor. A pivotal moment for Mock was her befriending and helping George Walker's lesbian sister after he had beaten her. Given Walker's well-known homophobia and his power as a policeman, Mock's act of kindness was very risky and, of course, led to her arrest. Given the antigay laws and ordinances as well as dangers inherent in lesbian bars in the 1950s, many lesbians would not have become involved in the problems between a homophobic policeman and his sister.[28]

Mock's sense of justice and love became most evident when she was the most vulnerable: while she was in jail, awaiting trial. When Johns Committee investigators asked her repeatedly for the name of her girlfriend, a public school teacher, Mock refused. Even with the incentive of having her sentence reduced through the committee's intervention, Mock still refused to betray her girlfriend. Eventually sentenced to three years at Lowell State Prison, Mock persisted in defying the Johns Committee. Again at her most vulnerable times while in prison—her parole hearings—Mock did not waver. The committee's repeated demands for her girlfriend's name—and the promises of Mock's immediate release as incentive—did not work. Also while at Lowell, Mock outmaneuvered chief investigator Strickland during interrogation. She gave him nothing of value, only names of known gays or ones beyond his reach, and even played dumb in order to divert him from further questions about teachers.[29]

After Mock left Lowell, she moved to Miami but continued to remain positively engaged with others around her: reconnecting with her daughter, moving back to Tampa because of the birth of her first grandchild, having a long-term relationship with another woman, and donating time and materials from her print shop to the burgeoning women's community in Tampa. Years later, when Hazel Storey located the anonymous woman who had testified against them, Mock, like Sig Diettrich, declined the opportunity for revenge and told Storey to let go of the past.[30]

For Mock, finding the love of her life—Linda Bothwell—must have caused Mock to wonder how her life might have been different had she met Bothwell sooner. Certainly, Bothwell's writing a brief story about her partner's moral courage would have created an additional bond between them. Finally, Mock continues to protect her girlfriend from the 1950s. Although the Johns Committee is no longer a threat to her former girlfriend, Mock's stand persists to this day, for she does not give the woman's name or talk about her in interviews.[31]

Unlike Sig Diettrich or G. G. Mock, Margaret Fisher's actions were not on behalf of another person but rather an institution. Raised in a "family in which every woman [was] supposed to be *somebody* [emphasis in original],"[32] Fisher certainly had the requisite preparation for leadership before coming to USF: graduate training, a doctorate, dual appointments as professor and administrator, and impressive work as a scholar. Serving as both a USF administrator and a faculty member gave her a vantage point from which to defend her university against the Johns Committee. She understood the role of such dual appointments as part of USF's interdisciplinary, All-University educational policy and relished putting that philosophy into action in the classroom. Thus she was quite capable of educating the Johns Committee while defending USF's approach to higher education; when her attorney advised her to "obfuscate; exercise your talents," she knew that she could do that also.[33]

Fisher and her colleagues were convinced that the Johns Committee did not understand USF and decided to teach the legislators about the university's mission and values in relation to reading materials, academic freedom, religious issues, public image, and accreditation. Still, after a team of administrators and faculty had bombarded the committee with such information for five and one-half days, Fisher tried a different approach. Following her lawyer's advice, Fisher sometimes bored committee members, but she repeatedly outmaneuvered and frustrated them. That she did so while addressing such a controversial issue as rumors about a gay USF employee approaching a student is impressive. Taking a different approach in her testimony did not diminish or contradict her colleagues' testimony. Thus she was, as the committee said, "an important witness" while still helping her colleagues.[34]

Fisher continued to function as a team player in the aftermath of the Johns Committee hearings. Admiring the AAUW's aggressive, proactive decision to investigate the committee, she joined the efforts of the organization's local and state committees to discontinue the Johns Committee. Such activity would most likely have given her a level of satisfaction that she had not experienced during the campus hearings. However, her work with a group of faculty and administrators on the Grebstein affair would have been frustrating for all concerned. Since Fisher and her colleagues were trying to devise a way to "get the politicians off the hook"[35] after a student objected to Grebstein's reading material, it is not surprising that she found the assignment, but not her colleagues, frustrating.[36]

•

Looking back on her experiences with the Johns Committee almost fifty years later, Fisher insisted that she and her colleagues were just ordinary people who were busy building a university.[37] Fisher's point merits further analysis because it leads to an interesting and circuitous irony. Since the five subjects of this book were ordinary people, hardly anyone would have known if they had not stood up to the Johns Committee, because these five were not major leaders. (Although famous in Florida because of his lawsuit, Hawkins was still not a recognized leader.) For example, if Robert Saunders, as head of the Florida NAACP, had cooperated with the committee, his capitulation would have made headlines. In defying the committee, these five ordinary people consciously chose to forfeit the protection of not being well known. Their defiance, in turn, made them both known and vulnerable.

Fisher's recollections raised another issue as well when she insisted that she and her colleagues were not heroes but were just trying to keep the Johns Committee's "Greek theater" from becoming a "quasi-judicial investigatory approach."[38] She insists that the real "honors belong to Miami."[39] Her assessment also reflects the committee's original purpose: ending or delaying integration by dismantling the Florida NAACP. Thus Fisher maintains that, if one is looking for heroes, one should look at the Miami NAACP, not USF.

However, there are heroes, and there are champions. Heroes are more likely to become famous because they tend to be charismatic. Also, heroes often believe that one person can change the world, while those who champion a cause tend to try to dispel old attitudes and awaken people to new truths. Upon that basis, Fisher was correct. She and her colleagues were not heroes; they were champions, as were Hawkins and Perry. Hawkins, Perry, and Fisher defended a cause, while Diettrich and Mock were champions who protected specific people. In creating their majorities of one, these five Floridians refused to place their government above their integrity and would surely have agreed with Thoreau: "The citizen [must never] resign his conscience to the legislator."[40]

# Appendix

Documents from the Florida Legislative
Investigation Committee Records

Document One

July 28, 1956

*ATTENTION*

ALL WHITE CITIZENS OF THE DAYTONA BEACH AREA

On last week the fine citizens of our area organized a chapter of the *White Citizens Council* in this section. Since that time we have been encouraged by the moral support of meany of the fine citizens of Daytona Beach, including such men as Rev. Ralph Todd of the First Methodist Church, Mr. Henry Coleman of the Commercial Bank, H. M. Bixler of the YMCA, Owen Eubanks of the Florida Loan, Rev. Jack Bryant of Port Orange, and City Manager Allen of Daytona Beach. Aside from this it has been heartening to know that our State legislature is with us, led by Gov. Collins. We feel that they will back any organization that is against the Negro and his mad craze for civil rights.

Our objectives are these:

1. To preserve segregation in the public schools, if this means closing the schools and using the money for private schools for White children.
2. To keep Negroes off the public beach and areas that immediatly join the beach.
3. To destroy the Intergrated Ministerial Association in Daytona Beach.

4. To institute a mild program of violence to frighten the Negro into submission, stopping only short of bombing their homes as we did at Mims in 1951, through the old KKK.

5. To demand the destruction of the NAACP, a step the legislature has already taken. Their records should be destroyed and their leaders defamed and prosecuted.

6. To work closly with the newly organized KKK. We feel that our Governor and legislature are with us, for they have not as yet mention the revival.

7. To force a city ordinance by which Negroes will not be granted the privilege of public protest on any matter.

8. To close all facilities to Negroes in the downtown area.

9. To ban through our legislature all mixed sports, including the baseball team that trains here in the winter and have already written the team of our distaste for Negroes on their teams.

10. To institute a program that will result in the investigation of Negroes churches. If the churches can't be banned, certinly their ministers can be prosecuted for advocating civil rights, and ultimately chased from the pulpits.

11. And finally, to follow Mississippi in Burning all Books that speak of interracial fellowship and teaches that the Negro should be granted first class citizenship.

Read the paper for our next meeting on Tuesday, and come and join us in this great crusade to preserve the power of the white race. The News Journal will be against us, but yhis will not matter. It is run by Jews who themselves are one step above Negroes. Rev. Todd will bring the prayer on next week, and a list of undesirable Negroes will be circulated.

THE WHITE CITIZENS COUNCIL OF DAYTONA BEACH
John Larsen, William Leonard, Eric _enner [illegible]

White Citizens' Council flyer. Note references to the Moore assassinations and to the Johns Committee at numbers 4 and 5, respectively. Box 17, file 19. By permission of the State Archives of Florida, Tallahassee. (Because of the poor reproduction quality of the original, this document was retyped, retaining the original document's typographical and spelling errors.)

# Document Two

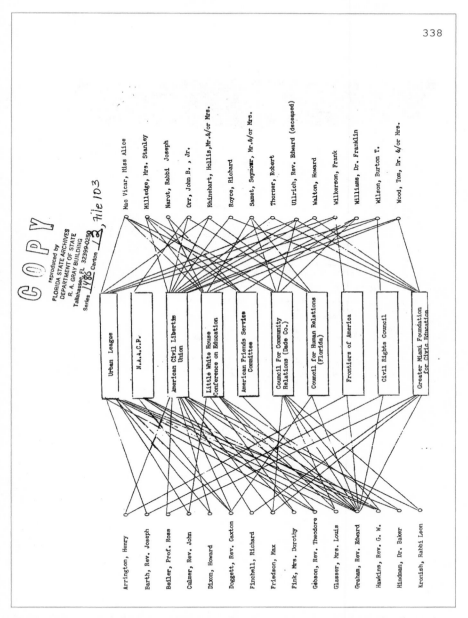

Committee-created chart, attempting to show connections among civil rights groups and activists. Box 12, file 103. By permission of the State Archives of Florida, Tallahassee.

# Document Three

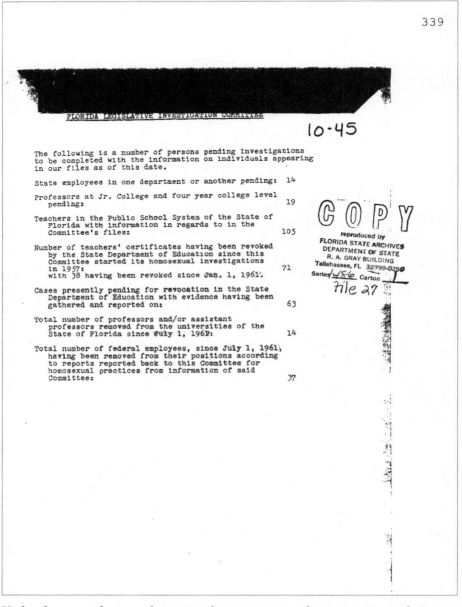

FLORIDA LEGISLATIVE INVESTIGATION COMMITTEE

10-45

The following is a number of persons pending investigations
to be completed with the information on individuals appearing
in our files as of this date.

State employees in one department or another pending:    14

Professors at Jr. College and four year college level
    pending:                                             19

Teachers in the Public School System of the State of
    Florida with information in regards to in the
    Committee's files:                                  105

Number of teachers' certificates having been revoked
    by the State Department of Education since this
    Committee started its homosexual investigations
    in 1957:                                             71
    with 38 having been revoked since Jan. 1, 1961.

Cases presently pending for revocation in the State
    Department of Education with evidence having been
    gathered and reported on:                            63

Total number of professors and/or assistant
    professors removed from the universities of the
    State of Florida since July 1, 1961:                 14

Total number of federal employees, since July 1, 1961,
    having been removed from their positions according
    to reports reported back to this Committee for
    homosexual practices from information of said
    Committee:                                           37

Undated memo referring to homosexual investigations as beginning in 1957, during
the Johns Committee's first full year of operations. Box 1, file 27. By permission of the
State Archives of Florida, Tallahassee.

# Notes

## Preface

1. The original version of the epigraph is "One man with courage makes a majority." It has been attributed to Andrew Jackson by both Robert Kennedy (foreword to *Profiles in Courage*, xi–xii) and by President Ronald Reagan in an October 10, 1987, speech ("Radio Address to the Nation on the Supreme Court Nomination of Robert H. Bork," The American Presidency Project, www.presidency.ucsb.edu/ws/?pid=33539) but has not been found in Jackson's writings. He may have adapted the quote from abolitionist Wendell Phillips—"One on God's side is a majority" (Boller and George, *They Never Said It*, 54), or from Henry David Thoreau—"Moreover, any man more right than his neighbors constitutes a majority of one already" ("Civil Disobedience," 43).

2. Stacy Braukman's *Communists and Perverts* focuses on the committee's pursuit of gays and studies the cold war anxieties that fueled the committee and paved the way for the rise of the evangelical Right. Braukman secondarily covers much of the committee's history. Karen Graves' *And They Were Wonderful Teachers* concentrates primarily on public school teachers.

3. The terms homosexual and gay or lesbian are used interchangeably throughout this book.

4. Johns Committee scholar Steven F. Lawson used the term "little McCarthyism" in reviewing the manuscript for this book.

## Chapter 1. Charley Johns and Virgil Hawkins

1. Brown v. Board of Education of Topeka, 347 U.S. 483 (1954); Johns quoted in *Dark Legacy*.

2. Johns quoted in Smith and Parks, "Desegregation in Florida," 55; Klein, "Guarding the Baggage," 251.

3. Klein, "Guarding the Baggage," 8–12.

4. "In Memoriam," 306; Johns, "Proctor Oral History Project"; Peggy O'Neal, "Former Acting Governor Charley Johns Has Made Career of Helping People," *Florida Times-Union*, November 1, 1976, sec. C; campaign biography, 2, box 263, Allen Morris Papers; Field, "Charley E. Johns," 3; "Acting Governor Charley E. Johns Wore Pork Chop Label Proudly," *Florida Times-Union*, January 24, 1990, n.p.

5. "Johns' Memory Is Paid Honor by Attorneys," *Florida Times-Union*, May 4, 1931, n.p. Senate presidents are elected during the current legislative session for the next session.

6. Johns, "Proctor Oral History"; "In Memoriam," 306.

7. Johns quoted in John Perry, "Charley Johns: The Controversial Candidate," *St. Petersburg Times*, March 6, 1954, sec. A, box 263, Morris Papers.

8. Field, "Charley E. Johns," 3.

9. "In Memoriam," 306; Field, "Charley E. Johns," 3; Plowden, Advance Wirescript, 1; *Journal of the Senate*, 1949, 1227, 1252–80, passim; *Journal of the Senate*, 1951, 1322, 1352–58, passim; campaign biography, 3, Morris Papers; Price, *Negro and Southern Politics*, 98; John Perry, "Charley Johns: Politician," *St. Petersburg Times*, March 7, 1954, sec. A, box 263, Morris Papers.

10. "In Memoriam," 306; editorial, *Tampa Tribune*, July 13, 1955; editorial, *Tampa Tribune*, July 10, 1955.

11. Klein, "Guarding the Baggage," 10, 12.

12. Havard and Beth, *Politics of Misrepresentation*, 64–65, 162, 171; Miller, "Pork Chop Gang," 2, 3.

13. Havard and Beth, *Politics of Misrepresentation*, 132–33; Price, *Negro and Southern Politics*, 104; Christie, "Collins–Johns Election," 8; Parsons, "Quasi-Partisan Conflict," 607–10. For more on the Pork Chop Gang, see Klein, "Guarding the Baggage."

14. Field, "Charley E. Johns," 3; Johns quoted in John Perry, "Charley Johns: The Controversial Candidate," *St. Petersburg Times*, March 6, 1954, 1, box 263, Morris Papers.

15. John Perry, "Charley Johns: The Controversial Candidate," *St. Petersburg Times*, March 6, 1954, 1, box 263, Morris Papers.

16. Plowden, Advance Wirescript, 1; *Journal of the Senate*, 1953, 770.

17. Stark, "McCarthyism in Florida," 6.

18. Plowden, Advance Wirescript, 1; "In Memoriam," 306. As Senate president, Johns was able to kill the bill by sending it to three different committees, thus preventing a vote on the bill (Dyckman, *Floridian of His Century*, 59).

19. Jacobstein, *Segregation Factor*, 16; Johns quoted in Collins, "Proctor Oral History Project," interview by Colburn and Scher.

20. Plowden, Advance Wirescript, 1; John Perry, "Charley Johns: Politician," *St. Petersburg Times*, March 7, 1954, sec. A, box 263, Morris Papers; "Statement by Acting Governor Charley E. Johns," October 23, 1953, 1–6, box 263, Morris Papers.

21. "Opinion with Reference to the Construction of Article 4, Section 19 of the

Constitution of Florida of 1885," 1, 15, box 42, Governor McCarty–Johns Correspondence. Although Florida's Constitution in 1953 prohibited a governor from succeeding himself, Johns could do so by serving as acting governor and then being elected to complete McCarty's term.

22. Christie, "Collins–Johns Election," 6; Plowden, Advance Wirescript, 1; Field, "Charley E. Johns," 3.

23. Dyckman, *Floridian of His Century*, 94; Clarke quoted in Klein, "Guarding the Baggage," 202.

24. Campaign biography, 1, Morris Papers.

25. Ibid., 3; Field, "Charley E. Johns," 3.

26. Christie, "Collins–Johns Election," 8, 13, 16; Field, "LeRoy Collins Story," 2; *Journal of the Senate*, 1949, 1227; Collins, "Proctor Oral History Project," monologue; Collins, "Proctor Oral History Project," interview by Washington; Bob Quinn to Leonard Pepper (telegram), April 3, 1954, box 2, Governor McCarty–Johns Correspondence; Wagy, *Governor LeRoy Collins*, 38.

27. Johns quoted in John Perry, "Charley Johns: Politician," *St. Petersburg Times*, March 7, 1954, sec. A, box 263, Morris Papers.

28. Christie, "Collins–Johns Election," 10.

29. Collins, "Proctor Oral History," interview by Colburn and Scher; ad quoted in "Video Clip 24, Governors Charley Johns–LeRoy Collins," Florida Memory Project, floridamemory.com/Collections/governors/johns.cfm.

30. "Video Clip 24, Governors Charley Johns–LeRoy Collins," Florida Memory Project, floridamemory.com/Collections/governors/johns.cfm; Collins, interview by Ice.

31. Christie, "Collins–Johns Election," 15–16; ad quoted in Klein, "Guarding the Baggage," 339.

32. Christie, "Collins–Johns Election," 16. When the Republican nominee died before the general election in November, the party did not provide another candidate (Tebeau, *History of Florida*, 439).

33. Tomberlin, "Florida Whites and *Brown*," 34; "Florida"; Smith and Parks, "Desegregation in Florida," 56–57.

34. Killian, "Florida's Citizens," 14.

35. Killian, *Black and White*, 81.

36. Killian, "Florida's Citizens," 12–14.

37. Florida, Attorney General, Amicus Curiae Brief, 43, 18.

38. Kluger, *Simple Justice*, 728.

39. Odum, "Summary of Segregation Brief," 27; Richard Ervin, speech, 10, box 272, Morris Papers; Smith and Parks, "Desegregation in Florida," 57.

40. Klein, "Guarding the Baggage," 163; *Journal of the Senate*, 1955, 1635.

41. Johns quoted in Plowden, Advance Wirescript, 1.

42. Johns quoted in Stark, "McCarthyism in Florida," 8.

43. Stewart, "The Law and Virgil Hawkins," 14–15.

44. Saunders, interview by Dubin; Rivers, "Everlasting Arms," 284–88.

45. Hawkins quoted in Stewart, "The Law and Virgil Hawkins," 16.

46. Stewart, "The Law and Virgil Hawkins," 14–16; Clendinen, "Victory in Sight," 22.

47. Selkow, "Hawkins and Justice," 97; Rivers, "Everlasting Arms," 290; Hawkins Sr. quoted in ibid., 295.

48. Julius Rosenwald, president of Sears and Roebuck Company, established his foundation in 1917 to construct schools for African Americans in the South. Rivers, "Everlasting Arms," 288–89, 294; Stewart, "The Law and Virgil Hawkins," 15; Selkow, "Hawkins and Justice," 97.

49. "February 4, 1957, Transcripts" file, 2, 10, box 3, Florida Legislative Investigation Committee (hereafter cited in notes as FLIC) Records; Stewart, "The Law and Virgil Hawkins," 15.

50. Bennett, "South's Most Patient Man," 44; Selkow, "Hawkins and Justice," 97; Rivers, "Everlasting Arms," 301; Brazeal, "Some Problems," 356. Sources differ on Hawkins' age at various points, even on a personal information form from his attorney's files (Personal Information Form, 1, box 15, FLIC Records) as well as in interviews of Hawkins in 1958 and 1987. However, he testified in the first Johns Committee hearing in 1957 that he was forty-seven years old ("February 4, 1957, Transcripts" file, 2, box 3, FLIC Records).

51. Florida A&M College gained university status in 1953 but is referred to as FAMU throughout this book. Also, the law school is referred to as FAMU College of Law or FAMU law school throughout. Paulson and Hawkes, "Desegregation of University of Florida," 59; State ex Rel. Hawkins v. Board of Control of Florida et al., 47 So. 2d 608 (1950; cited hereafter as *Hawkins v. Board of Control*); "A Certified Copy of Excerpts Taken from the Official Minutes of a Meeting of the Board of Control Held in Tallahassee, Florida, December 21, 1949," 1–2, box 117, Governor LeRoy Collins Correspondence. The other applicants (Oliver Maxey, Benjamin Finley, Rose Boyd, and William Lewis) later withdrew from the case, at different times, because of threats against themselves, their families, and their employers ("Plaintiffs in Virgil Hawkins Case," January 25, 1957, 1, box 13, FLIC Records; Cooper, "*Brown v. Board of Education*," 1); "February 5, 1957, Transcripts" file, 253–66, 274–96, 615–26, box 3, FLIC Records; Daniels, *Florida's First Black Lawyers*, vi. A detailed discussion of all legal aspects of Hawkins' case is beyond the scope of this work. For more in-depth information on the case, see Dubin, "One-Man Civil Rights Movement"; Selkow, "Hawkins and Justice"; Brazeal, "Some Problems"; Paulson and Hawkes, "Desegregation of University of Florida"; and Cooper, "*Brown v. Board of Education*"; as well as Whittington Johnson, "A Near Decade," 55–71; and case summaries and court decisions available through www.lexis-nexis.com.

52. John Blair to L. L. Fabisinski, June 12, 1956, box 33, Governor Collins Correspondence; Hill quoted in Stewart, "The Law and Virgil Hawkins," 15.

53. *Hawkins v. Board of Control*, passim, box 15, FLIC Records; Virgil Hawkins

to Alex Akerman, August 1, 1950, box 15, FLIC Records; Brazeal, "Some Problems," 356–57; Davis, *Half Century of Struggle*, 154. Akerman, a Republican, had served a term in the state legislature and was one of the defense attorneys in the 1949 Groveland case. He selected Horace Hill, who had recently graduated from Howard University Law School, as an assistant in the case. Hill later became active in the Daytona Beach NAACP, leading the legal challenge to integrate local beaches while also representing Virgil Hawkins (Lawson, Colburn, and Paulson, "Groveland," 10–11; Green, *Before His Time*, 92; Daniels, *Florida's First Black Lawyers*, 19).

54. Horace Hill, interview by Dubin.

55. *Hawkins v. Board of Control*, FLIC Records; William Gray to Virgil Hawkins, April 11, 1949, box 15, FLIC Records; "Shape of Things," 269; Paulson and Hawkes, "Desegregation of University of Florida," 59–60; Harley Herman, "Anatomy of a Bar Resignation," 89; "February 5, 1957, Transcripts" file, 216–17, box 3, FLIC Records.

56. Sweatt v. Painter, 339 U.S. 629 (1950); Kluger, *Simple Justice*, 259, 261, 266, 268, 278; Motley, *Equal Justice under Law*, 65, 114. Ada Sipuel entered the University of Oklahoma Law School in 1949, and both Herman Sweatt and George McLaurin won their U.S. Supreme Court cases on the same day in 1950 (Kluger, *Simple Justice*, 282–83).

57. McLaurin quoted in Kluger, *Simple Justice*, 268; Hawkins quoted in Stewart, "The Law and Virgil Hawkins," 15.

58. John Blair to L. L. Fabisinski, June 12, 1956, box 33, Governor Collins Correspondence; Paulson and Hawkes, "Desegregation of University of Florida," 61.

59. Jo Becker, "State Court Honors Civil Rights Pioneer," *St. Petersburg Times*, May 26, 1999, sec. B; Martin Dyckman, "After Brown, the Law Was on His Side, But the Florida Supreme Court Wasn't," *St. Petersburg Times*, May 16, 2004, 22; Barton, interview by Dubin; Saunders, interview by Dubin.

60. Anonymous source quoted in Stewart, "The Law and Virgil Hawkins," 15.

61. Dubin, "One-Man Civil Rights Movement," 916.

62. Brazeal, "Some Problems," 357; Moore quoted in Stewart, "The Law and Virgil Hawkins," 16.

63. Bethune quoted in Bennett, "South's Most Patient Man," 50.

64. "February 4, 1957, Transcripts" file, 10, box 3, FLIC Records; Davis, *Half Century of Struggle*, 11, 132, 154; Porter and Neyland, *Florida State Teachers Association*, 102; Brazeal, "Some Problems," 357.

65. Paulson and Hawkes, "Desegregation of University of Florida," 62; Puryear, "Desegregation of Public Education," 221; Stewart, "The Law and Virgil Hawkins," 16. In the fall of 1955, the IRS liquidated Hawkins' bank account without notifying him. His creditors pressured him and almost repossessed his car for delinquent payments; after making the missed payments, he put the vehicle in his wife's name but was still in debt to the IRS (Stewart, "The Law and Virgil Hawkins," 15–16).

66. Brazeal, "Some Problems," 357; "February 5, 1957, Transcripts" file, 219–27, box 3, FLIC Records.

67. *Journal of the Senate*, 1955, 60, 568.

68. Smith and Parks, "Desegregation in Florida," 57, 59; Brown v. Board of Education of Topeka, 349 U.S. 294 (1955).

69. Paulson and Hawkes, "Desegregation of University of Florida," 62, 64, 66; Cooper, "*Brown v. Board of Education*," 6, 8; Porter, "Status of Educational Desegregation," 247–48; Board of Control, "Study on Desegregation," 4–5, 12–13. One of the Florida supreme court justices who concurred in the "public mischief" ruling was Stephen O'Connell, future president of UF (Pleasants, *Gator Tales*, 56).

70. Allen Morris, Cracker Politics (syndicated column), n.p., March 17, 1956, Allen Morris Collection; Smith and Parks, "Desegregation in Florida," 60; LeRoy Collins, press release, March 12, 1956, 1, box 116, Governor Collins Correspondence.

71. Paulson and Hawkes, "Desegregation of University of Florida," 65–66; "February 5, 1957, Transcripts" file, 239, box 3, FLIC Records; Hawkins quoted in Bennett, "South's Most Patient Man," 46.

72. *St. Petersburg Times* quoted in Morris, Cracker Politics, March 17, 1956, n.p., Morris Collection. Allen Morris' Cracker Politics column was Florida's first syndicated political column (Danese, *Claude Pepper and Ed Ball*, 201).

73. "Memo to the State Board of Education for Meeting with Governor Collins on March 21, 1956," 2–3, box 116; "Resolution, March 21, 1956," 2, box 116, both in Governor Collins Correspondence; Paulson and Hawkes, "Desegregation of University of Florida," 65; John Blair to L. L. Fabisinski, June 12, 1956, 2, box 33, Governor Collins Correspondence; "Florida across the Threshold," 55; LeRoy Collins to L. L. Fabisinski, April 17, 1956, 1–2, box 116; LeRoy Collins, speech to Fabisinski Committee, May 1, 1956, 1, box 116, both in Governor Collins Correspondence; Rabby, *Pain and Promise*, 214.

74. Jakes, "Civil Rights Heroine"; Jakes, "Woman's Bus Ride"; Metz Rollins quoted in Rabby, *Pain and Promise*, 12.

75. Rabby, *Pain and Promise*, 12–17, 214–15.

76. "Special Committee to Recommend Legislative Action," 2–3; Rabby, *Pain and Promise*, 215.

77. Schnur, "Cold Warriors," 41–42; Collins, "How It Looks," 96; Collins, interview by Ice; note attached to Interposition Resolution, box 117, Governor Collins Correspondence; Collins, interview by Colburn and Scher.

78. *Journal of the Senate*, 1956, 27.

79. Ibid.; Johns quoted in *Dark Legacy*. Johns' attitude toward investigating Communists had been inconsistent. While acting governor, he told a reporter that congressional committees were "doing a wonderful job in *trying* [emphasis added] to weed out spies and Communists." He also said that the government should reinforce federal laws as a protection against Communists yet added that the laws probably could not be "strengthen[ed] . . . enough to do that" ("Facts Forum: State of Nation," typescript, n.d., 7–8, box 263, Morris Papers).

80. "Senate Finishes Job on Segregation Bills, Group to Probe NAACP," *Tallahas-*

*see Democrat*, July 25, 1956, sec. A; Johnson quoted in "6 Senators Switch Votes," *Tallahassee Democrat*, July 26, 1956, sec. A.

81. Saunders, *Bridging the Gap*, 76; Steele, Appendix, 257; Marshall quoted in Saunders, *Bridging the Gap*, 76.

82. Saunders, "Continuing the Legacy"; Ruth Perry, speech 5, n.d., 5, box 1, Perry Papers; Emmons, "Flame of Resistance," 219; Thurgood Marshall to Ruth Perry, July 17, 1956, box 1, Perry Papers.

83. *Journal of the Senate*, 1956, 27; Jack Musselman to LeRoy Collins, June 14, 1956, box 33, Governor Collins Correspondence. Despite his concerns about the makeup of the investigation committee, Musselman still saw it as a way to combat integration, Communism, and the NAACP (Jack Musselman to LeRoy Collins, June 14, 1956, box 33, Governor Collins Correspondence).

84. Mahon quoted in "Bills to Abolish Public Schools Pass First Test, Committee Rules against Bill to Probe NAACP," *Tallahassee Democrat*, July 30, 1956, sec. A.

85. "Broader Interposition Bloc Wins 45–42 Test in House, House Votes Recess," *Tallahassee Democrat*, August 1, 1956, sec. A; "NAACP Probing Bill Becomes Law," *Tallahassee Democrat*, August 21, 1956, sec. A. In retrospect, this line of reasoning became more important when Johns Committee targets felt that their only recourse was the judicial branch.

86. "Members" file, 1–3, box 1, FLIC Records; Schnur, "Cold Warriors," 12–13; Klein, "Guarding the Baggage," 12–13.

87. "Minutes" file, September 11, 1956, 4, FLIC Records.

88. "Minutes" file, October 18, 1956, 2; November 13, 1956, 2; December 11, 1956, 2, all minutes in box 1, FLIC Records; Bartley, *Rise of Massive Resistance*, 214, 216–19; Jack Greenberg, *Crusaders in the Courts*, 229; Patricia Sullivan, *Lift Every Voice*, 425; Lawson, "Florida Legislative Investigation Committee," 298–99; "Attorney General Opinions" file, 1, box 2, Governor McCarty–Johns Correspondence; Mike Pope, "Red Scare, White Supremacy, Purple Haze: Joe McCarthy, Charley Johns, and the Ripples of Fanaticism," *Tallahassee Democrat*, May 11, 2003, sec. E. The states with legislative committees similar to the Johns Committee were Louisiana, Mississippi, South Carolina, Georgia, Virginia, and Arkansas (Bartley, *Rise of Massive Resistance*, 222). The Virginia laws were ruled unconstitutional by the U.S. Supreme Court seven years later in *NAACP v. Button*. (See *NAACP v. Button* in *Legal Information Institute*, www.supct.law.cornell.edu/supct/cases/historic.html.)

89. Mark Hawes to Henry Land, September 19, 1956, box 9, Clerk of the House of Representatives (hereafter cited in notes as CHR) Papers; *Dark Legacy*; "Organization of Attorney General's Office," 1953, box 2, Governor McCarty–Johns Correspondence; "Report to the Legislature," January 17, 1957, 14, box 1, FLIC Records.

90. "Court Cases, Miscellaneous" file, 1, box 15; "Memo on Material from the Attorney General's Files, Virgil Hawkins Case," n.d., box 15; "Memo of Investigation," n.d., box 15; "Minutes" file, September 11, 1956, 4, box 1; John Cheasty form letter, October 23, 1956, box 3; Mark Hawes form letters, January 11, 16, and 17, 1957, box 3; R.

J. Strickland form letter, December 31, 1956, box 3, all in FLIC Records; Mike Pope, "Red Scare, White Supremacy, Purple Haze: Joe McCarthy, Charley Johns, and the Ripples of Fanaticism," *Tallahassee Democrat*, May 11, 2003, sec. E.

91. *Dark Legacy*; "Minutes" file, October 10, 1956, 1, box 1, FLIC Records; Braukman, *Communists and Perverts*, 60, 62; Mohl, *South of the South*, 26. Although the Communist strategy is reflected in the committee's October 10, 1956, meeting minutes, the committee was not authorized to investigate subversives (Communists) until 1958, so chair Henry Land's 1957 report devoted only half a page to the Communist threat (Henry Land, "Report of the Florida Legislative Investigation Committee," n.d., 13, box 1, FLIC Records).

92. Mark Hawes, "Progress Report," January 17, 1957, 2, 9–10, box 1, FLIC Records. Chair Henry Land's later report was similar to Hawes' (Henry Land, "Report of the Florida Legislative Investigation Committee," n.d., passim, box 1, FLIC Records).

93. Richard Ervin to Henry Land, October 4, 1956, box 3; Richard Ervin to Mark Hawes, February 8, 1957, box 3, both in FLIC Records.

94. "February 4–7, 1957, Transcripts" files, i, passim, box 3, FLIC Records.

## Chapter 2. Virgil Hawkins

1. *Dark Legacy*; Saunders, interviews by author, December 18, 1998; March 24, 2001; and February 15, 2002.

2. "February 4, 1957, Transcripts" file, 1, passim, box 3; Mark Hawes, "Progress Report," January 17, 1957, 2, 9–10, box 1, both in FLIC Records; Saunders, *Bridging the Gap*, 159.

3. Berg, *Ticket to Freedom*, 72, 74–75; Lawson, Colburn, and Paulson, "Groveland," 8, 25; Saunders, *Bridging the Gap*, 116.

4. List of Exhibits, n.d., 1–8; Harry T. Moore to Ed Davis, October 5, 1949; Ed Davis, Steering Committee flyer, May 8, 1951; "Florida State Conference of Branches, Resolutions" file, n.d., 3; Horace Hill to Ed Davis, February 4, 1952; E. E. Broughton, financial statement, April 17, 1952; Horace Hill to Robert Carter, August 6, 1954; Horace Hill, itemized expense statement, June 7, 1955; Ed Davis to Ruth Perry, November 16, 1955; Ed Davis to Horace Hill, November 17, 1955; Ruth Perry to Ed Davis, November 23, 1955; Ed Davis, financial statement, n.d., all in box 14; "February 4, 1957, Transcripts" file, 2, 6, 10, and 22, box 3, all in FLIC Records.

5. "February 4, 1957, Transcripts" file, 13–14, box 3, FLIC Records.

6. Ibid.

7. Ibid., 17–18.

8. Ibid., 19.

9. Ibid., 20–22.

10. Ibid.

11. Ibid., 23.

12. Ibid., 40–41. When Ed Davis was later recalled and agreed to turn over his and Harry T. Moore's UF files to the committee ("February 5, 1957, Transcripts" file, 269,

272, box 3, FLIC Records), most likely Davis removed all significant documents, just as Robert Saunders did about a week later (Saunders, *Bridging the Gap*, 165).

13. "February 4, 1957, Transcripts" file, 56, 58, 61, 65, 72, 85–92, box 3, FLIC Records; Saunders, *Bridging the Gap*, 66, 127. For more on Ruth Perry, see chapter 3.

14. "February 4, 1957, Transcripts" file, 123, 126, box 3, FLIC Records.

15. Ibid., 127, 130–31; "Legislators Eye Hawkins Case: Negro Leader Says Probers Trying to Outlaw NAACP," *Florida Times-Union*, February 5, 1957, sec. B.

16. "February 4, 1957, Transcripts" file, 164–202; Mark Hawes to Frank Massari, January 17, 1957; H. W. Warentine to Mark Hawes, January 31, 1957, all in box 3, FLIC Records; Emmons, "Flame of Resistance," 225; Hill, interview by Dubin; *Hawkins v. Board of Control*; Horace Hill, itemized expense statement, June 7, 1955, box 14; "NAACP Bank Accounts Checks" file, check to Horace Hill, March 11, 1952, box 13; E. E. Broughton, financial statement, April 17, 1952, box 14, all in FLIC Records; "Legislators Eye Hawkins Case: Negro Leader Says Probers Trying to Outlaw NAACP," *Florida Times-Union*, February 5, 1957, sec. B.

17. "February 4, 1957, Transcripts" file, 203–6, box 3, FLIC Records. For more discussion of testimony by Davis, Fordham, Hill, and other witnesses, see Saunders' firsthand account in *Bridging the Gap*, 162–66.

18. John Cye Cheasty, Status Report, December 11, 1956, 5; Memo of Investigation, n.d., 1–5, box 9, both in CHR Papers.

19. Hawes quoted in "Minutes" file, December 11, 1956, 1, box 9, CHR Papers.

20. "Minutes" file, December 11, 1956, passim, box 9, CHR Papers.

21. "Hawkins Due at NAACP Probe Meet," *Florida Times-Union*, February 4, 1957, sec. B.

22. "February 5, 1957, Transcripts" file, 213–14, box 3, FLIC Records.

23. Ibid., 216–18.

24. "February 5, 1957, Transcripts" file, 236–39, box 3, FLIC Records.

25. Although it was drawn from contributions to the Steering Committee (and not to the NAACP), the check was from an NAACP account (Saunders, *Bridging the Gap*, 163).

26. "February 5, 1957, Transcripts" file, 218, 242, box 3, FLIC Records.

27. Ibid., 244–46.

28. Ibid., 247.

29. Ibid., 248.

30. Ibid., 248–49.

31. The remainder of day two and most of day three of the hearing were devoted to questioning on the Tallahassee bus boycott.

32. "February 7, 1957, Transcripts" file, 606–10, 611, box 3; agreement, May 1951, 1, box 14, both in FLIC Records.

33. "February 7, 1957, Transcripts" file, 652–59, 656, box 3, FLIC Records.

34. Ibid., 656–59.

35. Ibid., 557–60, 564–70, 572; Horace Hill to William Fordham, December 9, 1955, box 14; Ed Davis to Horace Hill, December 29, 1955, box 14, all in FLIC Records.

36. "February 7, 1957, Transcripts" file, 573–75, box 3, FLIC Records.

37. Ibid., 668. The first witness asked was one of the students involved in the bus boycott ("February 6, 1957, Transcripts" file, 447, box 3, FLIC Records).

38. "February 7, 1957, Transcripts" file, 576–79, box 3, FLIC Records.

39. Ibid., 704.

40. Ibid., 704–5.

41. Ibid., 706, 709–11, 713; Ruth Perry to Ed Davis, November 23, 1955, box 3, FLIC Records; Rawls quoted in "NAACP Accused of Stirring Up Lawsuits," *Tallahassee Democrat*, February 8, 1957, sec. A.

42. "Control Board Asks Hawkins Suit Deferment," *Orlando Sentinel*, February 20, 1957, sec. A; "Supreme Court Lets Verdict on Hawkins Stand; Ervin Denied," *Orlando Sentinel*, February 27, 1957, sec. A.

43. Hawes quoted in Henry Land, "Report of the Florida Legislative Investigation Committee," 10, box 1, FLIC Records.

44. Saunders, *Bridging the Gap*, 166–68; Stark, "McCarthyism in Florida," 26. Since 1950, the Florida Bar and the Florida State Bar Association have been synonymous because lawyers admitted to the Bar are required to join the Florida Bar Association, which was renamed the Florida Bar in 1950 ("History of the Florida Bar," The Florida Bar, floridabar.org).

45. *Journal of the Senate*, 1957, 370, 724, 787, 1338, 1742; Karl, *The 57 Club*, 134–35; Lawson, "Florida Legislative Investigation Committee," 301.

46. Paulson and Hawkes, "Desegregation of University of Florida," 64, 66–67; George W. Gore Jr., "Some Important Trends in the Integration Process," 1956, 3, Gore Papers; affidavit of James Love, February 6, 1958, box 117, Governor Collins Correspondence.

47. Motley, *Equal Justice under Law*, 113–16. Motley, an NAACP attorney from the organization's New York headquarters, was co-counsel for the *Hawkins* case.

48. "Minutes" file, January 17, 1958, 4–5, box 9, CHR Papers; Lawson, "Florida Legislative Investigation Committee," 302.

49. Robert Saunders, annual report, 1958, 7, NAACP Papers; McCall quoted in Saunders, *Bridging the Gap*, 156. McCall later arrested a mentally handicapped teenager, Jesse Daniels, for the alleged rape (Saunders, *Bridging the Gap*, 156).

50. Saunders, *Bridging the Gap*, 156. Daniels was institutionalized for fourteen years, then freed and compensated by the legislature (Martin Dyckman, "After Brown, the Law Was on His Side, But the Florida Supreme Court Wasn't," *St. Petersburg Times*, May 16, 2004, sec. B).

51. DeVane quoted in Dubin, "One-Man Civil Rights Movement," 941.

52. Saunders, interview by Dubin; Motley, *Equal Justice under Law*, 116; Paulson and Hawkes, "Desegregation of University of Florida," 68.

53. *Hawkins v. Board of Control*, Brief of Respondents, January 1958, 30–31, box 14, FLIC Records; Paulson and Hawkes, "Desegregation of University of Florida," 69; Selkow, "Hawkins and Justice," 100; Sasscer, "Justice Delayed," 135, 147; Robert Saunders, annual report, 1958, 4, NAACP Papers.

54. Bennett, "South's Most Patient Man," 44; Stewart, "The Law and Virgil Hawkins," 16; Meek, interview by Dubin; Robert Saunders, annual report, 1958, 4, NAACP Papers; Selkow, "Hawkins and Justice," 101.

55. Cooper, "*Brown v. Board of Education*," 3–10; Stewart, "The Law and Virgil Hawkins," 17; Selkow, "Hawkins and Justice," 100–101.

56. George H. Starke, "George H. Starke: In His Own Words," *UF Law* (Fall 2008), University of Florida College of Law, www.law.ufl.edu/uflaw/08/08fall/Related-Articles/George-h-starke-jr-in-his-own-words.html; Evans, "One of the First," 47; Robert Saunders, annual report, 1958, 4, NAACP Papers.

57. Clendinen, "Victory in Sight," 22; Selkow, "Hawkins and Justice," 100; Paulson and Hawkes, "Desegregation of University of Florida," 70; Martin Dyckman, "After Brown, the Law Was on His Side, But the Florida Supreme Court Wasn't," *St. Petersburg Times*, May 16, 2004, sec. B; Stewart, "The Law and Virgil Hawkins," 16; Dubin, "One-Man Civil Rights Movement," 12; George Allen, "Proctor Oral History Project."

58. "The Virgil Hawkins Story," Virgil Hawkins Chapter, National Bar Association, vhfcnba.org/VirgilHawkins.aspx; Paulson and Hawkes, "Desegregation of University of Florida," 70.

59. Stewart, "The Law and Virgil Hawkins," 16; Saunders, interview by Dubin.

60. Paulson and Hawkes, "Desegregation of University of Florida," 70; Cooper, "*Brown v. Board of Education*," 11; Stewart, "The Law and Virgil Hawkins," 16. Ervin, who turned out to have a very liberal voting record while on the Florida Supreme Court, later said that, although he felt it was his duty as attorney general at the time to oppose Hawkins, he later believed that he was wrong and that the court should correct its error (Clendinen, "Victory in Sight," 23).

61. Porter and Neyland, *Florida State Teachers Association*, 214; Hawkins quoted in Herman, "Anatomy of a Bar Resignation," 97.

62. Stewart, "The Law and Virgil Hawkins," 16; Hawkins quoted in Paulson and Hawkes, "Desegregation of University of Florida," 71.

63. "State's Highest Court to Allow Hawkins to Resign from Bar," *Tallahassee Democrat*, April 19, 1985, sec. A.

64. Herman, interview by Dubin.

65. Herman, "Anatomy of a Bar Resignation," 105; Stewart, "The Law and Virgil Hawkins," 17; "History Making Lawyer Resigns from State Bar," *Tampa Tribune*, April 19, 1985, sec. B.

66. "Our History," Virgil Hawkins Florida Chapter National Bar Association, vhfcnba.org/OurHistory.aspx; Hawkins quoted in Ross Burnarman, "Meek Wants FSU Building Named for Black Lawyer," *St. Petersburg Times*, April 19, 1983, sec. B.

67. "State's Highest Court to Allow Hawkins to Resign from Bar," *Tallahassee Democrat*, April 19, 1985, sec. A; Herman, "Anatomy of a Bar Resignation," 104.

68. Hawkins quoted in Stewart, "The Law and Virgil Hawkins," 17; Hawkins quoted in Burt, *The Tropic of Cracker*, 87.

69. Hawkins quoted in Burt, *The Tropic of Cracker*, 91.

70. Stewart, "The Law and Virgil Hawkins," 17–18; Hawkins quoted in ibid., 16.

71. The Florida Bar, In re Virgil Darnell Hawkins, 532 So. 2d 669 (1988 Fla.); Dubin, "One-Man Civil Rights Movement," 950, 955; Peters, interview by Dubin; Ramsey Campbell, "Monument Honors Black Law Pioneer," *Orlando Sentinel*, February 10, 1991, www.articles.orlandosentinel.com.

72. Susan O'Reilly, "Posthumous Honors Eyed for Activist," *Tampa Tribune*, June 12, 1988, sec. A; Brent Kallestad, "Equal Justice: Black Man Posthumously Reinstated to Bar," *Tallahassee Democrat*, October 21, 1988, sec. B; "Virgil Hawkins, Honor Due the Unknown Gator," *Tallahassee Democrat*, May 3, 1989, sec. B; Rabby, *Pain and Promise*, 190; Herman, "Anatomy of a Bar Resignation," 111; D'Elosua, "Browner Speaks at Graduation," 1, 4.

Chapter 3. Ruth Perry

1. John B. McDermott, "10 More Cited in Reds Hunt," *Miami Herald*, February 28, 1958, sec. A, Ruth Perry Papers (contained in one box); *Dark Legacy*; Saunders, interviews by author; Saunders, *Bridging the Gap*, 168. Portions of this chapter appeared previously as "One Woman's Courage: Ruth Perry and the Johns Committee" in *Making Waves: Female Activists in Twentieth Century Florida*, edited by Jack Davis and Kari Frederickson (Gainesville: University Press of Florida, 2003) and as "Raising Her Voice: Ruth Perry, Activist and Journalist for the Miami NAACP," in the *Florida Historical Quarterly* 84, no. 4 (Spring 2006).

2. Perry quoted in Robert Saunders, "The NAACP Report," *Pittsburgh Courier*, April 10, 1954, sec. A, Perry Papers.

3. Perry-Kilburg, interviews by author, July 29 and August 31, 2002; Caroline Perry-Kilburg, e-mail to author, September 10, 2005; Ruth Perry, Along Freedom's Road, *Miami Times*, September 19, 1959, Perry Papers. Most of Perry's columns are included in the Perry Papers at the USF Tampa Library. The remaining columns were obtained from microfilm or from the private papers of Caroline Perry-Kilburg. Perry's column, Along Freedom's Road, ran in section 1 of the *Miami Times*, a sixteen-page newspaper, from October 6, 1956, to April 6, 1963. Autobiographical notes, speeches, letters, broadcasts, and comments are also from the Perry Papers unless otherwise noted.

4. Perry-Kilburg, interviews by author; Willard Austen, Cornell University, to Ruth Willis, June 13, 1929; R. H. Edwards, Cornell University, to Ruth Willis, September 3, 1929; Francis Willis to Ruth Willis, July 21, 1929, all from the private papers of Caroline Perry-Kilburg.

5. Perry-Kilburg, interviews by author.

6. "Presentation," *Florida Sun*, December 7, 1951, n.p., Perry Papers; Perry, Along Freedom's Road, *Miami Times*, May 18, 1957; Perry-Kilburg, interviews by author; Perry, speech 7, n.d., 5–6.

7. Perry quoted in Ronald York, "A Witness Eye-View," *Miami Herald*, March 1, 1958, sec. A, Perry Papers; Perry, Along Freedom's Road, *Miami Times*, July 15, 1961.

8. Emmons, "Flame of Resistance," 22, 242. Only fifty members were required in order to have an NAACP chapter (Robert Saunders to Lucille Black, October 7, 1964, box 2, Saunders Papers). See Dunn, *Black Miami*, 220–21; Perry, Along Freedom's Road, *Miami Times*, June 15, 1957.

9. Bartley, *Rise of Massive Resistance*, 201–10; Emmons, "Flame of Resistance," 6, 157–58; Mohl, "'South of the South?,'" 5–6.

10. Green, *Before His Time*, 171, 186. For discussion of this violence from an NAACP perspective, see the analysis by Robert Saunders, Moore's successor, in Saunders, *Bridging the Gap*, 111–19. In addition to Saunders, both Mohl and Green name the Klan or the White Citizens' Council, or both, as the assassins (Mohl, "'South of the South?,'" 6; Green, *Before His Time*, 195–98, 200–206).

11. Perry, Along Freedom's Road, *Miami Times*, December 23, 1961.

12. Perry, Along Freedom's Road, *Miami Times*, October 27, 1956.

13. Perry-Kilburg, interviews by author; Perry, autobiographical notes, n.d.; "Miami Branch Committees" file, April–May 1957, Saunders Papers.

14. "March 13, 1957, Transcripts" file, 2058–59, box 3, FLIC Records; Perry, speech 12, July 5, 1953.

15. "NAACP Leader," 5; Rose, "'Jewel' of the South," 53; Perry, speech 12, July 5, 1953.

16. Perry, comments 4, n.d. Comments are undated broadcasts.

17. Anonymous to Perry, August 24, 1954.

18. Perry, speech 6, December 1955.

19. Perry-Kilburg, interviews by author.

20. Perry-Kilburg, interviews by author; Perry, speech 9, November 22, 1955.

21. Broadcast 2, August 22, 1956. Despite the bomb threats, Perry continued her civil rights work, although the danger to her family was surely a concern. In fact, her daughter was a teenager at the time of the threats. One of Perry's female NAACP colleagues recognized that Perry's political work had the support of her family: "It is wonderful . . . that the family is willing to share you to give so many, many hours to the freedom of all people." (Perry-Kilburg, interviews by author; Pearl Mitchell to Perry, April 16, 1956, 2).

22. Perry, autobiographical notes, n.d.; Association Resolution, box 13, FLIC Records; Perry, Along Freedom's Road, *Miami Times*, November 17, 1956; comments 2, February 1956.

23. Emmons, "Flame of Resistance," 218–19; Saunders, *Bridging the Gap*, 83; Dunn, *Black Miami*, 182, 191.

24. Dunn, *Black Miami*, 213; Perry, Along Freedom's Road, *Miami Times*, January 12, 1957.

25. Saunders, *Bridging the Gap*, 83; Perry, Along Freedom's Road, *Miami Times*, January 12, 1957; Emmons, "Flame of Resistance," 229. In 1958, the Miami branch won again in the federal appeals court. This victory left the city with only one recourse, an appeal to the U.S. Supreme Court, which Miami's city attorney said would not be successful (Along Freedom's Road, *Miami Times*, April 19, 1958).

26. Thurgood Marshall to Perry, July 17, 1956; Perry, speech 5, n.d.

27. Perry, Along Freedom's Road, *Miami Times*, November 13, 1956; Mohl, *South of the South*, 26.

28. Perry, broadcast 2, August 22, 1956; "March 13, 1957, Transcripts" file, 2053–58, box 3, FLIC Records.

29. Perry, Along Freedom's Road, *Miami Times*, October 6, 1956. For further analysis of Perry's growth as a journalist, see Poucher, "Raising Her Voice," 517–40.

30. Perry, Along Freedom's Road, *Miami Times*, October 6, 1956; October 27, 1956.

31. Perry, Along Freedom's Road, *Miami Times*, February 16, 1957.

32. Perry, Along Freedom's Road, *Miami Times*, February 23, 1957. See also Poucher, "One Woman's Courage," 229–49.

33. Perry, autobiographical notes, n.d., 5.

34. Jack Greenberg, *Crusaders in the Courts*, 229; Bartley, *Rise of Massive Resistance*, 83–85, 125; Brady, "Black Monday," passim.

35. Bartley, *Rise of Massive Resistance*, 98–99; McMillen, *Citizens' Council*, 101–2; White Citizens' Council of Daytona Beach, "Attention All White Citizens of the Daytona Beach Area," July 28, 1956, box 17, FLIC Records. The WCC flyer also touted the support of local white ministers and businessmen as well as close ties with the "newly organized KKK." Three local men were listed as the leaders of the WCC of Daytona Beach. However, neither Saunders, Emmons, Mohl, nor Green named the three as being involved in the Moores' assassinations.

36. White Citizens' Council, box 17, FLIC Records.

37. "The Daring Plot against Miami Negroes," *Jet*, March 28, 1957, 12–14, Perry Papers; Saunders, *Bridging the Gap*, 161; Dunn, *Black Miami*, 210; Saunders, interview by author.

38. "February 25, 1957, Miami Transcripts" file, 48, 95–97, 129, box 4, FLIC Records.

39. Emmons, "Flame of Resistance," 223; Lawson, "Florida Legislative Investigation Committee," 303; Gibson quoted in Jack Mann, "Gibson Breaks Witch Hunt by Charley Johns," *Miami Herald*, December 5, 1958, sec. A, Perry Papers. Gibson did not take sole legal possession of the membership files until after the hearings, by which time the files were kept in New York (Lawson, "Florida Legislative Investigation Committee," 303).

40. Bartley, *Rise of Massive Resistance*, 214–16; Patricia Sullivan, *Lift Every Voice*, 425; Jack Greenberg, *Crusaders in the Courts*, 624.

41. Saunders, *Bridging the Gap*, 168; Saunders, interviews by author; "February 25, 1957, Miami Transcripts" file, 132, 140–49, 150–51, box 4, FLIC Records.

42. Ibid., 135, 137–39.

43. Ibid., 155–57, 160–63, 166–68.

44. Ibid., 171–75. However, Graves actually sent a telegram to Marshall on the first day of the hearings, recommending that the Miami chapter records be sent to New York immediately (Emmons, "Flame of Resistance," 229).

45. "February 26, 1957, Miami Transcripts" file, 76–77, 157–60, box 4, FLIC Records; McMillen, Citizens' Councils, 108, 326; Bartley, Rise of Massive Resistance, 148.

46. Perry, Along Freedom's Road, Miami Times, March 9, 1957.

47. Ibid.

48. Ibid.

49. Ibid.

50. Ibid.

51. "March 13, 1957, Transcripts" file, 2077, box 3, FLIC Records.

52. Saunders, Bridging the Gap, 168; Saunders, "Continuing the Legacy"; Saunders quoted in Emmons, "Flame of Resistance," 230.

53. Perry, Along Freedom's Road, Miami Times, June 8, 1957; Perry, comments, July 28, 1957. In late 1959, the school board lost the suit. African Americans were admitted to Miami's Orchard Villa Elementary School at the start of the next school year, but whites soon withdrew from the school. By December of 1959, it was virtually an all–African American school (Perry, Along Freedom's Road, Miami Times, September 12, 1959).

54. Perry, Along Freedom's Road, Miami Times, May 4, 1957; November 23, 1957.

55. Perry, Along Freedom's Road, Miami Times, October 26, 1957.

56. Perry, Along Freedom's Road, Miami Times, February 8, 1958.

57. Perry, Along Freedom's Road, Miami Times, February 22, 1958.

58. Ibid.

59. Lawson, "Florida Legislative Investigation Committee," 303; Erika L. Burroughs, "Robert William Saunders and a Memoir of the Civil Rights Movement in Florida" (master's thesis, University of South Florida, 1996), University of South Florida www.lib.usf.edu/spccoll/guide/s/rsaunder.html; Saunders, interviews by author.

60. "Minutes" file, December 11, 1956, 1, box 9, CHR Papers; "Members" file, 3; "Memos" file, January 8, 1958, 1–3, box 1, FLIC Records.

61. Schrecker, Age of McCarthyism, 17; and Schrecker, Many Are the Crimes, 44; Berg, "Black Civil Rights," 10; Jack Greenberg, Crusaders in the Courts, 110; Patricia Sullivan, Lift Every Voice, 374; White quoted in Green, Before His Time, 184.

62. Dewey Johnson quoted in Lawson, "Florida Legislative Investigation Committee," 301.

63. Robert Delaney, "Probe's Part-Time Attorney Is Paid More than Most of Ervin's Aides," Miami News, December 3, 1957, sec. B, box 9, CHR Papers.

64. "Minutes" file, July 24, 1957, 2, box 1, FLIC Records.

65. "February 26, 1958, Miami Transcripts" file, 183–89, box 4, FLIC Records.

66. Ibid., 331–59; Saunders, interviews by author.

67. Perry, autobiographical notes, n.d.; Jack Mann, "Gibson Breaks Witch Hunt by Charley Johns," *Miami Herald*, December 5, 1958, sec. A, Perry Papers; Saunders, *Bridging the Gap*, 168–69; Saunders, interviews by author; "February 27, 1958, Miami Transcripts" file, 391–93, box 4, FLIC Records. Perry also refused to answer when Hawes asked her about getting NAACP records back from the national office, which she said, during the 1957 hearings, that she would try to do ("February 27, 1957, Transcripts" file, 394–415, box 3, FLIC Records).

68. Perry quoted in Jack Mann, "Gibson Breaks Witch Hunt by Charley Johns," *Miami Herald*, December 5, 1958, sec. A, Perry Papers.

69. Herrell quoted in "February 27, 1958, Miami Transcripts" file, 419, box 4, FLIC Records.

70. Navasky, *Naming Names*, 28.

71. Ibid., 34.

72. "February 27, 1958, Transcripts" file, 429, box 4, FLIC Records.

73. Saunders, interviews by author.

74. Erika L. Burroughs, "Robert William Saunders and a Memoir of the Civil Rights Movement in Florida" (master's thesis, University of South Florida, 1996), University of South Florida, www.lib.usf.edu/spccoll/guide/s/rsaunder.html; Saunders, interviews by author; Gibson quoted in Jack Mann, "Gibson Breaks Witch Hunt by Charley Johns," *Miami Herald*, December 5, 1958, sec. A, Perry Papers.

75. Saunders, interviews by author.

76. "February 27, 1958, Miami Transcripts" file, 431, 433–35, box 4, FLIC Records.

77. Erika L. Burroughs, "Robert William Saunders and a Memoir of the Civil Rights Movement in Florida" (master's thesis, University of South Florida, 1996), University of South Florida, www.lib.usf.edu/spccoll/guide/s/rsaunder.html; "February 27, 1958, Transcripts" file, 467, box 4, FLIC Records.

78. "February 27, 1958, Transcripts" file, 468–70; "February 28, 1958, Miami Transcripts" file, 492–96, box 4, both in FLIC Records.

79. Perry quoted in Ronald York, "A Witness Eye-View," *Miami Herald*, March 1, 1958, sec. A, Perry Papers.

80. Ibid.

81. Anonymous to Ruth Perry, March 3, 1958.

82. Ibid.; Robert Carter to Ruth Perry, March 7, 1958. According to one historian, a prominent Miami politician offered to protect Perry's job, but there is no further evidence of this possibility (Emmons, "Flame of Resistance," 233).

83. Perry, Along Freedom's Road, *Miami Times*, March 8, 1958.

84. Ibid.

85. Perry, Along Freedom's Road, *Miami Times*, June 28, 1958.

86. Perry, Along Freedom's Road, *Miami Times*, November 1, 1958; August 9, 1958.

87. Perry, Along Freedom's Road, *Miami Times*, October 11, 1958.

88. Braukman, *Communists and Perverts*, 53; Lawson, *Civil Rights Crossroads*, 198; Perry, Along Freedom's Road, *Miami Times*, April 18, 1959.

89. Jack Mann, "Gibson Breaks Witch Hunt by Charley Johns," *Miami Herald*, December 5, 1958, sec. A, Perry Papers; Saunders, interviews by author; "Background Information," n.d., 1; "List of Witnesses in Miami Case," n.d., 1, box 13, both in FLIC Records; Lawson, "Florida Legislative Investigation Committee," 303.

90. Lawson, "Florida Legislative Investigation Committee," 303. For a full explanation of Gibson's legal battles, Lawson's essay is a very good source. Although written before the FLIC Records were unsealed in 1993, his essay uses the Florida Bar files and is an excellent study of associational privacy. Perry, Along Freedom's Road, *Miami Times*, November 14, 1959; Saunders, interviews by author; Perry, autobiographical notes, n.d., 5.

91. Perry, Along Freedom's Road, *Miami Times*, November 14, 1959; August 6, 1960; February 25, 1961.

92. "February 27, 1958, Miami Transcripts" file, 418, box 4, FLIC Records.

93. Perry, Along Freedom's Road, *Miami Times*, March 24, 1962.

94. Perry, Along Freedom's Road, *Miami Times*, May 19, 1962.

95. Perry, Along Freedom's Road, *Miami Times*, August 5, 1961; Danese, *Claude Pepper and Ed Ball*, 227–29. Pepper won by only 59 votes (Danese 228–29).

96. Perry, Along Freedom's Road, *Miami Times*, January 12, 1963.

97. Perry, Along Freedom's Road, *Miami Times*, September 10, 1960; June 4, 1960; September 24, 1960; May 13, 1961; December 2, 1961; April 29, 1961.

98. Perry-Kilburg, interviews by author.

99. Lawson, "Florida Legislative Investigation Committee," 315; Perry-Kilburg, interviews by author. The U.S. Supreme Court also ruled in favor of the NAACP in 1958 in *NAACP v. Alabama*, 357 U.S. 449, 466 (1958); see Jack Greenberg, *Crusaders in the Courts*, 231. For a discussion of the Gibson case in relation to freedom of association, see also Randall Kennedy, "Contrasting Fates," 265–73. Lawson, "Florida Legislative Investigation Committee," 315–16; Dunn, *Black Miami*, 222; and Perry, Along Freedom's Road, *Miami Times*, April 6, 1963, Perry-Kilburg Papers.

100. Perry-Kilburg, interviews by author; Perry, Along Freedom's Road, *Miami Times*, April 6, 1963.

101. Henry Land, 1957 Report to the Legislature, 10, 13; Charley Johns, 1959 Report to the Legislature, Part I, 2–3, both in box 1, FLIC Records.

## Chapter 4. Sig Diettrich

1. Sig Diettrich to Ray Crist, March 24, 1959, Diettrich Papers. This five-page, single-spaced letter contains detailed information not available in other sources about Diettrich's interrogation as well as his reactions to his forced resignation. The Diettrich Papers are contained in one box. Unless otherwise noted, author information and all letters to and from Diettrich are contained in the Diettrich Papers.

2. Diettrich to Crist, March 24, 1959.

3. Walter J. Matherly to J. Ridgell, November 12, 1931, box 2, UF College of Business

Administration Archives; "Stanley, Diettrich Made Citizens of US," *Gainesville Sun,* December 14, 1938, sec. A; author information, correspondence on *Greater Miami* booklet, 1; "About Clark," *Clark University,* www.clarku.edu/aboutclark/timeline; "Ph.D. Dissertations," 216.

4. Prunty, "Geography in the South," 55; Diettrich to Matherly, July 4, 1932, box 2, UF College of Business Administration Archives.

5. Diettrich to Fr. Joe Curtin, May 7, 1959; "Sigismond deRudesheim Diettrich," obituary, *Gainesville Sun,* May 21, 1987, sec. B; "Gainesville Community Playhouse History," *Gainesville Community Playhouse,* www.gcplayhouse.org/data/history/history/.htm.

6. "Gainesville Community Playhouse History," *Gainesville Community Playhouse,* www.gcplayhouse.org/data/history/history/.htm; Diettrich to Wallace Atwood, October 17, 1936, May 15, 1939; Atwood to Diettrich, October 8, 1942.

7. "Stanley, Diettrich Made Citizens of US," *Gainesville Sun,* December 14, 1938, sec. A; Diettrich to Atwood, May 15, 1939; Atwood to Diettrich, May 18, 1939; "January 19, 1959, Transcript" file, 1282, box 7, FLIC Records.

8. Diettrich to Atwood, March 22, 1943; Diettrich to Atwood, July 23, 1943. Rollin Atwood was still chair but had left UF to serve in the war and would not return, choosing to pursue a career in the State Department (Prunty, "Geography in the South," 55).

9. Diettrich to Atwood, March 20, 1944; Harris, "Geographers in the U.S. Government," 249; Diettrich, "Florida's War Economy," 1–4; Matherly, Editor's Note, 1; Diettrich to Atwood, January 6, 1943; Diettrich, "Florida's Transition," 1–4; Diettrich, "Florida's Regional Economy," 1–4.

10. Atwood to Diettrich, April 20, 1946; Diettrich to Atwood, July 9, 1946; Diettrich to Atwood, October 29, 1946; Diettrich to Crist, March 24, 1959; Pleasants, *Gator Tales,* 32; Diettrich to Atwood, n.d.; Diettrich to Atwood, May 15, 1939; "January 19, 1959, Transcripts" file, 1283–85, box 7, FLIC Records; Diettrich to Crist, March 24, 1959.

11. "January 19, 1959, Transcripts" file, 1284, box 7, FLIC Records.

12. "Geographic Record," 329; Diettrich to Atwood, May 1, 1946; Schwendeman, "Directory of College Geography," 149; Diettrich, "Florida's Metropolitan Growth," 1–4; Diettrich, "Florida's Climatic Extremes," 68–74.

13. Diettrich to Reitz, December 3, 1958, box 26, Reitz Papers; "News from Geographic Centers," 1960, 25; Don Dyer to Diettrich, March 9, 1959; Diettrich to Father Joe Curtin, April 8, 1959.

14. R. J. Strickland, Statements of Fact, December 5 and 12, 1958, 2–3, box 1, FLIC Records.

15. R. J. Strickland, Progress Report, September 29–October, 16, 1958, 1–3, box 1, FLIC Records.

16. Schnur, "Cold Warriors," 34; David Johnson, *The Lavender Scare,* 22; D'Emilio,

*Making Trouble*, 58–59, 64; U.S. Senate Committee on Expenditures in Executive Departments quoted in D'Emilio, *Making Trouble*, 59.

17. D'Emilio, *Making Trouble*, 60, 64.

18. Braukman, "Nothing Else Matters," 571–72; Faderman, *Odd Girls*, 146–47.

19. D'Emilio, *Making Trouble*, 60, 66; Braukman, "Nothing Else Matters," 554.

20. Florida Statutes, Chapter 800.01 (1957); Fejes, "Murder, Perversion, and Moral Panic," 4, 315, 343–44; Eskridge, "Privacy Jurisprudence," 830. In 1971, the Florida Supreme Court invalidated the crime against nature law because it was too vague. Three years later, the legislature decriminalized the same law (Graves, *And They Were Wonderful Teachers*, 167–68).

21. "Members" file, 3; "Minutes" file, July 24, 1957, 1, both in box 1, FLIC Records. Griffin was the grandfather of former Florida secretary of state and congresswoman Katherine Harris.

22. "Minutes" file, July 24, 1957, 1, box 1, FLIC Records; Stark, "McCarthyism in Florida," 28–31; memo, January 8, 1958, 1–3, box 1, FLIC Records.

23. "Minutes" file, October 2, 1957, 1, box 9, CHR Papers.

24. Robert Delaney, "Secret Sessions Held by Probers," *Miami Herald*, November 7, 1957, sec. A, box 9, CHR Papers; memo, January 8, 1958, 1–2, box 1, FLIC Records.

25. Memo, January 8, 1958, 1–2, box 1, FLIC Records.

26. Although undated, the report clearly was written some time in 1958 or later because the report referred to the 1957 investigations in the past tense and to other developments in July 1961 (Staff Report, ca. July 1961, 1, box 1, FLIC Records).

27. Stark, "McCarthyism in Florida," 92–93. UF administrators had briefly dealt with the issue of gay students in 1954 when a student withdrew after being involved in sexual relations at a chicken ranch near Gainesville. However, there was no follow-up investigation by UF. A year later, the editor of the UF *Alligator* planned to infiltrate a gay party at the ranch and then write a story about it, but there appears to have been no response from the administration (Braukman, "Anticommunism," 135).

28. Stark, "McCarthyism in Florida," 92–95; Dauer, "Proctor Oral History Project."

29. FLIC, "1959 Report to the Legislature," 3, box 1, FLIC Records.

30. Matthews had an extensive collection of left-wing letterheads and party literature (Schrecker, *No Ivory Tower*, 72; Schrecker, *Age of McCarthyism*, 17, 90).

31. J. B. Matthews to Mark Hawes, June 18, 1958, box 3; R. J. Strickland, Statement of Fact, August 14, 1958, 1, box 1, both in FLIC Records; "Minutes" file, September 27, 1958, 2, box 9, CHR Papers; "Reitz to Get University of Florida Probe Report," *Tampa Tribune*, January 13, 1959, sec. A.

32. FLIC, "1959 Report," 1–2, box 1, FLIC Records; "Senator Quiet on Probe Here," *Gainesville Sun*, October 28, 1958, sec. A; "Investigating Group Checking on Faculty," *University of Florida Alligator*, October 31, 1958, sec. A; "Campus Cloak and Dagger," editorial, *University of Florida Alligator*, November 7, 1958. Starke was the only African American among UF's twelve thousand students. He experienced no demonstrable

opposition but left the university after one semester (Stephanie Evans, "One of the First," 47).

33. Subpoenas, August 8, 1958, 1, box 1, FLIC Records; Jack Detweiler, "Reactions at Gainesville Hint Johns' Investigator Inquiring about Faculty," *Tampa Tribune*, October 29, 1958, sec. A; Frances Reitz, "Proctor Oral History Project"; "Wayne Reitz History," *University of Florida*, www.union.ufl.edu/history.asp; Wayne Reitz quoted in Pleasants, *Gator Tales*, 50).

34. Johns Correspondence, passim; Johns to Reitz, October 23, 1956; Reitz to Johns, December 16, 1955; Johns to Reitz, January 6, 1964, box 40, Reitz Papers.

35. Reitz to Johns, January 29, 1964, box 40, Reitz Papers.

36. Johns to Reitz, July 15, 1964, box 40, Reitz Papers.

37. Reitz to Johns, July 29, 1964, box 40, Reitz Papers.

38. "Senator Quiet on Probe Here," *Gainesville Sun*, October 28, 1958, sec. A; Jack Detweiler, "Reactions at Gainesville Hint Johns' Investigator Inquiring about Faculty," *Tampa Tribune*, October 29, 1958, sec. A ; "Investigating Group Checking on Faculty," *University of Florida Alligator*, October 31, 1958, sec. A; Kepner, *Rough News*, 302; Stark, "McCarthyism in Florida," 96.

39. Rick Tuttle, "Strickland Profile," *Miami Herald*, March 26, 1963, 1–4, typescript, box 263, Morris Papers.

40. Ibid.

41. Stark, "McCarthyism in Florida," 93.

42. R. J. Strickland, Statement of Fact, August 12, 1958, 3, box 1, FLIC Records; Braukman, "Anticommunism," 136; Loughery, "Hunting Gays in Gainesville," 18; R. J. Strickland, Statement of Fact, August 19, 1958, 1, box 1, FLIC Records.

43. Art Copleston, "My Experiences during the Inquisition," *James T. Sears*, www.jtsears.com/johnsrec2.htm; *Behind Closed Doors*; "October 16, 1958, Transcripts" file, 1–4, box 6; "January 20, 1958, Transcripts" file [*sic*, should be 1959], 1295–1316, box 6, both in FLIC Records; Megan Seery, "For Some Bill Sparks Johns Committee Déjà Vu," *Florida Alligator*, April 14, 2005, sec. A; "UF Apologizes for Honoring Anti-Gay Alumnus," *The Advocate*, July 1, 2005, www.advocate.com; R. J. Strickland, Statement of Fact, October 2, 1958, 2, box 1, FLIC Records.

44. R. J. Strickland, Statements of Fact, November 20 and 21, 1958, 1; December 5 and 12, 1958, 2–3, all in box 1, FLIC Records.

45. R. J. Strickland, Progress Report, September 29–October 16, 1958, 1–3, box 1, FLIC Records.

46. The interrogations took place in closed meetings, not open to the public or the press, in which sworn testimony might be taken by a notary or court reporter.

47. "Legislative Probe Chairman Huddles Here with Top Aides," *Gainesville Sun*, January 6, 1959, sec. A.

48. "January 5, 1959, Transcripts" file, passim, box 6; "January 6–9, 1959, Transcripts" file, passim, box 7, both in FLIC Records; Carleton, *Freelancing through the Century*, 147. The transcripts cited here are also labeled as "Crimes against Nature at

the University of Florida" and are most likely the Johns Committee's "Crimes against Nature" report on UF, long thought to be missing. For more on the chicken ranch owners, see Sears, *Lonely Hunters*, 76–77.

49. "Reitz to Get University of Florida Probe Report," *Tampa Tribune*, January 13, 1959, sec. A; "Staff Member Tells Reitz Johns' Investigator Tried to 'Coerce, Intimidate,'" *Tampa Tribune*, January 20, 1959, sec. A.

50. "Staff Member Tells Reitz Johns' Investigator Tried to 'Coerce, Intimidate,'" *Tampa Tribune*, January 20, 1959, sec. A.

51. "January 19, 1959, Transcripts" file, passim, box 7, FLIC Records.

52. Diettrich to Ray Crist, March 24, 1959; "January 19, 1959, Transcripts" file, 1228–33, box 7, FLIC Records.

53. Hawes quoted in "January 19, 1959, Transcripts" file, 1233, box 7, FLIC Records.

54. Ibid., 1228–36,; Hawes quoted in ibid., 1237.

55. Ibid., 1237–39.

56. Ibid., 1252–60, 1277–79.

57. Ibid., 1262–67; Hawes quoted in ibid., 1268.

58. Ibid., 1281.

59. Ibid., 1282–83.

60. Ibid., 1284.

61. Herrell quoted in "February 27, 1958, Miami Transcripts" file, 418, box 4 FLIC Records.

62. Navasky, *Naming Names*, 317–18.

63. See "January 5–9, 1959, Transcript" file, passim, boxes 6 and 7, as well as other UF transcripts in the same boxes, all in FLIC Records.

64. FLIC, "1965 Report to the Legislature," 4–5, box 1; "Minutes, Advisory Committee to the Florida Legislative Investigation Committee," June 29–30, 1964, passim, box 1; "January 19, 1959, Transcripts" file, 1287, box 7, all in FLIC Records.

65. Diettrich to Crist, March 24, 1959; Hawes quoted in "January 19, 1959, Transcripts" file, 1287, box 7, FLIC Records.

66. Reitz to Johns, January 22, 1959, box 26, Reitz Papers; "August 19, 1958–January 22, 1959, Transcripts" files, passim, boxes 6 and 7, FLIC Records.

67. Diettrich to Crist, March 24, 1959.

68. Ibid.

69. Ibid.

70. "Active Members, 1958," 3, box 6; meeting notice, January 20, 1959, 1, box 3, both in AAUP Papers, UF Chapter; "January 21, 1959, Transcripts" file, 1422–25, box 7, FLIC Records; Carleton, *Freelancing through the Century*, 148; anonymous quoted in Jack Detweiler, "Professors to Probe Senator Johns' Investigation," *Tampa Tribune*, January 29, 1959, sec. A.

71. Jack Detweiler, "Professors to Probe Senator Johns' Investigation," *Tampa Tribune*, January 29, 1959, sec. A.

72. Winston Ehrmann, "UF Chapter Newsletter," October 16, 1959, 1–2, box 3;

Summary of Discussion and Action by AAUP Committee on Legislation, 1–4, box 6, both in AAUP Papers, UF Chapter. For a national response to the Johns Committee by the AAUP, see chapter 6.

73. Diettrich to Crist, March 24, 1959; Diettrich to Crist, n.d.

74. "Johns' Group Gives Findings to University," *University of Florida Alligator*, February 17, 1959, sec. A. Reitz wisely asked that J. J. Daniel, vice chair of the Board of Control, be present when the Johns Committee submitted its report to Reitz (Reitz to Johns, January 22, 1959, box 26, Reitz Papers).

75. Reitz quoted in Diettrich to Crist, March 24, 1959.

76. Diettrich to Crist, March 24, 1959.

77. Ibid.

78. Ibid. This long letter is very emotional as Diettrich freely shares his feelings with his friend and colleague.

79. Ibid.

80. Ibid.

81. Ibid.

82. Ibid.

83. Ibid.

84. Ibid.

85. Ibid.

86. "J. E. Congleton Resigns from UF," *Gainesville Sun*, March 18, 1959, sec A. The documents from the University Archives are titled as "Resignations," but, in the space allotted for the reason for each person's resignation, only the word "terminated" is given (Carl Van Ness to Louis Lavelle, June 10, 1993, 1–6, Diettrich Papers).

87. Diettrich to Crist, March 24, 1959.

88. Ibid.

89. Ibid.

90. Reitz quoted in "UF Completes Study of Johns Probe Report," *Gainesville Sun*, March 19, 1959, sec. A.

91. Ibid.

92. Diettrich to Crist, March 24, 1959.

93. Ibid.; Diettrich to Bob and Muriel (no last name given), April 27, 1959; "Charley Johns 'Pleased' with UF Cleanup," *Gainesville Sun*, March 24, 1959, sec. A. Not wanting to risk his fellowship, Diettrich did not make his resignation public until after he was in Pakistan (Diettrich to Bob and Muriel, April 27, 1959).

94. Diettrich to Crist, March 24, 1959. For a different interpretation, see Braukman, "Anticommunism," 144. Braukman sees not only Diettrich's sexual encounters with men as evidence of his being gay but also his description of homoerotic urges as a denial of his true sexuality. However, Braukman's analysis is based upon only one of Diettrich's letters (albeit his most important one), written to one of his best friends shortly after Diettrich resigned. Braukman does not cite his Johns Commit-

tee testimony or any of his other letters in the Diettrich Papers. Despite this one flaw, her work on the Johns Committee is excellent.

95. Iren had spent two weeks with Rosemary and Charles when the baby was born (Diettrich to Bob and Muriel, April 27, 1959).

96. Diettrich to Father Joe Curtin, April 8, 1959; Don and Marilyn Dyer to Diettrich, March 31, 1959; Crist to Diettrich, March 27, 1959; "Iren Dokupil Diettrich," obituary, *Gainesville Sun*, November 3, 2006, sec. B.

97. "14 Leave UF in Morals Cleanup, Reitz Reveals," *Gainesville Sun*, April 3, 1959, sec. A; "Reitz Tells Action on Johns' Report," *University of Florida Alligator*, April 7, 1959, sec. A; Diettrich to Curtin, April 8, 1959; Diettrich to Crist, April 8, 1959.

98. Diettrich to Bob and Muriel, April 27, 1959; Diettrich to Rosemary Diettrich Leedham and Charles Leedham, May 16, 1959; Diettrich to Crist, March 24, 1959; Crist to Diettrich, March 27, 1959; Diettrich to Crist, April 8, 1959; Don Dyer to Diettrich, March 31, 1959; Nathan Starr to Diettrich, April 26, 1959; Erwin Raisz to Diettrich, April 29, 1959; Crist to Diettrich, April 4, 1959.

99. Diettrich to Curtin, April 8, 1959; Diettrich to Dyer, April 27, 1959; Diettrich to Crist, April 8, 1959; Diettrich to Crist, April 27, 1959.

100. Diettrich to Neil Sager, April 29, 1959; Diettrich to Father Thomas Gross, April 25, 1959; Diettrich to Harwood and Olive Dolbeare, April 24, 1959.

101. Diettrich to Gross, April 25, 1959; Diettrich to Curtin, May 7, 1959.

102. Diettrich to Rosemary Diettrich Leedham and Charles Leedham, May 16, 1959; Diettrich to Leedhams, May 19, 1959.

103. "Minutes" file, April 14, 1959, 1–2, box 1, FLIC Records.

104. Ibid. The committee's concept that gay professors would recommend their gay students for teaching positions in the public schools originated with the Florida Sheriffs Bureau's 1957 hunt for gays at the Southwest Tuberculosis Hospital (Florida Sheriff's Bureau, "Investigative Report: Southwest Florida Tuberculosis Hospital," 1–94, box 1, FLIC Records). For more on the Southwest Tuberculosis Hospital investigation, see chapter 5.

105. FLIC, "1959 Report," 3–7, 9, box 1, FLIC Records.

106. Quoted in Weitz, "Bourbon, Pork Chops," 188.

107. Ibid., 186–88.

108. "News from Geographic Centers," 1959, 22–23; "News from Geographic Centers," 1960, 25.

109. "Minutes" file, September 22, 1961, 6–7, box 9, CHR Papers; Johns to Reitz, November 9, 1961, box 2, FLIC Records; Reitz to Johns, November 18, 1961; "Policy on Morals and Influences," attachment in Baya Harrison Jr. to Johns, November 18, 1961, both in box 26, Reitz Papers.

110. Didio and Lottie Graeffe quoted in Stark, "McCarthyism in Florida," 93, 99. Didio and Lottie Graeffe taught at UF then, and many of their friends were fired.

111. Carl Van Ness to Louis Lavelle, June 10, 1993, Diettrich Papers.

112. Seaburg, "Proctor Oral History Project."

113. Hart, "Proctor Oral History Project."

114. Woodward, "Unreported Crisis," 83; Stark, "McCarthyism in Florida," 97–98.

115. "Reitz Brands as False Story on Morals Probe," *Gainesville Sun*, February 18, 1959, sec. A.; Stark, "McCarthyism in Florida," 107–8.

116. "University Professors" file, passim, box 13, FLIC Records.

117. Johns quoted in Pleasants, *Gator Tales*, 49.

118. Johns to Reitz, December, 12, 1959, box 40, Reitz Papers.

119. Diettrich to Crist, March 24, 1959; "Our Mission," Foundation for the Promotion of Music, www.thefpm.org; "Sigismond deRudesheim Diettrich," obituary, *Gainesville Sun*, May 21, 1987, sec. B.

120. Crist to Diettrich, April 4, 1959; Raisz, "The Atlas," 208. Diettrich's work is noted on the acknowledgements page, but "Erwin Raisz and Associates" are listed as the author with "text by John R. Dunkle," who was Diettrich's student (Raisz and Associates, *Atlas of Florida*, title page). Reitz successfully marketed the *Atlas*, prepublication, to insurance companies, large businesses, and some government agencies (Reitz, form letter, January 11, 1960, box 64, Reitz Papers). Only three years after the *Atlas of Florida* was published, the director of the University of Florida Press reported monthly sales of over seventy-six thousand dollars (William Harvey to Reitz, August 7, 1967, box 64, Reitz Papers).

121. "Sigismond deRudesheim Diettrich," obituary, *Gainesville Sun*, May 21, 1987, sec B.

## Chapter 5. G. G. Mock

1. "August 18, 1959, Transcripts" file, 10, box 7, FLIC Records.

2. Ibid. An alias is substituted for the policeman's real name because it was blacked out in the deposition, as were most names in the FLIC transcripts before they were released to the public. See chapter 6 for more information.

3. "August 18, 1959, Transcripts" file, 3, 9–10; Walker quoted in ibid., 10, box 7, FLIC Records.

4. Ibid., 19, 26, 36; policeman quoted in ibid., 10.

5. Schnur, "Cold Warriors," 123; McGarrahan, "Florida's Secret Shame," 12; Mock, interview by author. Former House speaker Mallory Horne later told reporters that the committee hired five lesbian informants (McGarrahan, "Florida's Secret Shame," 11). The interview of G. G. Mock would not have been possible without invaluable help from Caroline Bloodworth, who responded to a notice in a national lesbian publication and then encouraged Mock to consent to the interview.

6. For more on Florida's crimes against nature laws, see chapter 4.

7. Eskridge, "Privacy Jurisprudence," 829–30; Fejes, "Murder, Perversion, and Moral Panic," 344. Unfortunately for Florida historians, there are very few local gay and lesbian publications from the 1950s and 1960s to document responses to such ordinances, as well as other aspects of early, local gay rights movements. At that time, even the

national gay and lesbian press was in its infancy. Also, events in Florida's larger cities were covered only occasionally in Jim Kepner's columns in *ONE* magazine, starting with the murder of a gay man in Miami in 1954. (See Loftin, *Letters to ONE*, 116–17; and Kepner, *Rough News*, 49. Kepner also wrote under three pen names: Dal McIntire, Lyn Pedersen, and Frank Golovitz.) Such paucity of locally based gay and lesbian sources illustrates the difficulty of preserving the documents of a people who are invisible, whether it is because they feared to self-identify as gay or lesbian or because the dominant culture chose to disregard or eradicate them (Knowlton, "Documenting the Gay Rights Movement," 18, 20).

8. Eskridge, "Privacy Jurisprudence," passim; Sears, *Lonely Hunters*, 91; "January 26, 1960, Transcripts" file, passim, box 7, FLIC Records; Mock, interview by author; Faderman, *Odd Girls*, 161. Even softball was connected with the bars because their owners often sponsored the teams, and players, in turn, would patronize the bar that sponsored them (Faderman, *Odd Girls*, 161–62).

9. Faderman, *Odd Girls*, 126, 162, 168–69.

10. Ibid., 177–83; Daughters of Bilitis quoted in ibid., 180.

11. Daughters of Bilitis quoted in ibid., 181.

12. D'Emilio, *Sexual Politics*, 186; Mock, interview by author; Rudy, "Radical Feminism," 2–3.

13. Faderman, *Odd Girls*, 126, 162, 168–69, 177–83; D'Emilio, *Sexual Politics*, 186; Rudy, "Radical Feminism," 2–3.

14. Faderman, *Odd Girls*, 163; D'Emilio, *Sexual Politics*, 98. Two other tactics used against gay men were spying on them and using male decoys to entice gay men into sexually compromising behavior. Spies were rarely used against lesbians because they usually did not have sex in public or semipublic places and police lacked enough female officers to work as decoys (Eskridge, "Privacy Jurisprudence," 722).

15. Eskridge, "Privacy Jurisprudence," 721.

16. Faderman, *Odd Girls*, 163–66.

17. Gerard Sullivan, "Political Opportunism," 62–63; Kepner, *Rough News*, 52; Sears, *Lonely Hunters*, 12–17. For more on this murder, see Sears, *Lonely Hunters*, 12–17, 24; Kepner, *Rough News*, 49–52, 58; and Loftin, *Letters to ONE*, 116–17.

18. Johns quoted in Sears, *Lonely Hunters*, 22.

19. Police chief quoted in Kepner, *Rough News*, 51. However, in a cautionary tone that foreshadowed the warnings of legislators who later opposed creation of the Johns Committee, Rayman noted that the clean-up effort would result in lawful citizens being interrogated, which could lead to costly lawsuits (Sears, *Lonely Hunters* 23; Kepner, *Rough News*, 53).

20. Kepner, *Rough News*, 117.

21. Sears, *Lonely Hunters* 28–30; "Memos" file, report by L. J. Vanbuskirk and M. Bromley, January 30, 1957, passim, box 1, FLIC Records.

22. Mike Wells, "Following the Coldest Trail," *Tampa Tribune*, January 15, 2006, sec. A, mikewellsfiles.wordpress.com/2008/011506-following-the-coldest-trail.doc. For

more on this murder, see Wells, ibid. Three months after the murder, five teenage boys received three-year sentences for robbing and "rolling sex perverts" that they had met at the Knotty Pine Bar, which the victim frequented. After the sentences, Assistant Solicitor James Parham added that a gay man had been killed in the fall of 1956; the murder victim was attacked in October of the same year (McIntire, Tangents, 18).

23. Florida Sheriffs' Bureau, Investigative Report, June 3, 1957–June 8, 1957, cover letter, box 1; "February 6, 1959, Transcripts" file, 2–21, box 7; 1959 Report to the Legislature, 4, box 1, all in FLIC Records. At about the same time that the investigation of Hillsborough County schools began, Florida politicians also began to move against gay and lesbian teachers. A legislative committee on education met with the Florida Education Association to discuss the lack of a system for removing teachers for immoral conduct. This was before the Johns Committee brought the issue to the 1959 legislature (Graves, "Doing the Public's Business," 84). An analysis of the committee's hunt for gay and lesbian teachers is beyond the intended scope of this work. For more on this, see Graves' article cited above; her recent book, *And They Were Wonderful Teachers*; and Schnur, "Cold Warriors," chapter 3.

24. Florida Sheriffs' Bureau, Investigative Report, June 3, 1957–June 8, 1957, cover letter, box 1; "February 6, 1959, Transcripts" file, 8, 9, 11, 19–20, 36–38, box 7, both in FLIC Records.

25. 1959 Report to the Legislature, part I, 4, box 1, FLIC Records.

26. Stark, "McCarthyism in Florida," 111.

27. Deputy quoted in "February 6, 1959, Transcripts" file, 38–39, box 7, FLIC Records.

28. The woman arrested for her masculine dress, Florene Fleischman, later became a minister and served as president of the International Gay and Lesbian Association (Kepner, *Rough News*, 403).

29. Detective quoted in Chuck Hendrick, "13 Nabbed in Crackdown on Morals Offenders Here," *Tampa Tribune*, July 13, 1957, sec. A.

30. Detective quoted in ibid.

31. Ibid.

32. Judy Ausley, "Tired Old Dyke: Florida, 1963–1968," July 7, 2009 blog, *Stereotypd*, www.stereotypd.com; McIntire, Tangents, 19; Eskridge, "Privacy Jurisprudence," 722–24; detective quoted in Chuck Hendrick, "13 Nabbed in Crackdown on Morals Offenders Here," *Tampa Tribune*, July 13, 1957, sec. A.

33. Mock, interview by author; North, "Lesbians," 6–8.

34. Ausley, "Florida: 1963–1968"; Merril Mushroom, letter to author, September 14, 2009, 3; Mushroom, "Bar Dyke Sketches," 17–21; North, "Lesbians," 4.

35. Sears, *Rebels, Rubyfruit, and Rhinestones*, 82; Mushroom, "Bar Dyke Sketches," 17–21; captain quoted in Chuck Hendrick, "13 Nabbed in Crackdown on Morals Offenders Here," *Tampa Tribune*, July 13, 1957, sec. A. See also Mushroom, "Gay Kids and Johns Committee."

36. Captain quoted in Chuck Hendrick, "13 Nabbed in Crackdown on Morals Of-fenders Here," *Tampa Tribune*, July 13, 1957, sec. A.

37. Mock, interview by author.

38. "August 18, 1959, Transcripts" file, 2, 4, 10–11, 29–31, 35, box 7, FLIC Records.

39. Ibid., 36.

40. Ibid., 41, 46–47; Mock, interview by author.

41. North, "Lesbians," 6; "August 18, 1959, Transcripts" file, 10–13, box 7, FLIC Records.

42. "August 18, 1959, Transcripts" file, 39, box 7, FLIC Records.

43. Ibid.

44. Ibid., 41–42.

45. Ibid., 39–42.

46. "September 27, 1959, Transcripts" file, 3, 5–8, box 7, FLIC Records; clerk quoted in ibid., 8.

47. "August 18, 1959, Transcripts" file, 4–5, 14–18, 30, 37, 43–44, 46–47, box 7, FLIC Records.

48. Ibid., 30; attorney quoted in ibid., 26–27.

49. Ibid., 31.

50. Mock, interview by author.

51. Ibid.

52. Ibid.

53. "August 18, 1959, Transcripts" file, 1–2, 26, 36, box 7, FLIC Records; Mock, in-terview by author.

54. R. J. Strickland to W. C. Herrell, July 18, 1959, box 3; "August 18 and 19, 1959, Transcripts" file, passim, box 7, both in FLIC Records. As with other FLIC tran-scripts, the names are blacked out within the Lowell depositions. However, a Johns Committee memo with no blackouts, titled "Contents of This File Drawer," lists the names of those interrogated at Lowell by date as well as names and dates for other transcripts ("Contents of This File Drawer" memo, n.d., 1–2, box 13, FLIC Records).

55. Strickland neglected to ask one woman for what offense she was serving time, but she described herself as a "confirmed homosexual" ("August 19, 1959, Transcripts" file, 102, passim, box 7, FLIC Records).

56. Stark, "McCarthyism in Florida," 111.

57. Strickland quoted in "August 18, 1959, Transcripts" file, 16, box 7, FLIC Records.

58. Ibid., 3–9.

59. Ibid., 3–9.

60. Ibid., 7.

61. Ibid., 3–9.

62. Ibid., 11–16, 19, 21–26, 31.

63. Ibid., 46–47.

64. Although Strickland actually asked if Storey knew any school personnel, she

replied as if he had asked for names of gays or lesbians ("August 18, 1959, Transcripts" file, 29–30, box 7, FLIC Records), most likely because she was serving time for a crime against nature. Also, Mock may have been able to communicate with Storey about Strickland's line of questioning, or the women interrogated may have known beforehand the reason for their being questioned.

65. "August 18, 1959, Transcripts" file, 32–35, 51, box 7, FLIC Records.

66. Ibid., 6, 42–45, 50–51.

67. Ibid., 35–36; Strickland quoted in ibid., 35–36.

68. Ibid., 35, 42–45, 50–51.

69. Ibid., 45.

70. Ibid., 51.

71. Ibid., 58–67.

72. Ibid., 76–91.

73. Ibid., 95–100, 105–21; Braukman, "'Nothing Else Matters,'" 3.

74. "January 11, 1961, Transcripts" file, 2, 8, 11–12, box 8; "August 18, 1959, Transcripts" file, 139–48, box 7, FLIC Records.

75. "August 18, 1959, Transcripts" file, 150–65, box 7, FLIC Records. Although not required by Florida's sunshine laws, aliases are substituted for the teacher's and the last inmate's names.

76. R. J. Strickland to Charley Johns, August 24, 1959, box 3, FLIC Records.

77. Mock, interview by author.

78. Conversation quoted in ibid.

79. Ibid.

80. Ibid.

81. Ibid.

82. Ibid.; "May 1983 to May 2008," 1, 4; "Village Printer," 8.

83. Mock, interview by author.

84. Bothwell quoted in ibid.

85. Unfortunately, *Stonewall* ceased publication after a few years, and all attempts to locate a copy of the article, even from Mock herself, have failed.

86. Braukman, "'Nothing Else Matters,'" 557–58, 560, 571–72; Lynch, "What We Feared," 24.

## Chapter 6. Margaret Fisher and Her University of South Florida Colleagues

1. Fisher, interview by author.

2. "May 30, 1962, Transcripts" file, 1101, box 5, FLIC Records; Fisher, interview by author.

3. Fisher, interview by author; Cutler quoted in ibid.

4. Columbia questionnaire, 1–5, box 4, Margaret Fisher Papers.

5. "Beginning with a Bang," University of South Florida, http://usfweb2.usf.edu/

History/fisher.html; "University Professors" file, 7, box 13, FLIC Records; Margaret Fisher, Columbia University placement file, passim, box 4; Fisher, curriculum vitae, 1–2, box 4; self-study, 1–2, 5–6, box 2; Columbia questionnaire, 1–5, box 4, all in Fisher Papers; Fisher, "Oral History," interview by Gaskins.

6. Fisher, curriculum vitae, 1–2, box 4; self-study, 2, box 2; Margaret Fisher to Margaret Mead, March 1, 1960, 1–4, box 4, all in Fisher Papers.

7. Fisher, "Oral History," interview by Gaskins; Fisher, "USF Silver," interview by Hewitt; John Allen to Margaret Fisher, September 7, 1960, box 4, Fisher Papers.

8. Fisher, "USF Silver," interview by Hewitt; 1962–63 correspondence, passim, box 4, Fisher Papers.

9. Margaret Fisher to Mr. and Mrs. J. Olcutt Sanders, September 14, 1961, box 4; Margaret Fisher to Dr. and Mrs. Sadek Samaan, January 16, 1961, box 4, both in Fisher Papers.

10. John Allen quoted in Lowell Brandle, "Bricks, Books, and Brains Building Blocks for Allen," *St. Petersburg Times*, September 3, 1957, sec. B.

11. Ibid.; Lowell Brandle, "A 'Storehouse of Knowledge' for Suncoast," *St. Petersburg Times*, September 4, 1957, sec. B; "The John Allen Legacy," University of South Florida, usfweb2.usf.edu/History/allen_legacy.html; Lowell Brandle, "Huge Challenge Faces University's President," *St. Petersburg Times*, September 1, 1957, sec. A; Pleasants, *Gator Tales*, 41.

12. "Early Days," University of South Florida, www.usf.edu/department/history/ch1; Grace Allen, "USF Silver," interview by Hewitt; Lowell Brandle, "'Exciting,' Multi-Storied Library To Be Hub of New State University," *St. Petersburg Times*, September 2, 1957, sec. B; Lowell Brandle, "Bricks, Books, and Brains Building Blocks for Allen," *St. Petersburg Times*, September 3, 1957, sec. B. Another recruiting advantage for Allen was the Board of Control's quota system, which allowed for only a certain number of full, associate, and assistant professors. This system made UF top heavy, leaving no hope of promotion, even for younger associate and assistant professors who were prize-winning authors. One UF dean told Charles Arnade that he would not be promoted to associate, "even if [he] won the Nobel Prize." Allen used the situation to USF's advantage and brought in young, promising professors from UF, including Arnade (Arnade, "USF Silver").

13. Grace Allen, "USF Silver."

14. Cooper and Fisher, *Vision of a Contemporary University*, 17, 25; Mayhew, "Intellectual Tone," 1–3; Lowell Brandle, "Bricks, Books, and Brains Building Blocks for Allen," *St. Petersburg Times*, September 3, 1957, sec. B.

15. USF, *Accent on Learning*, 6. USF's official motto on the university seal is "Truth and Wisdom," but "Accent on Learning" has also been used frequently since USF was founded (Mark Greenberg, *University of South Florida*, 26, 29, 31, 34).

16. Cooper and Fisher, *Vision of a Contemporary University*, 18–32, passim; Fisher, "USF Silver"; John Allen, "The Task of a University, *USF Educational Review* (Fall 1962): 27, box 1, John Egerton Papers; Mark Greenberg, *University of South Florida*, 35.

17. Cooper and Fisher, *Vision of a Contemporary University*, 23–24, 113; "The John Allen Legacy," University of South Florida, usfweb2.usf.edu/History/allenlegacy.html.

18. Grace Allen, "USF Silver."

19. Schnur, "Cold Warriors," 197; FLIC, "Report from the Florida Legislative Investigation Committee to the State Board of Control and the State Board of Education: Investigation of the University of South Florida" (hereafter cited as "Report from FLIC"), 1, box 1; Robert Rendueles to President of Manatee Junior College, January 11, 1961, box 3, both in FLIC Records.

20. Mayhew, "Intellectual Tone," 4–7.

21. "June 4, 1962, Transcripts" file, 1642–44, passim, box 5; "May 30, 1962, Transcripts" file, 961–71, box 5, both in FLIC Records; Jane Smith, "Report on USF," 5, box 1, Egerton Papers.

22. George Stallings to Charley Johns, November 28, 1961, box 2, FLIC Records.

23. Charley Johns to George Stallings, December 5, 1961; Charley Johns to R. J. Strickland, December 4, 1961, both in box 2, FLIC Records.

24. "June 4, 1962, Transcripts" file, 1652, box 5, FLIC Records.

25. Jane Smith, "Report on USF," 3–4, box 1, Egerton Papers; Julian Lane to Charley Johns, April 13, 1962, box 2, FLIC Records.

26. Julian Lane to Charley Johns, April 13, 1962, box 2, FLIC Records.

27. "April 26, 1962, Transcripts" file, 1–4, box 9, FLIC Records; Schnur, "Cold Warriors," 209.

28. See chapter 3.

29. "Members" file, 1–4, box 1; staff memo, March 8, 1962, 1, box 1, both in FLIC Records.

30. Other members of the inner group, in addition to Johns Committee members and staff, included Representative Joe McClain of Pasco County; Edward Whittlesey, former head of UF public relations under Allen (and described as disliking him); and Fred Turner, assistant to state superintendent of education Thomas Bailey, also described as an Allen foe (staff memo, April 18, 1962, 1, box 1, FLIC Records).

31. Ibid.

32. Ibid.

33. "May 19, 1962, Transcripts" file, 1–5, box 10, FLIC Records.

34. Stark, "McCarthyism in Florida," 136–37; "AAUP Position Paper," May 25, 1962, 1–2, box 4, John Allen Papers; Harkness, "USF Silver."

35. "May 7–May 18, 1962, Transcripts" file, passim, box 10, FLIC Records.

36. Harkness, "USF Silver"; Stark, "McCarthyism in Florida," 138–39; Grace Allen, "USF Silver"; "The John Allen Legacy," University of South Florida, usfweb2.usf.edu/History/allen_legacy.html.

37. John Allen, "Speech to Faculty, Staff, and Students," May 21, 1962, 1–4, box 4, John Allen Papers.

38. Strickland quoted in Stark, "McCarthyism in Florida," 150.

39. Fisher, interview by author.

40. The other three were Robert Warner, professor and chair of The American Idea course; Russell Cooper, dean of liberal arts; and Henry Winthrop, professor in The American Idea course as well as in psychology ("May 23–June 6, 1962, Transcripts" files, passim, boxes 5 and 10, FLIC Records).

41. Fisher, "USF Silver."

42. Fisher quoted in Graves, "Confronting," 160.

43. Eleven witnesses testified prior to Fisher, six administrators and five faculty. (This does not include professors Sy Kahn and John Caldwell, whose transcripts are not in the Johns Committee's files.) Excluding Professor Henry Winthrop, administrators were interrogated about twice as long as faculty ("May 23–June 1, 1962, Transcripts" file, passim, box 5, all in FLIC Records).

44. "University Professors," 8, 20, box 13; "May 23, 1962, Transcripts" file, 2–40, 196–98, box 5; Johns quoted in "May 23, 1962, Transcripts" file, 197, box 5, all in FLIC Records.

45. "May 23, 1962, Transcripts" file, 198–227, box 5, FLIC Records; Johns quoted in Sears, *Lonely Hunters*, 22; Johns quoted in "May 23, 1962, Transcripts" file, 247, box 5, FLIC Records.

46. "May 23, 1962, Transcripts" file, 247, box 5, FLIC Records.

47. "May 30, 1962, Transcripts" file, 967–71, box 5, FLIC Records.

48. "University Professors," 13, box 13; "May 30, 1962, Transcripts" file, 1008, 1030, box 5, both in FLIC Records.

49. "May 30, 1962, Transcripts" file, 979–83, 984, box 5, FLIC Records.

50. Ibid., 999–1000.

51. "University Professors," 4, box 13; "May 23, 1962, Transcripts" file, 72, box 5, FLIC Records.

52. Ibid., 95–105.

53. "May 23–June 1, 1962, Transcripts" file, passim, box 5, FLIC Records.

54. The name is blacked out, but it is clear from the context that Hawes is asking about Caldwell and, most likely, Wayne Hugoboom. Unfortunately, John Caldwell's interrogation transcript is not in the Johns Committee's records or USF's Johns Committee files ("May 30, 1962, Transcripts" file, 1008–14, 1090, box 5, FLIC Records). Hawes quoted in "May 30, 1962, Transcripts" file, 1090, box 5, FLIC Records.

55. "May 30, 1962, Transcripts" file, 1106–15, box 5, FLIC Records.

56. Ibid., 1096–1101. The Johns Committee had included a portion of Winn's statement "for the Board of Control's information," in the hearing record immediately after dismissing Johnshoy (1101).

57. "May 30, 1962, Transcripts" file, 1120–22, box 5, FLIC Records. However, Cooper and French said that they did not receive a report from Caldwell ("June 1, 1962, Transcripts" file, 1521, box 5; "May 30, 1962, Transcripts" file, 958, box 5, both in FLIC Records).

58. "May 30, 1962, Transcripts" file, 1122–29, 1133–54.

59. Ibid.

60. Ibid.

61. Johns quoted in ibid., 1154.

62. Ibid., 1154–55.

63. Ibid., 1153–69, 1170.

64. Ibid., 1185–86.

65. Fisher referred once to the chance of reprisals against Winn if there had been an investigation but made no further mention of it, nor was this pursued by Hawes ("May 31, 1962, Transcripts" file, 1327–34, box 5, FLIC Records).

66. "June 6, 1962, Transcripts" file, 31, 124–25, 130, box 5, FLIC Records.

67. "Report from FLIC," 13–18, box 1; "June 6, 1962, Transcripts" file, 168–70, box 5, both in FLIC Records.

68. "June 6, 1962, Transcripts" file, 105–8, 115–16, FLIC Records.

69. Hawes quoted in ibid., 143–44; ibid., 144.

70. Ibid., 145–48. Toward the end of the campus hearings, the Johns Committee interviewed some of its friendlier witnesses at the Hillsborough County courthouse on June 4, 5, and 7. "June 4, 1962, Transcripts" file, 1614–89, box 5; "June 5, 1962, Transcripts" file, 2–3, 14–25, box 5, all in FLIC Records.

71. Fisher, interview by author; Fisher, "Oral History." Later, as president of a small college, Johnshoy was serving on a special commission in Vietnam when he and four other college presidents were killed in a plane crash (Fisher, interview by author).

72. Fisher, "USF Silver."

73. Grace Allen, conversation with author, February 15, 2002.

74. Ibid.

75. Charley Johns, press conference transcript, June 6, 1962, 1; Charley Johns, press release, June 7, 1962, 2, both in box 4, John Allen Papers.

76. "Report of the Special Committee of the Board of Control," September 14, 1962, 1, box 1, File 2, FLIC Records.

77. "Minutes" file, August 8, 1962, 1, box 1, FLIC Records; John Allen, statement to the press, August 27, 1962, 1, box 4, Egerton Papers; "Report of the Special Committee," 1, box 1, FLIC Records; Stark, "McCarthyism in Florida," 153–54. Johns had actually decided to release the report the week before August 24, 1962, telling his secretary to make enough copies "for the last of next week for the press" (Charley Johns to Myra White, August 18, 1962, box 2, FLIC Records).

78. "Report from FLIC," 12–14, 17, box 1, FLIC Records.

79. John Egerton, "The Controversy: One Man's View of Politics in the Making of a University," 107–13, box 3, Egerton Papers.

80. "Report from FLIC," 30–41, 43, box 1; "June 6, 1962, Transcripts" file, 146, box 5, both in FLIC Records.

81. "Report from FLIC," 44, box 1, FLIC Records.

82. Ibid., 45–48.

83. Stark, "McCarthyism in Florida," 159; "Johns Committee Investigation, 1962, News Clippings," box 4, John Allen Papers.

84. Stark, "McCarthyism in Florida," 158; Fisher, interview by author.

85. Allen, statement to the press, August 27, 1962, box 4, Egerton Papers.

86. Margaret Fisher to John Allen, August 31, 1962, box 4, John Allen Papers; Fisher, interview by author.

87. Graves, "Confronting," 165.

88. Elizabeth S. Hohnadel to John Allen, April 8, 1963, box 4, John Allen Papers; Carol S. Scott to John Egerton, April 25, 1963, box 3, Egerton Papers; Fisher, "USF Silver"; Fisher quoted in Graves, "Confronting," 168.

89. "Report to President Allen from James Parrish on John Caldwell Hearing," 1–3, box 4, John Allen Papers; Bertwell, "A Veritable Refuge," 422–25; Stark, "McCarthyism in Florida," 166–72.

90. "Board of Control Policies," October 19, 1962, 1–5, box 1, FLIC Records; John Egerton, "The Controversy: One Man's View of Politics in the Making of a University," 152–61, box 3, Egerton Papers; Margaret Fisher to Boris Nelson, November 6, 1962, box 4, Fisher Papers.

91. John Egerton, "The Controversy: One Man's View of Politics in the Making of a University," 152–61, box 3, Egerton Papers.

92. "Comments from the Public," passim, box 4, John Allen Papers; Statement by Faculty, December 7, 1962, 1–2, box 1, FLIC Records.

93. Stark, "McCarthyism in Florida," 180–81, 183; Board of Control, "Policy on Morals and Influences," 1–2, box 1, FLIC Records.

94. Sam Mase, "Homecoming Skits Lampoon Johns, Kennedy, Smathers," *Tampa Tribune*, October 21, 1962, box 3, Egerton Papers.

95. Stark, "McCarthyism in Florida," 186; John Egerton, "The Controversy: One Man's View of Politics in the Making of a University," 168–70, box 3, Egerton Papers; G. C. Eichholz to John Allen, n.d., box 4, John Allen Papers.

96. Randolph Pendleton, "Committee's Actions Left Journalist Broken," *Florida Times-Union*, July 11, 1993, sec. A; *Dark Legacy*; McGarahan, "Florida's Secret Shame," 12, 15; Peter, "Florida's Sinner Safari," 14.

97. Graves, *And They Were Wonderful Teachers*, 118–19, 125; Lawson, "Florida Legislative Investigation Committee," 315–16; Ruth Perry, Along Freedom's Road, *Miami Times*, April 6, 1963, n.p., Perry Papers.

98. Senate Executive Session Transcript, April 18, 1963, 1, 6–7, 30–31, box 1, FLIC Records; John Allen, "Address to the State Legislature," April 24, 1963, 1–7, 10, box 1, Egerton Papers.

99. "Members" file, 1–4, box 1, FLIC Records; "Minutes" file, August 8, 1964, 4; November 10, 1963, 2; January 29, 1964, 7; June 5, 1964, 2, all in box 9, CHR Papers.

100. FLIC, "Homosexuality and Citizenship in Florida," January 1964, passim, i, box 1, FLIC Records. The Purple Pamphlet can be viewed in its entirety at ufdc.ufl.edu/UF00004805/.

101. Ibid., A-7.

102. Ibid., A-6.

103. McIntire, Tangents. "'John' Like Report," 9–13; Gerstein quoted in "Representative R. O. Mitchell," editorial, WFLA Radio, March 19, 1964, box 19, FLIC Records.

104. D'Emilio, *Sexual Politics*, 174; Call, "An Open Letter," 85. For more on the Purple Pamphlet, see Braukman, *Communists and Perverts*, 169–72.

105. C. William Heywood and Robert M. Wallace, "Academic Freedom and Tenure: The University of South Florida," *AAUP Bulletin* (Spring 1964): 44–57, box 1, FLIC Records.

106. Anonymous professor quoted in John Egerton, "The Controversy: One Man's View of Politics in the Making of a University," 270, box 3, Egerton Papers.

107. Ibid., 267–71; staff report no. 5, April 3, 1964, 1, box 1, FLIC Records.

108. Mark Greenberg, *University of South Florida*, 72.

109. McGarahan, "Florida's Secret Shame," 18; "Members" file, 1–4, box 1; Walter Stokes to John Evans, September 18, 1964, box 2, both in FLIC Records.

110. Stark, "McCarthyism in Florida," 189.

111. Ibid., 230, 238; Schnur, "Cold Warriors," 316, 318–20. The Senate secretary's staff blacked out names on the original FLIC Records before making a copy of the records. Thus (as staff member Charles Frier explained to the author), no pristine version of the FLIC Records now exists, and the State Archives' collection of the records is identical to those stored in the Senate Office Building. Booth Gunter, "State Releases Once-Secret Johns Records," *Tampa Tribune*, July 2, 1993, n.p.; "Florida Examines Era of Suspicion," *New York Times*, July 4, 1993, n.p.

112. McGarahan, "Florida's Secret Shame," 17; Herrell quoted in *Dark Legacy*.

113. Strickland quoted in McGarahan, "Florida's Secret Shame," 15.

114. Fisher, "Oral History"; Margaret Fisher to Alvin Scaff, February 18, 1965, box 4; program for Conference on Continuing Education for Women, March 20–21, 1966, box 2; program for National Association of Women Deans Conference, September 1974, box 4, all three in Fisher Papers.

115. Mark Greenberg, *University of South Florida*, 73–84; Fisher, "Margaret Fisher Oral History," interview by Greenberg.

116. Arnade, "USF Silver"; "Beginning with a Bang," University of South Florida, usfweb2.usf.edu/History/fisher.html.

117. Fisher, interview by author.

118. Steven Northcutt, "Fisher Quits USF to be Self-Employed," *The Oracle*, August 5, 1975, 13, box 1, Fisher Papers; "A Tribute," 8.

119. Fisher, interview by author.


## Chapter 7. Conclusion

1. Johns quoted in *Dark Legacy*.

2. Braukman, "'Nothing Else Matters,'" 571–73; Schnur, "Closet Crusaders," 145, 155; D'Emilio, *Making Trouble*, 64.

3. Braukman, *Communists and Perverts*, 15, 88.

4. Ibid., 88.

5. Stewart, "The Law and Virgil Hawkins," 16; Dunn, *Black Miami*, 222; Crist to Diettrich, April 4, 1959, Sigismond Diettrich Papers; Raisz, "The Atlas," 208; William Harvey to J. Wayne Reitz, August 7, 1967, box 64, J. Wayne Reitz Papers; Mock, interview by author; Fisher to Alvin Scaff, February 18, 1965, box 4, Margaret Fisher Papers.

6. The original version of this quote has been attributed to Andrew Jackson who may have adapted it from abolitionist Wendell Phillips (Boller and George, *They Never Said It*, 54) or Henry David Thoreau ("Civil Disobedience," 43).

7. Thoreau, "Civil Disobedience," 43.

8. Ibid., 85.

9. Wells quoted in Duster, *Crusade for Justice*, 51.

10. Giddings, *When and Where I Enter*, 29; Royster, *Southern Horrors*, 40–41; "Senate Issues Apology over Failure on Lynching Laws," *New York Times*, June 1, 2005, www.nytimes.com.

11. Stevens, *Jailed for Freedom*, 187–88, 113–18.

12. Mueller, "Ella Baker," 57, 62, 64, 67–68; Dreier, "The 50 Most Influential Progressives," September 15, 2010.

13. This portion of the chapter was influenced by the six major human values and their supporting strengths in the work of Christopher Peterson and Martin Seligman. For more on these values and strengths, see the Values in Action Institute's website (www.uat.viacharacter.org), which explains Peterson and Seligman's work in the field of positive psychology. I am indebted to Connie Cooper, LCSW, for introducing me to Peterson and Seligman's work.

14. "February 4, 1957, Transcripts" file, passim, box 3, FLIC Records.

15. Ibid., 19.

16. Ibid., 23.

17. Sasscer, "Justice Delayed," 135.

18. Hawkins quoted in Stewart, "The Law and Virgil Hawkins," 17.

19. Ruth Perry, Along Freedom's Road, *Miami Times*, October 27, 1956, Ruth Perry Papers.

20. Perry, broadcast, May 23, 1954, 5, Perry-Kilburg Papers.

21. "February 27, 1958, Miami Transcripts" file, 429, box 4, FLIC Records.

22. Ibid., 393.

23. John F. Kennedy, *Profiles in Courage*, 258.

24. "January 19, 1959, Transcripts" file, passim, 1284, 1287, box 7, FLIC Records.

25. Ibid., passim.

26. Ibid., 1285.

27. "Our Mission," Foundation for the Promotion of Music, www.thefpm.org; "Sigismond deRudesheim Diettrich," obituary, sec. B.

28. "August 18, 1959, Transcripts" file, 1–28, box 7, FLIC Records; Mock, interview by author.

29. Mock, interview by author; "August 18, 1959, Transcripts" file, 7, box 7, FLIC Records.

30. Mock, interview by author.

31. Ibid.

32. Columbia questionnaire, 1–5, box 4, Fisher Papers.

33. "University Professors" file, 7, box 13, FLIC Records; Ed Cutler quoted in Fisher, interview by author.

34. "May 30, 1962, Transcripts" file, passim, 1101, box 5, FLIC Records.

35. Fisher to Boris Nelson, November 6, 1962, box 4, Fisher Papers.

36. Ibid.

37. Fisher, interview by author.

38. Ibid.

39. Ibid.

40. Misztal, *Intellectuals and the Public Good*, 207; Thoreau, "Civil Disobedience," 13.

# Bibliography

Archival Sources, Interviews, and Unpublished Sources

Allen, George. "Proctor Oral History Project." Interview by Joel Buchanan. July 22, 1996. University of Florida. http://ufdcweb1.uflib.ufl.edu/ufdc.

Allen, Grace. "USF Silver Anniversary Oral History Project." Interview by Nancy Hewitt. July 23, 1985. University of South Florida. http://purl.fcla.edu/usf/dc/.

Allen, John. Papers. University of South Florida Library, Tampa.

American Association of University Professors (AAUP). University of Florida Chapter. Papers. University of Florida Library, Gainesville.

Arnade, Charles. "USF Silver Anniversary Oral History Project." Interview by Nancy Hewitt. August 21, 1985. University of South Florida. http://purl.fcla.edu/usf/dc/.

Barton, Gloria. Interview by Lawrence Dubin. N.d. Transcript in files of the *Florida Law Review*, Gainesville.

Board of Control. "Study on Desegregation." May 1956. State Library of Florida, Tallahassee.

Brady, Tom P. "Black Monday: Segregation or Amalgamation, America Has Its Choice." Winona, Miss.: Association of Citizens' Councils, 1954.

Braukman, Stacy. "Anticommunism and the Politics of Sex and Race in Florida, 1954–1965." PhD diss., University of North Carolina at Chapel Hill, 1999.

Brown v. Board of Education of Topeka. 347 U.S. 483 (1954).

Brown v. Board of Education of Topeka. 349 U.S. 294 (1955).

Clerk of the House of Representatives (CHR). Papers. RG 920. Florida State Archives, Tallahassee.

Collins, Governor Leroy. Correspondence. RG 102. Florida State Archives, Tallahassee.

Collins, Leroy. Interview by Jackson Ice. July 27, 1978. Jackson Ice Papers. Florida State University Library, Tallahassee.

———. "Proctor Oral History Project." Interview by David Colburn and Richard Scher. April 10, 1976. University of Florida. http://ufdcweb1.uflib.ufl.edu/ufdc.

———. "Proctor Oral History Project." Interview by Ray Washington. March 1979. University of Florida. http://ufdcweb1.uflib.ufl.edu/ufdc.

———. "Proctor Oral History Project." Monologue. April 10, 1976. University of Florida. http://ufdcweb1.uflib.ufl.edu/ufdc.

Dauer, Manning J. "Proctor Oral History Project." Interview by Jorge Guira. March 28, 1982. University of Florida. www.uflib.ufl.edu/UFDC/.

Diettrich, Sigismond deRudesheim. Papers. University of Florida Library, Gainesville.

Egerton, John. Papers. University of South Florida Library, Tampa.

Emmons, Caroline. "Flame of Resistance: The NAACP in Florida, 1910 to 1960." PhD diss., Florida State University, 1998.

Fisher, Margaret. Interview by author. August 16, 2008.

———. "Margaret Fisher Oral History." Interview by Yael Greenberg. July 11, 2003. University of South Florida. http://scholarcommons.usf.edu/usfhistinfo_oh/95.

———. "Oral History Program, USF Tampa Library." Interview by Stephanie Gaskins. August 7, 1998. University of South Florida. http://digital.lib.usf.edu/?u30.4.

———. Papers. University of South Florida Library, Tampa.

———. "USF Silver Anniversary Oral History Project." Interview by Nancy Hewitt. August 7, 1985. University of South Florida. http://purl.fcla.edu/usf/dc.

Florida. Attorney General. Amicus Curiae Brief of the Attorney General of Florida. Brown v. Board of Education of Topeka. 347 U.S. 483 (1954).

———. Governor (1953–1955: Johns). "A Report to the People of Florida." Tallahassee: 1955.

———. Governor (1955–1961: Collins). "Florida across the Threshold: The Administration of Governor LeRoy L. Collins, January 4, 1955, to January 3, 1961, a Report." Tallahassee: 1961.

———. Special Committee to Recommend Legislative Action Relating to Public School Education and Other Internal Affairs of Such State Deemed Expedient after Consideration of Recent Decisions of the Supreme Court of the United States. Report. Tallahassee: 1956.

The Florida Bar. In re Virgil Darnell Hawkins. 532 So.2d 669 (Fla. 1988).

Florida Legislative Investigation Committee (FLIC). Records. RG 940. Florida State Archives, Tallahassee.

Florida Legislature. *Journal of the Senate.* 32nd Regular Session, April 5th through June 3rd, 1949.

———. *Journal of the Senate.* 33rd Regular Session, April 6th through June 4th, 1951.

———. *Journal of the Senate.* 34th Regular Session, April 7th through June 5th, 1953.

———. *Journal of the Senate.* 35th Regular Session, April 5th through June 3rd, 1955.

———. *Journal of the Senate.* Extraordinary Session, July 23rd through August 1st, 1956.

———. *Journal of the Senate.* 36th Regular Session, April 8th through June 3rd, 1957.

———. Florida Statutes, Chapter 800.01 (1957).

Gore Jr., George W. Papers. Black Archives, Florida A&M University, Tallahassee.

Harkness, Donald. "USF Silver Anniversary Oral History Project." Interview by Nancy Hewitt. August 5, 1985. University of South Florida. http://purl.fcla.edu/usf/dc/.

Hart, Thomas A. E. "Proctor Oral History Project." Interview by R. T. King. February 24, 1977. University of Florida. www.uflib.ufl.edu/UFDC/.

Herman, Harley. Interview by Lawrence Dubin. August 4, 1992. Transcript in files of the *Florida Law Review*, Gainesville.

Hill, Horace. Interview by Lawrence Dubin. August 7, 1992. Transcript in files of the *Florida Law Review*, Gainesville.

Ice, Jackson. Papers. Florida State University Library, Tallahassee.

Jakes, Wilhemina. "Civil Rights Heroine, It Started with a Bus Ride." Interview by Kathleeen Laufenberg. *Tallahassee Democrat*, May 25, 1997, sec. B.

———. "Woman's Bus Ride Launched City Boycott." Interview by Eugene Morris. *Tallahassee Democrat*, January 15, 1990, sec. B.

Johns, Charley. "Proctor Oral History Project." Interview by Ray Washington. N.d. University of Florida. http://ufdcweb1.uflib.ufl.edu/ufdc.

Klein, Kevin. "Guarding the Baggage: Florida's Pork Chop Gang and Its Defense of the Old South." PhD diss., Florida State University, 1995.

McCarty, Governor Dan, and Governor Charley Johns. Correspondence. RG 102. Florida State Archives, Tallahassee.

Meek, Congresswoman Carrie. Interview by Lawrence Dubin. August 6, 1992. Transcript in files of the *Florida Law Review*, Gainesville.

Mock, G. G. Interview by author. August 13, 2009.

Morris, Allen. Collection. State Library of Florida, Tallahassee.

———. Papers. Florida State University Library, Tallahassee.

National Association for the Advancement of Colored People (NAACP). Papers. Part III, Series C. University of Florida Library, Gainesville.

Perry, Ruth. Papers. University of South Florida Library, Tampa.

Perry-Kilburg, Caroline. Interviews by author. July 29, 2002, and August 31, 2002.

———. Private Papers.

Peters, Donald. Interview by Lawrence Dubin. N.d. Transcript in files of the *Florida Law Review*, Gainesville.

Plowden, Gene. Advance Wirescript, March 15, 1960. Biographical Files. State Library of Florida, Tallahassee.

Reitz, Frances. "Proctor Oral History Project." Interview by Emily Ring. N.d. University of Florida. www.uflib.ufl.edu/UFDC/.

Reitz, J. Wayne. Papers. University of Florida Library, Gainesville.

Saunders, Robert. Interviews by author. December 18, 1998, March 24, 2001, and February 15, 2002.

———. Interview by Lawrence Dubin. August 7, 1992. Transcript in files of the *Florida Law Review*, Gainesville.

————. Lecture: "Continuing the Florida NAACP Legacy of Harry T. Moore." Resource Center for Florida History and Politics. University of South Florida, Tampa, February 15, 2002.

Saunders, Robert, and Helen Saunders. Papers. University of South Florida Library, Tampa.

Schnur, James. "Cold Warriors in the Hot Sunshine: The Johns Committee's Assault on Civil Liberties in Florida, 1956–1965." Master's thesis, University of South Florida, 1995.

Seaburg, Lillian. "Proctor Oral History Project." Interview by Tom King. March 30, 1976. University of Florida. www.uflib.ufl.edu/UFDC/.

Stark, Bonnie. "McCarthyism in Florida: Charley Johns and the Florida Legislative Investigation Committee, July 1956 to July 1965." Master's thesis, University of South Florida, 1985.

State ex Rel. Hawkins v. Board of Control of Florida et al. 47 So. 2d 608–17 (Fla. 1950).

Sweatt v. Painter. 339 U.S. 629 (1950).

University of Florida. College of Business Administration Archives. University of Florida Library, Gainesville.

University of South Florida. *Accent on Learning* 1, no. 1 (1960): 1–80.

Weitz, Seth. "Bourbon, Pork Chops, and Red Peppers: Political Immorality in Florida, 1945–1968." PhD diss., Florida State University, 2007.


Articles, Books, and Miscellaneous Sources

Bartley, Numan V. *The Rise of Massive Resistance: Race and Politics in the South during the 1950s.* Baton Rouge: Louisiana State University Press, 1997.

Beals, Melba Pattillo. *Warriors Don't Cry: A Searing Memoir of the Battle to Integrate Little Rock's Central High.* New York: Washington Square Press, 1994.

Becker, Jo. "State Honors Civil Rights Pioneer." *St. Petersburg Times Magazine*, May 26, 1999.

*Behind Closed Doors.* DVD. Directed by Alison Beutke. Gainesville: University of Florida, 1999.

Bennett, Lerone. "The South's Most Patient Man." *Ebony*, October 1958.

Berg, Manfred. "Black Civil Rights and Liberal Anti-Communism: The NAACP in the Early Cold War." *Journal of American History* 94, no. 1 (June 2007): 75–96.

————. *Ticket to Freedom: The NAACP in the Struggle for Black Political Integration.* Gainesville: University Press of Florida, 2005.

Bernstein, Mary. "Identity and Politics: Toward a Historical Understanding of the Lesbian and Gay Movement." *Social Science History* 26, no. 3 (Fall 2002): 531–81.

Bertwell, Dan. "'A Veritable Refuge for Practicing Homosexuals': The Johns Committee and the University of South Florida." *Florida Historical Quarterly* 83, no. 4 (Spring 2005): 410–31.

Boller, Paul, and John George. *They Never Said It*. New York: Oxford University Press, 1990.

Branch, Taylor. *Parting the Waters: America in the King Years, 1954–1963*. New York: Simon and Schuster, 1988.

Braukman, Stacy. *Communists and Perverts under the Palms: The Johns Committee in Florida*. Gainesville: University Press of Florida, 2012.

———. "'Nothing Else Matters But Sex': Cold War Narratives of Deviance and the Search for Lesbian Teachers in Florida, 1959–1963." *Feminist Studies* 27 (Fall 2001): 553–76.

Brazeal, B. R. "Some Problems in the Desegregation of Higher Education in the 'Hard Core' States." *Journal of Negro Education* 33 (Summer 1958): 352–72.

Burt, Al. *The Tropic of Cracker*. Gainesville: University Press of Florida, 1999.

Call, Hal. "An Open Letter to the Florida Legislature's 'Johns Committee.'" In *Speaking for Our Lives: Historic Speeches and Rhetoric for Gay and Lesbian Rights (1892–2000)*, edited by Robert Ridinger, 84–88. New York: Haworth Press, 2004.

Carleton, William G. *Freelancing through the Century*. Gainesville: Carleton House, 1988.

Carter, Robert L., and Thurgood Marshall. "The Meaning and Significance of the Supreme Court Decree." *Journal of Negro Education* 24 (Summer 1955): 397–404.

Christie, Terry. "The Collins–Johns Election, 1954: A Turning Point." *Apalachee* 6 (1963–67): 5–19.

Clark, Roy Peter, and Raymond Arsenault, eds. *The Changing South of Gene Patterson: Journalism and Civil Rights, 1960–1968*. Gainesville: University Press of Florida, 2002.

Clendinen, Dudley. "Is Victory in Sight for Virgil Hawkins?" *St. Petersburg Times Magazine*, March 21, 1976.

Colburn, David R. *From Yellow Dog Democrat to Red State Republican: Florida and Its Politics since 1940*. Gainesville: University Press of Florida, 2007.

Colburn, David R., and Lance DeHaven-Smith. *Government in the Sunshine State: Florida since Statehood*. Gainesville: University Press of Florida, 1999.

Collins, Leroy. *Forerunners Courageous: Stories of Frontier Florida*. Tallahassee: Colcade Publishers, 1971.

———. "How It Looks from the South." *Look*, May 27, 1958.

*The Committee*. DVD. Directed by Lisa Mills. Orlando: University of Central Florida, 2012.

Cooper, Algia. "*Brown v. Board of Education* and Virgil Darnell Hawkins: 28 Years and 6 Petitions to Justice." *Journal of Negro History* 64 (Winter 1979): 1–20.

Cooper, Russell, and Margaret Fisher. *The Vision of a Contemporary University*. Gainesville: University Presses of Florida, 1982.

Cramer, A. Richard. "School Desegregation and New Industry: The Southern Community Leaders' Viewpoint." *Social Forces* (May 1963): 384–89.

Crawford, Vicki L., Jacqueline Anne Rouse, and Barbara Woods, eds. *Women in the*

*Civil Rights Movement: Trailblazers and Torchbearers, 1941–1965*. Bloomington: Indiana University Press, 1993.

Danese, Tracy E. *Claude Pepper and Ed Ball: Politics, Purpose, and Power*. Gainesville: University Press of Florida, 2000.

Daniels, Janeia, ed. *Florida's First Black Lawyers*. Tallahassee: Virgil Hawkins Chapter, National Bar Association, 2009.

*Dark Legacy*. Videocassette. Directed by Chris Thompson. Tallahassee: WFSU Television, 1994.

Dauer, Manning J. "Florida: The Different State." In *The Changing Politics of the South*, edited by William C. Havard, 92–164. Baton Rouge: Louisiana State University Press, 1972.

Davis, Edward. *A Half Century of Struggle for Freedom in Florida*. Orlando: Drake Publishing, 1981.

Davis, Jack E., and Kari Frederickson, eds. *Making Waves: Female Activists in Twentieth Century Florida*. Gainesville: University Press of Florida, 2003.

D'Elosua, Christina. "Browner Speaks at Graduation, Hawkins Awarded Honorary Degree." *FlaLaw* (UF College of Law newsletter) 4, no. 28 (June 2001): 1–4.

D'Emilio, John. *Making Trouble: Essays on Gay and Lesbian History, Politics, and the University*. New York: Routledge, 1992.

———. *Sexual Politics, Sexual Communities*. Chicago: University of Chicago Press, 1983.

Diettrich, Sigismond. "Florida's Climatic Extremes: Cold Spells and Freezes." *Economic Geography* 25, no. 1 (January 1949): 68–74.

———. "Florida's Metropolitan Growth." *Economic Leaflets* 7, no. 12 (November 1948): 1–4.

———. "Florida's Regional Economy." *Economic Leaflets* 2, nos. 5 and 6 (April and May 1943): 1–4.

———. "Florida's Transition from Rural to Urban Economy." *Economic Leaflets* 2, no. 2 (January 1943): 1–4.

———. "Florida's War Economy: I. Population Changes." "II. Economic Changes." "III. Florida's Changing Position." *Economic Leaflets* 4, nos. 10–12 (September–November 1945): 1–4.

Dreier, Peter. "The 50 Most Influential Progressives of the 20th Century." *The Nation*, September 15, 2010.

Dubin, Lawrence. "Virgil Hawkins: A One-Man Civil Rights Movement." *Florida Law Review* 51 (1999): 913–56.

Dudziak, Mary. *Cold War Civil Rights: Race and the Image of American Democracy*. Princeton, N.J.: Princeton University Press, 2000.

Due, Tananarive, and Patricia Stephens Due. *Freedom in the Family: A Mother-Daughter Memoir of the Fight for Civil Rights*. New York: Ballantine, 2003.

Dunn, Marvin. *Black Miami in the Twentieth Century*. Gainesville: University Press of Florida, 1997.

Duster, Alfreda, ed. *Crusade for Justice: The Autobiography of Ida B. Wells*. Chicago: University of Chicago Press, 1972.

Dyckman, Martin. *Floridian of His Century: The Courage of Governor LeRoy Collins*. Gainesville: University Press of Florida, 2006.

Elkins, Charles. "From Plantation to Corporation: The Attack on Tenure and Academic Freedom in Florida." *Sociological Perspectives* 41, no. 4 (1998): 757–65.

Eskridge, William. "Privacy Jurisprudence and the Apartheid of the Closet, 1946–1961." *Florida State University Law Review* 24 (Summer 1997): 703–840.

Evans, Sara M. *Born for Liberty: A History of Women in America*. New York: Free Press, 1991.

Evans, Stephanie. "'I Was One of the First to See Daylight': Black Women at Predominantly White Colleges and Universities in Florida since 1959." *Florida Historical Quarterly* 85, no. 1 (Summer 2006): 42–63.

Faderman, Lillian. *Odd Girls and Twilight Lovers: A History of Lesbian Life in Twentieth Century America*. New York: Penguin, 1992.

———. *To Believe in Women: What Lesbians Have Done for America—a History*. New York: Houghton Mifflin, 1999.

Fejes, Fred. "Murder, Perversion, and Moral Panic: The 1954 Media Campaign against Miami's Homosexuals and the Discourse of Civic Betterment." *Journal of Homosexuality* 37 (1999): 305–47.

Field, Ben. "The Charley E. Johns Story." *Orlando Sentinel Magazine*, May 1, 1954.

———. "The LeRoy Collins Story." *Orlando Sentinel Magazine*, May 16, 1954.

"Florida." *Southern School News* 1, no. 4 (December 1, 1954): 5.

Franklin, John Hope, and Alfred A. Moss Jr. *From Slavery to Freedom: A History of African Americans*. New York: Knopf, 2000.

Gannon, Michael. *The New History of Florida*. Gainesville: University Press of Florida, 1996.

"Geographic Record." *Geographical Review* 37, no. 2 (April 1947): 319–31.

Giddings, Paula. *When and Where I Enter: The Impact of Black Women on Race and Sex in America*. New York: William Morrow, 1998.

Goldman, Roger. *Thurgood Marshall: Justice for All*. With David Gallen. New York: Carroll and Graf, 1993.

Graves, Karen. *And They Were Wonderful Teachers: Florida's Purge of Gay and Lesbian Teachers*. Urbana: University of Illinois Press, 2009.

———. "Confronting a 'Climate of Raucous and Carnival Invasion': The AAUW Takes on the Johns Committee." *Florida Historical Quarterly* 85, no. 2 (Fall 2006): 154–76.

———. "Doing the Public's Business: Florida's Purge of Gay and Lesbian Teachers, 1959–1964." *Educational Studies* 41, no. 1 (2007): 7–32.

Green, Ben. *Before His Time: The Untold Story of Harry T. Moore, America's First Civil Rights Martyr*. New York: Free Press, 1999.

Greenberg, Jack. *Crusaders in the Courts: Legal Battles of the Civil Rights Movement.* New York: Twelve Tables Press, 2004.

Greenberg, Mark. *The University of South Florida: The First Fifty Years.* Tampa: University of South Florida, 2006.

Halberstam, David. *The Fifties.* New York: Ballantine, 1993.

Harris, Chauncy. "Geographers in the U.S. Government in Washington, D.C., during World War II." *Professional Geographer* 49, no. 2 (1997): 245–56.

Havard, William C., and Loren P. Beth. *The Politics of Misrepresentation: Rural-Urban Conflict in the Florida Legislature.* Baton Rouge: Louisiana State University Press, 1962.

Heale, M. J. *McCarthy's Americans: Red Scare Politics in State and Nation, 1935–1965.* Athens: University of Georgia Press, 1998.

Herman, Arthur. *Joseph McCarthy: Re-examining the Life and Legacy of America's Most Hated Senator.* New York: Free Press, 2000.

Herman, Harley. "Anatomy of a Bar Resignation: The Virgil Hawkins Story." *Florida Coastal Law Journal* 2 (Fall 2000): 77–112.

"In Memoriam: Charley Everett Johns." *Journal of the Senate,* 1990, 306.

Jacobstein, Helen. *The Segregation Factor in the Florida Democratic Gubernatorial Primary of 1956.* Gainesville: University of Florida Press, 1972.

Johnson, David K. *The Lavender Scare: The Cold War Persecution of Gays and Lesbians in the Federal Government.* Chicago: University of Chicago Press, 2004.

Johnson, Whittington. "The Virgil Hawkins Case: A Near Decade of Evading the Inevitable: The Demise of Jim Crow Higher Education in Florida." *Southern University Law Review* 16 (Spring 1989): 55–71.

Karl, Fred. *The 57 Club: My Four Decades in Florida Politics.* Gainesville: University Press of Florida, 2010.

Kennedy, John F. *Profiles in Courage.* New York: Harper and Row, 1964.

Kennedy, Randall. "Contrasting Fates of Repression: A Comment on *Gibson v. Florida Legislative Investigation Committee.*" In *Secret Agents: The Rosenberg Case, McCarthyism, and Fifties America,* edited by Marjorie Garber and Rebecca L. Walk-Owitz, 265–73. New York: Routledge, 1995.

Kennedy, Robert F. Foreword to *Profiles in Courage.* New York: Harper and Row, 1964.

Kepner, Jim. *Rough News, Daring Views: 1950s Pioneering Gay Press Journalism.* New York: Haworth Press, 1998.

Killian, Lewis. *Black and White: Reflections of a White, Southern Sociologist.* New York: General Hall, 1994.

———. "Florida's Citizens and Desegregation in the Schools." *Florida School Bulletin* 17 (September 1954): 10–14.

Kluger, Richard. *Simple Justice.* New York: Random House, 1975.

Knowlton, Elizabeth. "Documenting the Gay Rights Movement." *Provenance* 5 (Spring 1987): 17–30.

Lawson, Steven F. *Civil Rights Crossroads: Nation, Community, and the Black Freedom Struggle*. Lexington: University of Kentucky Press, 2003.

———. "The Florida Legislative Investigation Committee and the Constitutional Readjustment of Race Relations, 1956–1963." In *An Uncertain Tradition: Constitutionalism and the History of the South*, edited by Kermit L. Hall and James W. Ely Jr., 296–325. Athens: University of Georgia Press, 1989.

Lawson, Steven F., David R. Colburn, and Darryl Paulson. "Groveland: Florida's Little Scottsboro." *Florida Historical Quarterly* 65, no. 1 (July 1986): 1–26.

Library of America. *Reporting Civil Rights: Part One, American Journalism, 1941–1963*. New York: Library of America, 2003.

Loftin, Craig, ed. *Letters to ONE*. Albany: State University of New York Press, 2012.

Loughery, John. "Hunting Gays in Gainesville." *Harvard Gay and Lesbian Review* 3 (Winter 1996): 17–18.

Lynch, Lee. "What We Feared." *Lesbian Connection*, July/August 2007.

Matherly, Walter. Editor's Note. *Economic Leaflets* 1, no. 1 (December 1941): 1.

"May 1983 to May 2008." *Womyn's Words*, May 2008.

Mayhew, Lewis, ed. "Intellectual Tone for a State University." *University of South Florida Bulletin* 3, no. 4 (June 1961): 1–28.

McGarrahan, Ellen. "Florida's Secret Shame." *Miami Herald Tropic*, December 8, 1991.

McIntire, Dal. Tangents. *ONE*, October–November 1957.

———. Tangents. "'John' Like Report of the Johns Committee." *ONE*, June 1964.

McMillen, Neil R. *The Citizens' Council: Organized Resistance to the Second Reconstruction, 1954–1964*. Urbana: University of Illinois Press, 1994.

Meyerowitz, Joanne. *Not June Cleaver: Women and Gender in Postwar America, 1945–1960*. Philadelphia: Temple University Press, 1994.

Miller, James Nathan. "How Florida Threw Out the Pork Chop Gang." *National Civic Review* 60, no. 7 (July 1971): 1–5.

Misztal, Barbara. *Intellectuals and the Public Good: Creativity and Civil Courage*. New York: Cambridge University Press, 2007.

Mohl, Raymond A. *South of the South: Jewish Activists and the Civil Rights Movement in Miami, 1945–1960*. Gainesville: University Press of Florida, 2004.

———. "'South of the South?': Jews, Blacks, and the Civil Rights Movement in Miami." *Journal of American Ethnic History* 18 (Winter 1999): 3–36.

Mormino, Gary. *Land of Sunshine, State of Dreams: A Social History of Modern Florida*. Gainesville: University Press of Florida, 2005.

Motley, Constance Baker. *Equal Justice under Law: An Autobiography*. New York: Farrar, Straus, and Giroux, 1998.

Mueller, Carol. "Ella Baker and the Origins of 'Participatory Democracy.'" In *Women in the Civil Rights Movement: Trailblazers and Torchbearers, 1941–1965*, edited by Vicki L. Crawford, Jacqueline Anne Rouse, and Barbara Woods, 51–70. Bloomington: Indiana University Press, 1993.

Mushroom, Merril. "Bar Dyke Sketches: 1959." *Common Lives, Lesbian Lives* no. 5 (Fall 1982): 17–22.

———. "The Gay Kids and the Johns Committee: 1956." In *Telling Tales out of School: Gays, Lesbians, and Bisexuals Revisit Their School Days*, edited by Kevin Jennings, 13–20. Los Angeles: Alyson Books, 1998.

Myrdal, Gunnar. *An American Dilemma.* 2 vols. New York: Harper and Row, 1969.

"NAACP Leader, Missing 3 Weeks, Reported 'Alive.'" *Jet*, August 13, 1953.

Navasky, Victor S. *Naming Names.* New York: Viking Press, 1980.

"News from Geographic Centers." *Professional Geographer* 11, no. 4 (July 1959): 22–24.

———. *Professional Geographer* 12, no. 5 (September 1960): 25–28.

Newton, Michael. *The Invisible Empire: The Ku Klux Klan in Florida.* Gainesville: University Press of Florida, 2001.

Neyland, Leedell. *Florida Agricultural and Mechanical University: A Centennial History (1887–1987).* Tallahassee: Florida A&M University Foundation, 1987.

North, Don. "Lesbians." *St. Petersburg Times Magazine*, November 9, 1969.

Odum, Ralph. "A Summary of the Segregation Brief of the Attorney General." *Florida School Bulletin* 17 (December 1954): 24–28.

Parks, Rosa. *Rosa Parks: My Story.* With Jim Haskins. New York: Penguin, 1992.

Parsons, Malcolm. "Quasi-Partisan Conflict in a One-Party Legislative System: The Florida Senate." *American Political Science Review* 56, no. 3 (September 1962): 605–14.

Paulson, Darryl, and Paul Hawkes. "Desegregation of the University of Florida Law School: *Virgil Hawkins v. Florida Board of Control.*" *Florida State University Law Review* 12 (1984): 59–71.

Peter, Emmett. "Florida's Sinner Safari." *New Republic*, April 27, 1963.

"Ph.D. Dissertations in Geography." *Annals of the Association of American Geographers* 25, no. 4 (December 1935): 215–18.

Plato. *Laches, or Courage.* Translated by Benjamin Jowett. Project Gutenberg, 2008. Apple iBook.

Pleasants, Julian. *Gator Tales: An Oral History of the University of Florida.* Gainesville: University Press of Florida, 2006.

Porter, Gilbert. "The Status of Educational Desegregation in Florida." *Journal of Negro Education* 25 (Summer 1956): 246–53.

Porter, Gilbert, and Leedell Neyland. *The History of the Florida State Teachers Association.* Washington, D.C.: National Education Association, 1977.

Poucher, Judith. "One Woman's Courage: Ruth Perry and the Johns Committee." In *Making Waves: Female Activists in Twentieth Century Florida*, edited by Jack E. Davis and Kari Frederickson, 229–49. Gainesville: University Press of Florida, 2003.

———. "Raising Her Voice: Ruth Perry, Activist and Journalist for the Miami NAACP." *Florida Historical Quarterly* 84, no. 4 (Spring 2006): 517–40.

Price, H. D. *The Negro and Southern Politics.* New York: New York University Press, 1957.

Prunty, Merle. "Geography in the South." *Annals of the Association of American Geographers* 69, no. 1 (March 1979): 53–58.

Puryear, R. W. "Desegregation of Public Education in Florida—One Year Afterward." *Journal of Negro Education* 24 (Summer 1955): 219–27.

Rabby, Glenda Alice. *The Pain and the Promise: The Struggle for Civil Rights in Tallahassee, Florida.* Athens: University of Georgia Press, 1999.

Raisz, Erwin. "The Atlas of Florida." *Annals of the Association of American Geographers* 49, no. 2 (June 1959): 168–222.

Raisz, Erwin, and Associates. *Atlas of Florida.* Gainesville: University of Florida Press, 1964.

Rivers, Larry O. "Leaning on the Everlasting Arms: Virgil Darnell Hawkins' Early Life and Entry into the Civil Rights Struggle." *Florida Historical Quarterly* 86, no. 3 (Winter 2008): 279–308.

Robinson, Jo Ann. *The Montgomery Bus Boycott and the Women Who Started It: The Memoir of Jo Ann Gibson Robinson.* Knoxville: University of Tennessee Press, 1993.

Rose, Chanelle. "The 'Jewel' of the South?: Miami, Florida and the NAACP's Struggle for Civil Rights in America's Vacation Paradise." *Florida Historical Quarterly* 86, no. 1 (Summer 2007): 39–69.

Royster, Jacqueline Jones, ed. *Southern Horrors and Other Writings: The Anti-Lynching Campaign of Ida B. Wells, 1892–1900.* Boston: Bedford Books, 1997.

Rudy, Kathy. "Radical Feminism, Lesbian Separatism, and Queer Theory." *Feminist Studies* 27, no. 1 (2001): 190–227.

Sasscer, Amy. "Justice Delayed Is Justice Denied: Florida's 'Public Mischief' Defense and Virgil Hawkins' Protracted Legal Struggle for Racial Equality." In *Old South, New South, or Down South: Florida and the Modern Civil Rights Movement,* edited by Irvin S. Winsboro, 134–54. Morgantown: West Virginia University Press, 2009.

Saunders, Robert. *Bridging the Gap: Continuing the Florida NAACP Legacy of Harry T. Moore.* Tampa: University of Tampa Press, 2000.

Schnur, James. "Closet Crusaders: The Johns Committee and Homophobia, 1956–1965." In *Carryin' On in the Gay and Lesbian South,* edited by John Howard, 132–63. New York: New York University Press, 1997.

Schrecker, Ellen. *The Age of McCarthyism.* Boston: Bedford/St. Martin's, 2002.

———. *Many Are the Crimes: McCarthyism in America.* Princeton, N.J.: Princeton University Press, 1998.

———. *No Ivory Tower: McCarthyism and the Universities.* New York: Oxford University Press, 1986.

Schwan, Gesine. "Civil Courage and Human Dignity: How to Regain Respect for the Fundamental Values of Western Democracy." *Social Research* 71, no. 1 (Spring 2004): 107–16.

Schwendeman, J. R. "The Directory of College Geography of the United States: Its Origin, Purpose, and Publication." *Professional Geographer* 19, no. 3 (May 1967): 149–50.

Sears, James T. *Lonely Hunters: An Oral History of Lesbian and Gay Southern Life, 1948–1968*. Boulder, Colo.: Westview Press, 1997.

———. *Rebels, Rubyfruit, and Rhinestones*. New Brunswick, N.J.: Rutgers University Press, 2001.

Selkow, Samuel. "Hawkins, the United States Supreme Court, and Justice." *Journal of Negro Education* 31 (Winter 1962): 97–101.

"The Shape of Things." *The Nation*, October 6, 1951.

Smith, C. U., and A. S. Parks. "Desegregation in Florida—a Progress Report." *Quarterly Review of Higher Education among Negroes* 25, no. 1 (January 1957): 54–60.

Sparks, Holloway. "Dissident Citizenship: Democratic Theory, Political Courage, and Activist Women." *Hypatia* 12, no. 4 (Fall 1997): 74–110.

Steele, C. K. Appendix. "The Tallahassee Bus Protest Story." In *Bridging the Gap* by Robert Saunders, 257–64. Tampa: University of Tampa Press, 2000.

Stevens, Doris. *Jailed for Freedom: American Women Win the Vote*. Troutdale, N.Y.: New Sage Press, 1996.

Stewart, Barbara. "The Law and Virgil Hawkins." *Orlando Sentinel Magazine*, March 8, 1987.

Sullivan, Gerard. "Political Opportunism and the Harassment of Homosexuals in Florida, 1952–1965." *Journal of Homosexuality* 37, no. 4 (1999): 57–81.

Sullivan, Patricia. *Lift Every Voice: The NAACP and the Making of the Civil Rights Movement*. New York: New Press, 2009.

Swedburg, Richard. "Civil Courage (Zivilcourage): The Case of Knut Wicksell." *Theory and Society* 28, no. 4 (August 1999): 501–28.

Tebeau, Charlton. *A History of Florida*. Rev. ed. Coral Gables: University of Miami Press, 1988.

Thoreau, Henry David. "Civil Disobedience." Vook, Inc., 2011. Apple iBook.

Tomberlin, Joseph. "Florida Whites and the *Brown* Decision of 1954." *Florida Historical Quarterly* 51, no. 1 (July 1972): 22–36.

"A Tribute to Dean Margaret Fisher." *Alumni Voice*, October 2008.

"UF Apologizes for Honoring Anti-Gay Alumnus." *The Advocate*, July 1, 2005.

"The Village Printer." *Womyn's Words*, November 1984.

Wagy, Thomas. *Governor LeRoy Collins of Florida: Spokesman of the New South*. University: University of Alabama Press, 1985.

Walton, Douglas. *Courage: A Philosophical Investigation*. Berkeley: University of California Press, 1986.

Woodward, C. Vann. *The Burden of Southern History*. Third ed. Baton Rouge: Louisiana State University Press, 2008.

———. *The Strange Career of Jim Crow*. New York: Oxford University Press, 1974.

———. "The Unreported Crisis in the Southern Colleges." *Harper's*, October 1962.

# Index

Page numbers in italics refer to pages that contain photographs.

Taxes, Hawkins' troubles with, 16, 146, 161n65

Teacher assignment laws, 18–19

Teachers, gay witch hunt's focus on, 86, 89, 96, 103–6, 107–9, 182n23

Terminations. *See* Resignations, forced

Terrorism, acts of, 12, 44, 49–50, 144–45. *See also* KKK; WCC

Test standards, UF's, 33–34

Texas files, 21, 28, 55

Therapeutic value of Johns' name, 128

Thoreau, Henry David, 144, 152

Thorner, Robert, 155

Threats of violence. *See* Violence, threats of

Tigert, John, 67

Tileston, John, 74–75, 104

Tilley, B. R., 97

Todd, Rev. Ralph, 153

Tourism, concerns over, 5, 144

*Tribune* reports. See *Tampa Tribune*

Tuition handouts, Hawkins' rejection of, 12, 14, 31

Turner, Fred, 186n30

UF admission standards, 33–34

UF homecoming skit, 132–33

UF investigation: hunt for gays, 68, 70–75; interrogations, 75–80; report, 86

UF law school, beginning of Hawkins' fight to attend, 13

"Uncle Toms," Hawkins' view of, 39

Undercover agents, 95

University of Dacca. *See* Pakistan

University of Florida (UF). *See* UF investigation

"University of South Florida, Going Soft on Communism, The" (Wenner), 119

University of South Florida (USF). *See* USF investigation

University of Tampa (UT), 96

Unsealing of Johns Committee's records, 140

Urban League, 155

Urban university, USF's vulnerabilities as, 117

USF, opposition to establishment of, 117

USF investigation: campus hearings, 112, 121– 28; motel interrogations, 120–21; reports, 129–30, 134–35

USF's major policies for academics, 115–16

USF's vision. *See* "Accent on Learning"

U.S. Supreme Court cases. See *Brown v. Board of Education*; *Gibson v. Florida Legislative Investigation Committee*; *Hawkins v. Board of Control*; *NAACP v. Alabama*; *NAACP v. Button*; *Roth v. United States*; *Sipuel v. Oklahoma State Board of Regents*; *Sweatt v. Painter*

Vice squads, 98–99

Violence, KKK as organized structure for, 43

Violence, threats of, 15, 76–77, 144, 146, 160n51; against Perry, 41, 44–46, 50, 54, 169n21

Violence, use of, 49–50, 145, 153–54, 170n35; Moores' assassination, 43, 49–50, 147, 154, 169n10, 170n35; murders, 95, 96, 110, 182n22

"Virgil D. Hawkins Collection," 40

Virgil Hawkins Fellowships, 39, 147

Voter registration drives, 145

Vow to brother, Johns', 2, 4–5

Vulnerabilities, USF's, 117

Walker, George, 91, 102, 149, 180n2

Walker, May, 62

Walton, Howard, 155

Warner, Robert, 122–23, 187n40

Warren, Fuller, 17, 29

WCC (White Citizens' Council), 48, 49–50, 169n10; Daytona Beach WCC, 49–50, 153–54, 170n35; Miami WCC, 49–50, 53; Perry's would-be assassins, 41, 51, 57, 58

Webb, Cecil, 74

Wells, Ida B., 144–45

Wenner, Thomas, 119, 120

"We want Johns" protest, 86

Whitaker, Tom, 136

White, Walter, 56

White Citizens' Councils. *See* WCC

White supremacist organizations. *See* KKK; WCC

JUDITH G. POUCHER retired from teaching Florida history at Florida State College. Her previous work has appeared in the *Florida Historical Quarterly* and in *Making Waves: Female Activists in Twentieth-Century Florida*; she is currently a research consultant for *The Committee*, a new Johns Committee documentary, and for its companion website.

THE UNIVERSITY PRESS OF FLORIDA is the scholarly publishing agency for the State University System of Florida, comprising Florida A&M University, Florida Atlantic University, Florida Gulf Coast University, Florida International University, Florida State University, New College of Florida, University of Central Florida, University of Florida, University of North Florida, University of South Florida, and University of West Florida.